Look Out Below!

Look Out Below!

A Story of the Airborne by a Paratrooper Padre

Chaplain (Lt. Col.) Francis L. Sampson,
US Army

Introduction by Sean Brennan
Foreword by Philip Hannan

The Catholic University of America Press
Washington, D.C.

First published in 1958
Introduction Copyright © 2023
The Catholic University of America Press
All rights reserved

The paper used in this publication meets the minimum requirements of
American National Standards for Information Science—Permanence of
Paper for Printed Library Materials, ANSI Z39.48-1992.

∞

Cataloging-in-Publication Data is available from the Library of Congress

ISBN: 978-0-8132-3657-5
eISBN: 978-0-8132-3658-2

To

All the Men,

Living and Dead,

Who Have Ever Worn

the Wings

of a Paratrooper

in the United States Army

Contents

A Historical Introduction to the Memoirs of Lieutenant Colonel Francis L. Sampson

By Sean Brennan
Professor of History
University of Scranton

The third episode of the famous 2001 HBO miniseries *Band of Brothers,* "Carentan," depicts the Battle of Carentan. This battle lasted from June 6 to June 14, 1944, in a small French town near Normandy, where the American victory helped to secure the beachheads that had been won on D-Day. In the episode, privates Donald Malarkey and Warren "Skip" Munk observe a Catholic chaplain, identified as "Chaplain Maloney," praying with and performing last rites for wounded and dying American paratroopers, all the while German and American bullets are flying past him. After expressing incredulity at the chaplain's actions, Malarkey admits the Irish are "crazy fools," while Muck acknowledges Malarkey would know. The two then rush back into the battle. Another Irish-American US Army chaplain who exemplified the same incredible bravery as this Chaplain Maloney was Francis L. Sampson, who served as regimental chaplain of the 501st Parachute Regiment. The 501st, like the 506th Parachute Regiment depicted in the HBO miniseries, was part of the US Army's 101st Airborne Division, which served in some of the most intense battles on the Western Front from D-Day to the surrender of Germany eleven months later. Sampson would later serve as the regimental chaplain of the 11th Airborne Division, serving in the Korean War from 1950 to 1951, during the some of the heaviest fighting in that conflict. He wrote two memoirs concerning his time in combat: the first, *Paratroop Padre*, was written soon after the end of the Second World War, while the second, *Look Out Below!* was published in 1958 and not only expanded on his accounts of the Second World War but also included sections on the occupation duty in Germany and his service in the Korean War. What follows is a historical introduction to the latter, a remarkable memoir of spiritual service in two of the most significant conflicts of the twentieth century.

Francis L. Sampson, the son of immigrants from County Cork, Ireland, was born in Cherokee, Iowa in 1912.[1] Following graduation from high school, he traveled from northwestern Iowa to northern Indiana to attend the University of Notre Dame, the most famous and distinguished of the "Catholic Ivies." These universities had emerged mostly in the nineteenth and early twentieth centuries as alternatives to the traditional Ivies that predominately educated the white, Anglo-Saxon Protestant establishment.[2] Already preparing for the priesthood, Sampson studied theology and, following his graduation, attended Saint Paul Theological Seminary in Minnesota, where he graduated with a master's degree in Theology in 1941. Sampson was ordained a priest in the Diocese of Des Moines in June 1941. After his ordination, he briefly served as a parish priest in Neola, Iowa, in the southwestern part of the state, as well as a theology teacher in Dowling High School in Des Moines. However, events across the Atlantic and the Pacific took Sampson on a very different path of life, as the Japanese attack on Pearl Harbor on December 7, 1941 and the subsequent German declaration of war on the United States in support of their Japanese ally finally brought the United States into the largest conflict in human history.

Like thousands of other Catholic, Protestant, Orthodox, and Jewish clergy, Sampson desired to enter the US Armed Forces to provide spiritual leadership and support to the men soon to fight the Axis forces. Throughout the war, the US Armed Forces had a major shortage of chaplains, and thus chaplains had to provide spiritual assistance to soldiers from very different faith backgrounds. Despite having only been a priest for less than one year, Sampson's bishop,

---

1. From the mid- to late nineteenth century, Ireland's population dropped from eight million to four million. Between one and one and a half million died in the potato famine of the late 1840s, while the rest immigrated to various countries. The United States was the most popular destination for these immigrants, and Sampson's parents were among the approximately two million immigrants who came over during this time.

2. The others were Boston College, Holy Cross, Fordham, Villanova, and the oldest of them all, founded in 1789, Georgetown.

Gerald Bergan, gave him permission to enter in the US Military Ordinariate as part of the Chaplain's Corps. Sampson's memoir formally begins with this event. By his own admission, Sampson decided to serve as a chaplain for paratroopers on a whim, a decision that meant he would have to go through the same rigorous training all paratroop soldiers and officers endured.

The location for that training was in Fort Benning, Georgia, then as now a center for parachute training for the US Army. As Sampson correctly noted, only a third of those who began parachute training at Fort Benning actually finished Stage A, which emphasized physical conditioning and calisthenics. Those who completed the next three stages, the final of which actually involved parachute jumps from airplanes, were fewer still. For those who were part of the 501st Parachute Infantry Regiment (where Sampson was assigned), paratroop school at Fort Benning was followed by training at various military bases in North Carolina before the entire division was sent to England in the spring of 1944 to prepare for the invasion of Europe. This invasion was Operation Overlord, the fourth and final of the amphibious invasions on the Western front of the European theatre, following Torch (North Africa), Husky (Sicily), and Avalanche (Italy). Originally set for June 5, 1944, the invasion date of D-Day was postponed to the following day due to unfavorable weather. The invasion's objective was to attack and hold the northwestern French territory of Normandy and to use it as the initial staging ground for the Allied Expeditionary Force to liberate much of Western Europe from Nazi rule. Sampson would join 24,000 other parachute troopers from the American 101st and 82nd Airborne Divisions and the British Sixth Airborne Division in the drops into Normandy at midnight on the day of the invasion, June 6, 1944. Their aim was to seize several key German positions in the region and make way for the arrival of 165,000 soldiers on the beaches approximately six hours later. Sampson's experience following his parachute drop was typical of many of the men who parachuted out of their planes on that day of days.[3] He was separated

---

3. Many famous films on the Allied invasions of Normandy, such as *The Longest Day* and *Saving Private Ryan*, also touch on this theme of lost paratroopers during the D-Day landings.

from most of his unit following a landing in a place far from his intended arrival site, and he subsequently attempted to rejoin his unit with many other soldiers who had also become lost. While Sampson does not mention the risk involved, the parachute troopers showed a remarkable faith in their countrymen taking part in the amphibious landings, for if the landings at Omaha, Utah, Sword, Juno, and Gold beaches had failed, the paratroopers would have been stranded in German territory with little hope of anything besides a fight to the death or surrender.

During D-Day the chaplain had a brief experience of German captivity, as well as a narrow brush with death. As Sampson details, he and a few other soldiers were taken as prisoners to a nearby farmhouse by German *Fallschirmjagers* (literally, "parachute hunters," paratroopers preparing to execute them). A Catholic German sergeant, who recognized Sampson as a Catholic chaplain, ordered the other Germans to spare his and his companions' lives. Later the Germans simply abandoned their prisoners as they rapidly retreated from the advancing American infantrymen. In the complete chaos following the Allied invasion of Normandy, soldiers on both sides were captured and then often released, as paratroopers rarely had the numbers or equipment to guard their prisoners, nor the time and inclination to take them back to secured positions to be transported to POW camps. The darker side to this chaos, as Sampson acknowledged, was that Allied or Axis prisoners were often shot out of hand.

While it comprises only a few paragraphs in the fourth chapter of Sampson's memoir, one of the most influential sections of *Look Out Below!* concerns Sampson's encounter on Utah Beach a few weeks after D-Day with a private named Frederick "Fritz" Nyland. Nyland was a member of H Company of the 501st Parachute Infantry Regiment and had been separated from his unit. Sampson unfortunately gets a few details wrong, which later made their way into several historical and fictional accounts of the battle between Allied and German forces at Normandy. Nyland informed Sampson that the company commander of his brother "William," who was presumably serving in the 508th Infantry Regiment, had told him his brother was killed in action and buried in the Sainte-Mere-Eglise cemetery. Nyland and Sampson traveled to the cemetery, only to find the grave of his brother "Roland" as well, before also finding the grave of William a few minutes later. While Sampson is not clear if either he or Fritz Nyland knew this at the time, a third brother had been listed as KIA in the Pacific theatre of the war. Following this harrowing experience, Fritz informed Sampson that his mother, nicknamed "Butch" because of her love of gangster programs on the radio, would suffer horribly over the news. Nyland's mother did receive three telegrams at the same time informing her of the fate of her sons. Sampson helped get Nyland back to England, and back to the United Sates by filling out the paperwork for an honorable discharge due to Nyland's family circumstances. Shortly thereafter, Nyland was reunited with his parents.[4]

In reality, Nyland's brother who was also a paratrooper was named Robert "Bob" Nyland. Robert served in the 505th Parachute Infantry Regiment, which was part of the 82nd Airborne Division, and he was killed on D-Day helping hold off a German offensive at Neuvill-an-Plain. The other brother, whose real name was Preston Nyland, served with the 22nd Infantry Regiment, part of the Fourth Infantry Division, and was killed the day after D-Day on June 7, attacking an enormous German artillery position. The telegrams Nyland's mother received informed her of the deaths of Robert and Preston, but the oldest brother, Edward, was actually listed as missing in action (MIA) after his plane had been shot down by the Japanese over Burma. Edward miraculously survived several days wandering the jungles of Burma before being captured by the Japanese. Almost equally miraculously, Edward survived Japanese captivity in Burma before being liberated by the British army on May 4, 1945. Upon liberation, he rejoined his surviving brother and their parents at their home in Tonawanda, New York, a suburb of Buffalo. Fritz would later relocate to San Francisco, and both brothers married and had children. Robert and Preston Nyland were later reburied in the American Military Cemetery at Colleville-sur-Mer near the beaches of Normandy.

The story of Fritz Nyland was the inspiration for the famous 1998 film *Saving Private Ryan*, one of the most memorable films of

4. Since the end of the Second World War, the US military's sole-survivor policy would have allowed Fritz Nyland to return home after the fates of his brothers without any bureaucratic issues.

director Steven Spielberg. Nyland's story, as told by Sampson, was recounted in Steven Ambrose's book *D-Day, June 6, 1944*, with the same incorrect names from Sampson's account. Screenwriter Robert Rodat received the book as a present from his wife, and Nyland's story inspired Rodat's screenplay for the film. His screenplay eventually made its way to Spielberg and resulted in one of the most acclaimed and influential war films ever made. Matt Damon's character, James Francis Ryan, is roughly inspired by Fritz Nyland, although the circumstances of his return are less dramatic than depicted in the film.

A few weeks after the successful landings at Normandy, the 101st Airborne was sent back to England. Its next major endeavor, briefly detailed by Sampson in the fifth chapter, was Operation Market Garden in September 1944. Operation Market Garden features in many works on the Second World War, notably Richard Attenborough's 1978 war epic *A Bridge too Far* and *Band of Brothers'* fourth episode. Market Garden occurred just as the Nazis achieved their last string of successes. On July 20, 1944, Colonel Claus von Stauffenberg's plot to kill Hitler and overthrow his regime failed. In August, the Nazis crushed the Polish Home Army's uprising in their capital of Warsaw with exceptional brutality, even by Nazi standards. Enacted in September, Market Garden was the brainchild of Britain's Field Marshall Bernard Montgomery, designed to liberate the entirety of the Netherlands and seize a number of key bridges over the Rhine River and thus offer a pathway for Allied forces into Germany. Yet it ultimately failed to fully achieve either one of these objectives. While most of the American paratroopers who were not killed or captured in the battle were able to rejoin their units, the British First Airborne Division, at the front of the assault, was almost entirely wiped out.[5]

Germany's ability to consolidate its position following its retreat from France and the subsequent failure of Market Garden to win

---

5. Military historians have debated the failure of Market Garden, citing many causes: bad weather, missed drop spots, poor intelligence reports that underestimated the size and fighting ability of the German soldiers stationed in Holland, or Montgomery's overly ambitious plans and unrealistic timetables. Eisenhower was reluctant to greenlight Montgomery's plans but did so under pressure from Churchill and FDR.

the war by Christmas convinced AEF leadership that the direct attack on Germany itself would have to wait until the spring of 1945 (aside from the continual fighting in the Belgian/German border along the Hurtgen Forest which had turned into a WWI-style bloody stalemate). Most of the German military leadership desired to draw out the war by using Germany's central geographic position to hold back the AEF in the West and the Red Army in the East in the hope eventually the Grand Alliance against them would somehow collapse. Hitler, however, was much less inclined to listen to his military advisors following the July 20 plot and believed such a strategy would simply delay Germany's defeat, not reverse it. Instead, Hitler believed that Germany could still win the war through a smashing military victory, or at least believed that such a victory would improve Germany's eventual negotiating position. Thus he demanded a massive winter offensive in the West, with the goal of replicating Germany's success in the Ardennes campaign in May 1940.

Germany's goal would be to take the Belgian port of Antwerp, which, along with the French port of La Havre, was the main disembarking point for soldiers, vehicles, and supplies for the AEF. This action would hopefully divide the Allied position in the West in two, allowing the Germans to destroy both in turn. In theory the strategy was not a bad one, as few in the AEF command structure expected a winter offensive, and it potentially offered a morale boost to desperate German soldiers who had been retreating for months. However, this plan was completely divorced from the German military situation during the winter of 1944 to 1945. Germany was completely dependent on the happenstance that the weather would provide cloud cover, as German air power was nearly nonexistent. Additionally, most German officers did not believe it was possible to actually take Antwerp, and even lackeys such as Field Marshall Keitel who believed it was possible knew the Germans could not possibly hold against an inevitable Allied counteroffensive. Hitler was not deterred however, and in late December 1944, the Battle of the Bulge commenced.

This time, as Sampson admits, he was not lucky enough to avoid captivity. On December 20, while looking for the bodies of American paratroops who had been killed in the opening days of the

German offensive through Belgium and also for abandoned American medical equipment, Sampson and his driver, a Corporal Adams,
were captured by hundreds of German soldiers. Hitler's decision to
transfer hundreds of thousands of German soldiers to the West,
many of them battle-hardened veterans of combat with the Red
Army, temporarily created a German numerical advantage against
the AEF. Taking advantage of the cloud cover, the Germans took
the Americans, British, and Canadians completely by surprise,
taking tens of thousands of prisoners.

Sampson devotes two chapters of the memoir to his time as the
German POW. These chapters are among the darkest and most
intense of the memoir, as the German guards are often portrayed as
brutal thugs who enthusiastically steal from their American prisoners. At the same time, the Ardennes Offensive filled many German
soldiers with enthusiasm that the war could still be won, something
they never hesitated in reminding their prisoners of during December and early January. Discipline under their German captors could
be quite harsh, and as Sampson writes, at one point he had to stop
many of his fellow POWs from rioting against their German captors, which the chaplain was convinced would lead to a retaliatory
massacre by the Germans.[6] Upon arrival to Stalag II-A, located in
the southeastern part of the isolated and heavily forested German
province of Mecklenberg-Vorpommern, Sampson and his follow
Americans were imprisoned with 80,000 others from various Allied
nations. Sampson's claim the German authorities only barely
observed the Geneva Conventions during this stage of the war,
noting the camp conditions were filthy and rations were meager, has
also been verified by the research of many historians. As harrowing
as this account is, Sampson's portrayal of his experience as the POW
provides a realistic counterpoint to certain films and television shows
that depicted life in a German POW camp as little different from a
summer camp, often full of wacky adventures—the notorious 1960s
television show *Hogan's Heroes* being perhaps the best example.

---

6. Sampson was correct in this fear, as there were a few instances of German
soldiers, mostly Waffen SS veterans of the Eastern front, summarily executing
American POWs. The massacre of 84 American soldiers outside of the village of
Malmedy, Belgium, on December 15, 1944, was the most notorious example.

While Sampson and other prisoners were not aware of war's developments during their time at Stalag II-A until it neared its end, ultimately the Battle of the Bulge proved to be a failure for the Germans. Because of the ferocious defense of the key crossroad city of Bastogne by paratroops from the 101st Airborne Division and the lifting of the clouds, which allowed the AEF to use their considerable advantage in air power, the Germans were soon driven from their conquests in the initial week of the Ardennes Offensive, having never come close to taking their objective of Antwerp. Much of Germany's remaining reserves of ammunition and gasoline had been lost in the failed offensive, leaving the German forces in the East unable to resist a massive Red Army offensive that began in early February that enabled the Soviets to take Bucharest, Budapest, and Vienna, and by late April, had placed them at the gates of Prague and Berlin. In the West, the AEF finally succeeded in crossing the Rhine and began conquering large swaths of German territory. For Sampson and the other Allied prisoners at Stalag II-A in Neubrandenburg, their liberation was at hand.

The story of Sampson's liberation from Stalag II-A is one of the most important sections of the memoir, as it sheds light on an aspect of the end of the Second World War that is frequently overlooked by American audiences. Often films and television shows about the Second World War depict, or at least imply, American POWs' liberation from German camps at the hands of American or British armies. In fact, however, many of the Allied POW camps, such as Stalag II-A, located outside of Neubrandenburg, were in the eastern parts of Germany, and thus were liberated by the Red Army. The liberation of Sampson and his fellow prisoners occurred on April 28, in the closing weeks of the war. Sampson notes the German guards and camp staff had such a fear of the Russians at the end of the month they either fled in the direction of the Americans lines or, in an ironic twist of fate, turned themselves over for surrender to the American prisoners and were locked up in one of the barracks. Given the enormity of the crimes committed by the Germans during their invasion and occupation of the Soviet Union, they had a reason to be afraid, especially given the nature of their opponents from Stalin's regime.

The Red Army wreaked a horrible vengeance on the Germans at the end of the war, as well as on those they perceived to have aided them.[7] Sampson and the other Americans witnessed this vengeance almost immediately, as he notes that the Russian POWs, who were not enthusiastic about their liberation by their own countrymen, were forced to give up their fellow prisoners who were perceived to have collaborated with the Germans, and who were immediately executed. Several members of the German camp staff, including the commandant, were executed after being forced to dig their own graves, their strategy of surrendering to the Americans POWs first having proved to be unsuccessful. This violence was a foreshadowing of what was to come, as Sampson darkly portrays the destruction of Neubrandenburg by fires set by Red Army soldiers, the subsequent mass executions and suicides of German civilians in the town, and finally the looting conducted by Russian soldiers as well as French, Italian, and Serbian POWs who had been released from the camps. While Sampson does not go into detail about the fate of the surviving Russian POWs, they would have in all likelihood spent the next ten years in either isolated exile colonies or, if they were less lucky, the Gulag, as Stalin considered Russians taken prisoner by the Germans as guilty of cowardice at best or treason at worse. This policy was not reversed until the mid-1950s by Nikita Khrushchev.

Sampson and the men under his command were fortunate that their liberation was not delayed by months, unlike many of their fellow Allied POWs liberated by the Red Army. Per the agreements made at Yalta and renewed at Potsdam in January and July 1945 between Stalin and the Allied leaders, the American and British authorities in Germany and Austria, in order to facilitate the return of their own POWs held in Soviet custody, had to turn over Soviet and non-Soviet citizens who were accused of collaboration with the Axis powers. This included entire ethnic groups such as the Cossacks, many of whom had fled Russia to Yugoslavia, Austria, and Germany after the Bolsheviks had won the Russian Civil War. This process stretched into the fall of 1945 and, for many Soviet citizens who were turned over, meant either a death sentence or a twenty-

---

7. As detailed in the novels by the Red Army war correspondent Konstantin Simonov and historian Norman Naimark's still authoritative 1997 study, *The Russians in Germany: A History of the Soviet Zone of Occupation 1945–1949*, among many other works.

year sentence in the Gulag.[8] Sampson's account of the enormous physical destruction and the roads choked with desperate refugees and POWs darkly captures the apocalyptic environment in much of Europe at the end of the war. Additionally, his recollections also hint at the coming conflict of the Cold War: Sampson describes the American Army captain whose rescue of the American POWs from Stalag II-A in early May was actually the covert retrieval of a German scientist so that he could make his way to the American zone of Germany.[9]

Sampson returned to America in late May 1945 on a French ocean liner, and like many other military chaplains, he was eager to return to civilian life, at least for a time. A stereotype of American servicemen in the Second World War was that nearly all, including the chaplains, were desperate to finish the war, return to their civilian duties, and never put on a military uniform again. In reality, thousands of those who had served in the Second World War either decided to remain in the Armed Forces or returned to the service shortly thereafter. Such was the case for Sampson, who after a brief stint as a parish priest in Westphalia, Iowa, reenlisted in the US Military Ordinariate after receiving a letter detailing a chaplain shortage throughout the armed forces.

Sampson had yet seen the last of war. Still relatively young, he was reassigned to another parachute division, in this case the 11th Airborne Division, that had served in the Pacific theatre during the Second World War, specifically the liberation of the Philippine Islands, and that was currently occupying Hokkaido, the northernmost of the main islands of Japan. Like most servicemen at the time and since, Sampson enjoyed his tour in Japan, finding the popula-

---

8. Those who had survived the handover and Stalin's revenge, often nicknamed "Vlasovites" (referring to those who had fought with former Soviet general Andrei Vlasov's Russian Liberation Army on behalf of the Germans), were granted an amnesty by Khrushchev in 1956, part of what Soviet journalist Ilya Ehrenburg termed the *ottepel* or "the Thaw." It was referred to in the West as "de-Stalinization."

9. This endeavor was known as Operation Paperclip, conducted by the Army's Office of Strategic Services (OSS), the predecessor to the Central Intelligence Agency (CIA). The most famous retrieval, of course, was that of Wernher von Braun, the former chief designer of the V-2 Rocket *Wunderwaffen* ("Miracle Weapons"), who later became one of the main architects of the American NASA rocket program.

tion friendly and accommodating. It was also during this time that Sampson wrote and published the first edition of his memoirs, entitled *Paratrooper Padre,* with The Catholic University of America Press in 1948, which detailed his experiences in the Second World War. Nearly all the material in this edition is replicated in *Look Out Below!* The memoir was an immediate hit in its initial publication and raised Sampson's profile considerably throughout the country. In late 1949, the 11th Airborne, nicknamed the Angels, were sent back stateside to Fort Campbell, Kentucky, to conduct pioneering training work focused on using gliders to launch airborne assaults as opposed to parachute drops. It was an experience Sampson enjoyed considerably less than his time in Japan, although the environment for the Angels soon changed with the outbreak of the Korean War.[10]

Along with the Berlin Blockade, the Korean War was one of the pivotal events of the earliest stages of the Cold War, the four-decade-long political, economic, and military conflict between the former members of the Grand Alliance during the Second World War. The entire world, but especially Europe and eastern Asia, became the battleground between the Soviet Union and the West, in particular the United States and the United Kingdom. A former colony of China and later of Japan, Korea gained its short-lived independence following the unconditional surrender of Japan in 1945, as the country was divided along the 38th Parallel between the Soviets in the north and the Americans in south, per the agreements made between Stalin and Truman at Potsdam in August 1945. The Soviet-sponsored state in the north, with a provisional capital at Pyongyang, was led by Kim Il-Sung, who had fought with Soviet-sponsored partisans against the Japanese, while the American-constructed state in the south, with its capital in Seoul, was headed by Syngman Rhee, a conservative Methodist Korean nationalist who had spent many years in the United States. Original United Nations plans for elections toward a unified Korea never occurred, as neither Kim nor Rhee were willing to tolerate open and fair elections. By late 1948, both sides were sponsoring armed raids across the 38th Parallel and asked their respective patrons in Moscow and Washing-

---

10. Fort Campbell, Kentucky, remains in operation today, and was the birthplace of the author of this introduction.

ton for permission to unify the Korean peninsula through force of arms. Truman continually rejected these requests, as the State Department and the Pentagon disagreed on whether Republic of Korea was part of the American defensive perimeter in the Pacific. However, Kim's ambitions were ultimately supported by Stalin, and also by China's dictator Mao Zedong, who had overrun the *Kuomin-tang* (Nationalist) armies of Chiang Kai-Shek and had driven them to exile in Taiwan in 1949. As day broke on Sunday June 25, 1950, the North Korean Army crossed the 38th Parallel in a full invasion of South Korea. Two days later Syngman Rhee evacuated his government from Seoul and headed southwards to Pusan. When news of the invasion reached Washington, D.C., President Truman quickly determined, after discussing matters with Secretary of State Dean Acheson and Secretary of Defense George Marshall, to provide all aid necessary to repel the North Korean invasion. The invasion was seen as a battle of wills between the American government and the Soviet Union, as well as their Asian allies in Beijing and Pyongyang. If the West failed in this test of resolve, Truman believed, other Communist invasions elsewhere were sure to occur, the first certainly being in Germany.

Truman's UN ambassador, Warren Austin, took advantage of a Soviet boycott of the United Nations security council to pass a condemnation of the North Korean invasion in resolution 82, while the following resolution 83 called upon UN members to provide soldiers for a police action, authorized by the UN Secretary General Trygve Lie, to repel the North Korean armed forces north of the 38th Parallel. While over twenty countries would provide aid in some capacity, the two countries that contributed the majority of soldiers under the UN command were the United States and South Korea. Despite these developments, the South Korean forces, weakened by desertions and encirclements, as well as the undermanned American units rushed over from Japan, were only slowing the North Korean advance, and by the middle of August 1950 the UN forces had been pressed into a small perimeter in Pusan on the southeastern part of the peninsula.[11]

11. The Soviets had been boycotting the UN since January 1950 over American and French refusal to seat the delegates from Mao's regime in the UN Security Council to replace those of Chiang Kai-Shek's government, which had fled to Taiwan.

Sampson and the other members of the 11th Airborne were not among the first divisions of the US military sent over to fight in Korea following Kim Il-Sung's invasion. In fact, the Army had actually instructed Sampson to attend further graduate courses in theology at the University of Notre Dame in early August. As the situation on the Korean peninsula became progressively worse, however, more and more divisions stationed in the United States, including the 11th Airborne, were sent to the Pacific to prevent the North Korean army from overrunning the entire peninsula. One unique aspect of the Korean war was that many of the American soldiers were veterans of either the European or Pacific theatres of the Second World War and were now fighting alongside those who had served on the other end of the world just a few years before. One group of American servicemen who impressed Sampson were the US Marines, especially their discipline and patriotism, as he mentions several times in his chapter on his experiences in Korea.[12] A few weeks after the arrival of the 11th Airborne, General Douglas MacArthur, one of the architects of the defeat of the Empire of Japan during the Second World War and the Supreme Commander of the United Nations Command, launched an ambitious and ultimately successful attack on the North Korean position at the harbor of Inchon deep behind the enemy lines.

Shortly after this stunning victory in early September, as the UN forces marched to the Yalu River on the Chinese and Soviet borders with Korea, Sampson found himself taking part in an event unparalleled in the history of the Cold War: the liberation of a Communist capital by a Western coalition. Pyongyang fell to the UN Forces on October 19, 1950, and soon it was flooded with refugees fleeing Kim Il-Sung's regime. As Sampson mentions, he also had the grim task of traveling with the United Nations Atrocity Committee to visit the mass graves of the thousands of victims of Kim Il-Sung's government outside the city limits. Since some of the victims were

---

12. Another group of soldiers who made a clear impression on Sampson were those from Turkey, which had recently joined the NATO alliance. He noted they were ferocious fighters who never allowed themselves to be taken prisoner. The participation of Turkish soldiers in the Korean War was a plot point in the famous American sitcom *MASH,* specifically episode twelve of the third season, "A Full Rich Day."

identified as Christians, and thus enemies of the militantly atheistic North Korean regime, Sampson also performed last rites for them, along with other chaplains serving with the forces under United Nations command. While Lie, Truman, and MacArthur hoped the United Nations forces could soon unite Korea under Syngman Rhee's leadership following elections supervised by the United Nations, such was not to be the case. Mao was determined not to let Kim's regime fall, and, with significant military support from the Soviets, launched a major offensive, sending over a million soldiers across the Yalu River against the UN coalition.

The invasion took MacArthur completely by surprise, and soon the UN forces were on full retreat. Sampson recounts that he and the rest of the 11th Airborne were forced to abandon Pyongyang on December 6 and eventually retreat across the 38th Parallel. Seoul would fall to the Communists again shortly thereafter, and soon an increasingly desperate MacArthur got into a public dispute with Truman, calling both for the use of atomic weapons against Chinese military targets and sponsorship of an invasion of China itself, spear-headed by Chiang Kai-Shek's soldiers brought from Taiwan. Ulti-mately in March 1951 Truman removed MacArthur from command, leading to a public firestorm in America that dragged on for the rest of his presidency. It was arguably during this four-month period that the risk of a direct war between the Soviet Union and the United States was at its highest, as American and Soviet fighters actively tried to shoot each other down over the skies of Korea, and Sampson was right at the center of it.[13] In the late spring of 1951, MacArthur's replacement, General Matthew Ridgway, was able to retake Seoul and stabilize the front along the 38th Parallel, where the fighting would continue for the next two years until an armistice signed between the UN, North Korean, and Chinese delegations at the vil-lage of Panmunjom on July 27, 1953, brought an end to the war.

Unlike his experience in the Second World War, Sampson was not in the Korean conflict until its conclusion. Avoiding encir-

13. The Cuban Missile Crisis, often seen as the highpoint of tensions in the Cold War, lasted only two weeks in October 1962. In comparison, the period from Chinese intervention in the Korean War to the return of the UN forces to the 38th Parallel lasted almost six months.

clement and capture in the great retreat south ahead of the Chinese advance, Sampson was sent on leave to Tokyo in February, which was extended into March due to some medical issues. Following his discharge from the hospital, Sampson was sent back stateside, bringing an end to his second war. He was more fortunate than some of his fellow other officers in the Chaplain Corps. Another famous Army chaplain who had served in the Second World War was Father Emil Kapaun, a graduate of the Catholic University of America and a chaplain in the US Army's First Cavalry Division. Kapaun was among the tens of thousands of Americans captured by the Chinese and North Koreans in early November 1950. Held in atrocious conditions characterized by malnutrition, filth, and brutal cold, many of those taken prisoner by the Communist forces did not survive. Kapaun, like the four other American chaplains taken prisoner in 1950, died in captivity. Ultimately twelve other American chaplains would perish in Korea during the conflict.

Upon arrival home, Sampson then completed his graduate work in theology at Notre Dame, and, given his extensive combat experience in the Second World War and Korea, spent two years as an instructor for chaplains in training at Fort Slocum in Long Island, New York, until 1955. He then returned to Germany to spend the next three years with the 11th Airborne, which had once again been reassigned. By this point, the former Third Reich had been divided into two states. The Soviet occupation zone, founded in October 1949, became the German Democratic Republic, Germany's other dictatorship of the twentieth century, modeled on the Soviet Union such as similar regimes in Poland, Hungary, Czechoslovakia, Romania, and Bulgaria. A month earlier, the British, French, and American zones merged to become the Federal Republic of Germany, which, after a difficult birth marked by economic impoverishment and political paralysis, had stabilized by the time of Sampson's arrival. West Germany, as the Federal Republic was nicknamed, joined NATO as a full member and was allowed to create its own army, the *Bundeswehr,* the year of Sampson's arrival in 1955. As this army did not yet exist, soldiers from NATO allies France, Britain, and especially the United States protected West Germany. The 11th Airborne was stationed in a large military facility of *kaserne* (barracks) in the Bavarian city of Augsburg, which had been previously used by the German Army during the

Second World War. Sampson is diplomatic during this section of the memoir, admitting his mixed feelings about the Germans due to the Nazi atrocities during the Second World War, but expresses confidence to his readers that the German people had changed, and were not going to be a threat to the peace of the world any longer. It was during this time that Sampson wrote *Look Out Below!*, an expansion of his earlier work *Paratrooper Padre*, with extra material on the Second World War as well as his activities in Korea and West Germany. He concluded the memoir with a tribute to many of the soldiers he had served with throughout his military career.

Look Out Below! was published in 1958, the year Sampson returned to the United States. He spent another thirteen years in the US Army Chaplain Corps, eventually rising to the rank of Major General and serving as the Chief of Chaplains from 1967 to 1971 during the height of the Vietnam War. Upon his retirement, he had been awarded sixteen citations, including the highly prestigious Distinguished Service Cross for his actions at Normandy during D-Day. He then returned to his beloved Iowa to serve as a parish priest once again, in this case at Saint Mary's in Shenandoah, located in the southwestern part of the state. He also had stints as the head of the United Service Organization (USO) from 1974 to 1976, and in one of his last assignments, he spent the years of 1983 to 1987 as the director of ROTC back at the University of Notre Dame. Following this assignment, Sampson retired to Sioux Falls, South Dakota, and passed away of cancer on January 23, 1996. He was buried in Luverne, Minnesota, with the traditional American military grave marker that his service in the Second World War, Korea, and Vietnam, as well as the famous invocation of Saint Francis of Assisi to "Make Me an Instrument of Your Peace."

From the training facilities of Fort Benning to the gates of Stalag II-A in Mecklenburg-Vorpommern to the ruins of Pyongyang, Sampson led one of the most distinguished careers of any chaplain in the US military during the twentieth century. His writings, especially *Look Out Below!*, provide a unique and valuable insight into some of the most important events of the last one hundred years. Sampson's unsentimental yet fervent religiosity was the perfect anecdote to the dark times in which he served his fellow soldiers, his country, and his God.

Cardinals Residence
452 Madison Avenue
New York 22

February 8, 1958

Rev. Francis L. Sampson, Chaplain
Headquarters VII Corps
APO 107
New York, New York

Dear Father Sampson:

I am delighted to know that your book, which I read originally when it appeared as a serial in *The American Ecclesiastical Review* under the title of *Paratrooper Padre,* has been such a success that you are about to publish a new edition including additional chapters on the Korean conflict and on your occupation duties in Japan and postwar service in Germany.

The title *Look Out Below!* is indeed most appropriate and descriptive of the life of a paratrooper and a paratrooper padre. Congratulating you on your priestly zeal and soldierly heroism and asking God to continue to bless you and your works, and with kind regards and best wishes, I am

Very sincerely yours in Christ,

† F. Cardinal Spellman, *Archbishop of New York*

Foreword

The ascetic Cardinal Newman, when a young man, stated that the army life had a great attraction for him because it was essentially a life of service to an ideal, to the protection of others. The same appeal has motivated all truly Christian soldiers.

In fact, the idealism and sacred character of a soldier's life is embodied in our Christian terminology. In the Roman Empire, the most sacred oath was that taken by the soldier as he was admitted to the army. The word for that oath was *sacramentum.* The Christians, searching for the most sacred word to express the institutions of Christ whereby we secure grace, used that word to denote this concept.

Today, possibly more than ever, a soldier's devotion is needed to protect and to inspire our country. For in a materialistic society, where advance and success are measured largely in dollars, we need a soldiers devotion to an ideal to remind us that the basis of our national life is its devotion to principle, not to wealth. The armed forces are one of the few institutions in our country devoted entirely to the ideal of service to others. This nation, founded on the defense of our mutual rights, cannot survive without devotion to those principles and rights.

Obviously, this religious motivation and devotion cannot exist without the services of the chaplain. Christian virtue, sustained and nurtured by the sacraments, demands the devoted services of a priest. This is true in every Christians life but especially in the life of a soldier, particularly when his duty carries him into the valley of death.

Nowhere is that bond between soldier and priest-soldier closer and more tightly knit than in the airborne service. The morale and feeling of kinship in any unit spring from the sharing of common risks and dangers. Those who wear the jumpers boots belong to a group whose survival depends upon the unwavering courage of each man. The life of each is in the hands of his neighbor. Those who risk the dangers coming from "hitting the silk" form a society whose common loyalties and feelings are unknown to those who have never experienced them. It is a group in which pride of unit must be high, where top performance is accepted as commonplace, where each man is superior because unique courage is the price of admission. In such a unit, always in high gear, the chaplain is as indispensable as he is beloved.

To control and direct the spirit of the trooper is a mighty challenge to a chaplain. "To be all things to all men that I might gain all" is the necessary approach.

The amazing success of Father Sampson is explained by his uncanny ability to identify himself completely with the paratrooper and thus "gain all for Christ." His exploits and escapes were legendary, but these were secondary to his constant care of the souls of all his men.

† Philip M. Hannan
Auxiliary Bishop of Washington Chancellor

Acknowledgments

I wish to express my thanks to His Eminence Francis Cardinal Spellman for his Foreword to this book; to the Most Reverend Philip M. Hannan for his Preface; to Lieutenant General Thomas F. Hickey for his Introduction; and to Chaplain (Major General) Patrick J. Ryan for the tribute to the members of the Chaplains Corps which closes the book.

Declan X. McMullen Co., Inc., and Mrs. Lawrence Critchell graciously permitted me to quote the Introduction to the late Mr. Critchells *Four Stars in Hell* by Lieutenant General Lewis H. Brereton, now deceased.

The following present and former airborne commanders very kindly responded to my request that they write a paragraph or two on any aspect of airborne they might choose. These tributes to the trooper constitute Part V.

General Matthew B. Ridgway, US Army (Retired)
General Maxwell D. Taylor, US Army
General Anthony C. McAuliffe, US Army (Retired)
Lt General Joseph M. Swing, US Army (Retired)
Lt. General James M. Gavin, US Army (Retired)
Lt. General Lemuel Mathewson, US Army
Lt. General Frank W. Farrell, US Army
Major General William Miley, US Army (Retired)
Major General Joseph P. Cleland, US Army (Retired)
Major General Robert F. Sink, US Army
Major General Hugh P. Harris, US Army
Major General Thomas L. Sherburne, US Army
Brig. General James D. Alger, US Army
Colonel Edson D. Raff, US Army
Colonel Julian J. Ewell, US Army
Colonel H. W. O. Kinnard, US Army

I am grateful to the Army Signal Corps and to the 11th Airborne Division Public Information Office for permission to use the pictures that are in this book.

Reverend Edmond D. Benard of The Catholic University of America was kind enough to read the proofs of this book, and it was his encouragement that prompted me to write it.

The photographs on pages 2, 17, 37, 48, 73, 87, 96,148,186, and 188 are official US Army photographs.

Introduction

Little did the Apostles know, when they were sent out to bring the Word of God and the life of grace to all men until the consummation of the world, that some of their successors would ordain priests who would become airborne to continue this mission! The history of military chaplains in the Christian era is a glorious one, but one of its most remarkable chapters was written by the airborne chaplains of the United States Army in World War II and on Korean battlefields. They became, in a special sense, athletes for Christ.

Into the night skies over Normandy, over the lowlands of Holland, into the biting cold of Belgian winter winds, over the deep valleys of Luzon and Korea, they jumped with the troopers to bring them the life and strength that only religion can give. The physical bravery of the airborne chaplains, their supernatural courage, and their total devotion to their mission for God and country deserve the grateful admiration of their fellow soldiers and of all Americans.

Look Out Below! is, I believe, the first book about the airborne to be written by one of these remarkable priests of God who leaped behind enemy lines and into the midst of combat with no weapon other than the sword of the spirit, no protection other than the shield of faith. Here is the story of the airborne troopers told by the one who knew them best and with insights only a priest could possess. It is sometimes humorous, sometimes tragic, often heroic, but always honest and inspiring as seen through the understanding and sympathetic eyes of the paratrooper padre.

Thomas F. Hickey
Lieutenant General, US Army
Third Army Headquarters
Fort McPherson, Georgia

Author's Introduction

Following World War II and the conflict in Korea the book market was flooded with war accounts written from almost every point of view. Brass hats have given the public the "big picture." Their aides have tried to show the human side of the brass hats. Practically every corps, wing, division, and regiment has a book describing its part in the war. Each campaign, battle, operation, and engagement has been exploited in print with no tactical detail slighted. Ernie Pyle led a host of writers in giving to the public the GI point of view, paying proper tribute to the men who were represented in groups of thousands by tiny movable pins on the operational map, men who had no part in the conduct of the war except to do the fighting, the sweating, the bleeding, and the dying. Mauldins "Willie and Joe" and Bakers "Sad Sack," both now in book form, gave some comic relief by holding the mirror up to nature and making the soldier laugh at the reflection of his own experiences of frustration in the Army. Gruesome pictorial books have given to millions a vicarious experience of the sickening sensation of fear and a realistic glance at the ghastliness of the grim years 1939 through 1953 in war-torn countries.

Still the manuscripts keep pouring in, each with a new angle on the subject, with a new point of view, with the latest statistical data, something on the horrors of Dachau or of Pyongyang, a revelation of the brilliant tactical strokes of a hitherto obscure general, the mistakes of some great military leader, scandals in high places, the latest humorous side, the involved diplomatic phase, the ethical aspects, biographical sketches, autobiographical accounts. Generals, privates, war correspondents, Red Cross workers, doctors, patients, ex-Nazis, converted Communists, displaced persons, churchmen, Congressional representatives, playwrights, novelists, and poets have belabored World War II and Korea until one would think (and devoutly hope) that the depressing material has just about been exhausted.

What possible excuse can there be then, one might reasonably ask, for another book on the subject, especially a book by a priest whose calling might seem to dictate a more peaceable, more elevating theme? Another question might very logically suggest itself. If a priest is supposed to practice the virtue of humility, why should a Catholic chaplain write an autobiographical account of war experiences?

In answering the first question I should like to make the observation that a priest sees war from a standpoint different from that of anyone else. He is more interested in what is going on inside men than in what is going on outside them. To him the souls of men are even more involved in combat than their bodies; their spiritual resources are more vital to real success than any material factors. The eternal life of a man is as much at stake there as his physical life, and the sacraments of Penance and the Holy Eucharist were healing the wounds of his soul while blood plasma, penicillin, and the sulfa drugs were healing the wounds of his body. And it is quite possible that in the providence of God many a man was the better prepared for death that came, not as a thief in the night, but as an ever-expected guide to his eternal home. As a priest, I write from this point of view.

The second question is a bit more difficult to answer. I know a great many chaplains who, from the standpoint of background, experiences, ability, and spirituality, are far better equipped than I am to give an insight into the army priests thoughts and reactions in the service and in combat. Unfortunately for all of us, however, very few of these capable men have borne witness in print to their extraordinary experiences.

Like many a GI during World War II, I wrote in some detail to my family about the experiences we were having. There was never any thought at the time that those letters might one day be published. A member of the Faculty of Sacred Theology at The Catholic University of America happened to read the letters and asked if I would be willing to allow extracts from them to be published in *The American Ecclesiastical Review* in the form of a series of articles under the title, "Paratrooper Padre." The articles were favorably received, and I was urged to have them published in book form. In due course the book *Paratrooper Padre* was published. It has now been completely revised and brought up to date. New chapters have been added dealing with the Korean conflict and duty in post-war Germany. The final part of the book is composed of testimonials to the airborne soldier by some of the great generals who have been fortunate enough to command paratroopers, and by the Chief of Chaplains. I am grateful to these officers for responding to my request.

A personal narration of the war action I saw in Germany and in Korea must necessarily be autobiographical and may seem a bit egotistical because of the predominant use of the first person. Please remember that no pair of knees ever shook more than my own in times of danger and that the use of the pronoun T simply bears personal witness to the quiet heroism of those "devils in baggy pants" (as the Germans called them) who parachuted into combat, fought, bled, and died so bravely in Normandy, Holland, Bastogne, and Korea.

These pages may give you the false impression that combat life is always exciting. As a matter of fact, it is for the most part monotonous; the greater part of every soldier's job is mere routine. I have written down only the interesting incidents as I recall them and have not bothered about our plan or strategy or what we accomplished or failed to accomplish tactically. There were many days when nothing of great interest or import happened as far as my unit was concerned. These pages give you only the high-lights of my own limited view and experience in the war against Germany and in the "police action" of Korea.

F. L. S.

PART I

Airborne Training

Chaplain (Lt. Col.) Francis L. Sampson

CHAPTER 1

Parachute School at Fort Benning

I N 1942 the Chaplain School was located at Harvard University. Although I was only one year ordained, my bishop, Most Reverend Gerald T. Bergan of Des Moines, had granted me permission to enter the Army, and I was taking the indoctrination course for chaplains at Harvard. At this time the Army asked for volunteer chaplains for the paratroops. Like a zealous young business man starting out in a strange town, I was ready to join anything out of a sheer sense of civic duty. Frankly I did not know when I signed up for the airborne that chaplains would be expected to jump from an airplane in flight. Had I known this beforehand, and particularly had I known the tortures of mind and body prepared at Fort Benning for those who sought the coveted parachute wings, I am positive that I should have turned a deaf ear to the plea for airborne chaplains. However, once having signed up, I was too proud to back out. Besides, the airborne are the elite troops of the Army, and I already began to enjoy the prestige and glamour that goes with belonging to such an outfit.

I literally basked in the praise bestowed upon me by the other chaplains, who didn't know that I had signed up without realizing that I would be required to jump. Had they guessed my predicament, the whole school would have had a good laugh at my expense. It has remained, however, my own deep dark secret until now.

The day I arrived at Fort Benning to begin jump training, I received a wire from my brother in The Dalles, Oregon, stating that my mother was very ill. On my way west I called up from Chicago, only to learn that she had died that day. Her body was brought back to Luverne, Minnesota, the place of her birth and childhood; the place she always called "home," the place she loved above all others.

My mother had always worked hard, very hard. As dad was the manager of a small-town hotel, mother took care of the food end of the business and for years did the cooking. Her life was filled with many worries and heartaches, but she always kept her keen sense of humor and Irish wit. The help and guests of the hotel loved her, for her kind and affable nature made the place a home rather than a lodging house. With scarcely a wrinkle in her face or a grey hair in her head, she looked like a young girl as she lay in her coffin.

She had often expressed the wish that her hair might turn grey; she wanted to look matronly, like the mother of three grown men. The failure of her hair to turn grey can in no way be attributed to the boyhood behavior of her three sons, for if ever a mother had been given cause for worry, and if worry is truly the requisite for grey hair, then my mothers should have been as white as snow. She had often dwelt on the thought that I would one day say her Funeral Mass, and she had spoken of it in a manner of real anticipation and delight. I suppose only the mother of a priest can understand that.

After the funeral, I prepared to return to the Fort Benning jump school, and I discovered that the prospect of jumping from a plane did not seem nearly as hazardous as it had before my mothers death. I realized then that the great mental hazard in parachute jumping was more the subconscious concern for one's family and dependents than for one's own safety; not, of course, that the latter was ever absent. This fact has been demonstrated over and over again, and I think it could be authenticated by almost every parachutist. I am sure the wives and mothers of paratroopers suffered the fearful anticipation of the next jump more keenly than did the jumpers. As a matter of fact, after several successful jumps the paratrooper gains a certain degree of confidence that is not shared by those who must wait at the phone for the familiar voice, "Made it O.K., darling. The landing was perfect"; or for the dreaded professional voice, "This is the Fort Benning Station Hospital. Your husband . . . ."

I vowed when I was going through the agony of jump school that I would never say anything good about it. It was even tougher than it was reputed to be. In all fairness, however, it must be admitted that the desired results were actually obtained, and the qualities of physical fitness, determination, and aggressiveness nursed at Benning bore fruit in Normandy, in Holland, then at Bastogne, and much later, in another war, in Korea. I shall try in the next few pages to be as objective about the airborne jump school as the memory of my sweating body, bruised skin and bones, aching muscles, abused dignity, and deflated ego will permit. If a note of acidity is detectable in my description of the jump school, I would ask the reader kindly to remember that it is entirely premeditated and intentional.

When I reported in at the school, the adjutant told me that the two previous chaplains to enroll were now in the hospital, one with a broken leg, the other with an injured back. My expression must have been both comic and tragic, for he looked at me and laughed, then said encouragingly, "But three or four chaplains have already gone through the school successfully."

I made a noise in my throat that was meant to be a chuckle and said with an assurance I was far from feeling, "I guess if they can make it, I can."

The school was divided into four weeks of intensive training called Stages A, B, C, and D. With seventy-seven other officers I reported May first to the chief instructor of A Stage. The training was conducted by sergeants who gloried in the fulfillment of an enlisted mans dream . . . to be in a position of authority over commissioned officers. Most of the sergeants were former professional athletes or acrobats. The word and order of a training sergeant was as absolute as any order of a commanding officer to his subordinates. One lieutenant colonel who spoke sharply to a training sergeant and refused to obey the sergeant's orders was made to apologize in the presence of the entire class assembled and was then dismissed from the school. They meant business here; they played no favorites, and any man who failed to fulfill the rugged requirements was washed out. Colonels were dropped as readily as second looeys; doctors and chaplains were given the boot as ruthlessly as line officers. Those who failed thereafter spoke of the school in terms of bitterness and hatred; even those who eventually made the grade would always recall the four eternal weeks with more repugnance and revulsion than pride.

Calisthenics and long runs constituted A Stage. I thought that I was in fairly good physical condition when I arrived at Benning, but the first morning of calisthenics—more than three hours of it—convinced me that I was as flabby and soft as any sergeant-major in the

Quartermaster Corps. We finished the morning with a forty-minute run under a broiling Georgia sun, leaving almost a fourth of the class stretched out at intervals along the road. Some had quit in anger; others ran until physically incapable of going farther; some were out cold. The "meat wagon" (ambulance, to the civilian) picked them up. Those who finished the run arrived at the barracks at the stroke of twelve and, drenched in sweat, completely exhausted, tired, and worn out even beyond the ability to curse the school, flopped on their bunks, unable to make the effort to go across the road for dinner. Food wasn't interesting. A shower required energy to take off fatigues. We only wanted rest, *rest*, r-e-s-t. Most of us dozed in our sweaty and smelly fatigues until they blew that infernal whistle again at one p.m.

We had the same schedule in the afternoon as in the morning, except that there was a little judo thrown in, plus several tries at the obstacle course. We always finished up with the inevitable run. I did rather badly with the calisthenics. I never could seem to get the hang of climbing the rope, and the Indian-club exercises left my arms limp and lifeless long before the sergeant said, "Enough." I finally learned to do fifty push-ups, but I was almost the last man in the class to do it. I could recommend to the Trappist monks the duck-waddle and squat jumps as a penance more agonizing than any hair-shirt. The only thing that kept me from being washed out of A Stage was the fact that I never dropped out of a run.

Only the toughest of the students would sacrifice precious hours of sleep for a movie at night. In the evening after supper, saying the Breviary in the quiet of the chapel was restful; but I do hope there is some truth to the old legend about the angels finishing the rosary for those who fall asleep from fatigue while saying it. Mass at six a.m. would begin another day just like the last.

The crowded barracks of seventy-eight officers had slipped to a comfortable thirty-eight by the end of the first week. Many of them had quit the first couple of days, but not before telling the sergeants and everyone connected with the school what they thought of it— and in terms not permitted in these pages.

B Stage, the second week of training, was much more interest-ing. During this stage we employed the many ingenious gadgets designed to simulate parachute jumping. The first prop was the fuselage of a plane from which the wings had been removed. They seated twenty-two of us in it at a time, and we were shown how to stand up properly in a plane, how to hook up the strap that pulls the top off the parachute pack, how to check the equipment of the man in front of us, how to respond to the orders of the jump master, and how to make a proper exit from the plane. We began to get cocky; jumping was going to be simple.

Then they took us to the landing trainer. This is a fiendish device by which the student is hooked up in a jumpers harness attached to a roller that slides down a long incline. At any moment he chooses, and always when you least expect it, the sergeant pulls a lever that drops you to the ground while you are traveling about twenty miles an hour. The idea is to hang on to your risers, duck your head between your knees as soon as you touch the ground, and go rolling along like a ball. Failure to duck quickly enough means that you go sliding along the cinders on your face. If you displeased the sergeant by your performance, he generally made you double-time around the training area several times, holding your risers aloft and telling everyone what you did wrong. I was given eight laps and had to shout to every man I passed, "I'm a bad chaplain, I dropped my risers!"

At no time during jump school were we permitted to walk; always double-time. Nor were we allowed to lean against anything or have our hands in our pockets. For violations of these rules push-ups were the punishment. One morning while a sergeant was giving a demonstration, I happened to yawn. "All right, Chaplain, give me fifty push-ups." I got through forty-two and couldn't budge another muscle to save my life. I continued to lie on the ground exhausted, supremely indifferent to the jibes of the sergeant and the laughter of the other officers.

The mock-up tower was a thirty-eight foot platform with a long cable extending on an incline to a big soft pile of sawdust. After the hook-up to the cable, the sergeant would give the signal to jump. The exit, the drop, and the jerk from the cable closely simulated an actual jump. The ride to the sawdust pile was fun at first, but each succeeding jump from this tower seemed much farther from the ground. We had more men quit the school during this phase than we did later on during the actual jump from an airplane in flight. The sergeant failed to hook up one man properly for his jump from the tower, and the man fell all the way to the ground. Fortunately he only sustained a fractured foot, but our confidence in the sergeant in charge was considerably shaken.

The "trainasium" was another of the elaborate props—a forty-foot-high maze of bars, catwalks, ladders, and so forth. There was only one other in the world like it, and that was at the parachute school in Germany. We hoped the Germans had as many accidents on theirs as we had on ours.

The afternoons of B Stage were spent in the packing sheds, where we learned to pack our own chutes. This was supposed to give us confidence in the chutes, but most of us would have preferred to leave the job to a professional packer. Our first five jumps would be made with chutes we packed ourselves. This really worried me, for I had no confidence in the bulging, lopsided, twisted thing that had taken me an hour and a half to pack. The sergeant told us, however, that you could jump a chute thrown in a barracks bag and it would open. The occasional "streamers" in the preceding classes didn't seem to warrant such confidence.

C Stage and the 250-foot "free towers" were next. We took turns in being hoisted to the top of the tower and released. Floating down from that height is pleasant, but the closer you get to the ground the faster you seem to drop. The earth seems to be rushing up to meet you . . . must remember the proper landing technique . . . feet a few inches apart, toes pointing down, chin in, hands on risers, body neither tense nor relaxed. The instructors voice over the loudspeaker from the tower, "Don't stretch for the ground! Make a half turn to the right!" It was too late; I landed like a sack of flour. But the body is a wonderful thing; it can collapse and fold up like an accordion, thus absorbing without injury the greatest part of a bad landing. I was quite satisfied with myself even though the instructor was not, for I could get up and haul the chute back to the tower without help. I could speak with the voice of experience to the next fellow in line still sweating out his first drop from the free tower.

There was a young second lieutenant in our class, a Polish lad, who had taken the whole course in stride. He was small—about a hundred and thirty pounds I'd guess—and the calisthenics and runs had seemed ridiculously easy for him. When given fifty pushups for leaning against a post, he asked the sergeant, "With which hand do you want me to give them?" Most of us could scarcely do the required fifty with both hands, but he did them with his left hand and was almost as fresh when he finished as when he began.

On Saturday morning at the close of C Stage a two-hundred-pound rugged first lieutenant in charge of the officers going through this stage said that he would like to have the chance of separating the men from the boys in the judo pit; and that if any of us thought that we could stay with him three minutes, he'd be glad to give us the opportunity. The young Polish officer stepped out. "I'd like a chance to try, sir." We felt that he had gotten in over his head this time, for the instructor was really clever and fast and had about seventy pounds advantage. But in less than thirty seconds the instructor was flat on his back. Our morale jumped a hundred per cent, and the young lieutenant became the hero of the school, for no one, including the sergeant instructors, liked the arrogant instructor of C Stage. We learned later that after completing his jump training the young Polish officer became the instructor in charge of C Stage.

D Stage was devoted to actually jumping from a plane and qualifying with five such jumps as a parachutist. Confessions Saturday afternoon and evening were very heavy, for besides the officers class there was a class of 800 enlisted men prepared to make their five qualifying jumps. Many of the men a long time away from the sacraments began to see the light. I doubt that any sermon could more effectively bring men to a realization of the importance of being in the state of grace than the prospect of a jump. Communions on Sunday were an inspiration, and I thought that if this was the effect of the anticipated jump, then parachuting ought to be mandatory for all young men in the service. It was easy, too, to visualize hundreds of mothers and fathers, wives and sweethearts, brothers and sisters, friends and nuns, each remembering in Communion that morning the intention of some boy who was going to leap from a plane twelve hundred feet above the earth with nothing between himself and destruction but a piece of silk.

Monday morning dawned bright and warm. This was it! In an hour or two we would be experiencing the granddaddy of all thrills. We were "sweating the jump out," and none of us had slept very well that night; but we would have been really disappointed had the weather been bad and the jump postponed. Scarcely anyone touched his eggs at breakfast, and the usual jokes, about turning in your chute if it didn't open and getting a new one, were absent this morning. Even the jump school song, "Gory, Gory, What a Helluva Way to Die," sung to the tune of "The Battle Hymn of the Republic," was neglected. Each man was wrapped in his own thoughts as we marched to the packing sheds to pick up the chutes we had packed for ourselves. Each of us checked the all-important break cord on his chute over and over again. All sorts of tragic possibilities crowded in on our imaginations as we tried to concentrate on the jump masters instructions.

"Don't get excited. Stay cool!" he shouted. "Just remember what you have been taught. Don't stand up before you get the signal; don't crowd towards the door. Follow the man in front of you quickly, but don't go out on his back. Keep your chin in until the chute opens, and then check your canopy. If you should happen to have a streamer—you won't, these chutes always open—*but if you should have a streamer,* just pull your reserve and throw it away from your body so you wont get tangled in the suspension lines. Now listen, you men, you're a good class, and I don't think there is a yellow guy here. I don't want anyone freezing in the door; I don't want any quitters! Now put on your helmets and line up."

They divided us up so that one officer would lead each group or "stick" of ten enlisted men. As I left the officers to join the ten enlisted men in my stick, a lieutenant who had often said to me that he wished that he had been brought up in some religion, quipped, "I hope your Boss isn't mad at us today, Chaplain."

Just before we boarded the plane, a little red-headed fellow next to me said, "Father, I was on duty Saturday night and didn't get a chance to go to confession. It has only been a couple of weeks, but I sure would like to go."

"But the motors will start up in a minute," I replied. "You had better make it snappy." With the rest of the men wondering what was going on, he leaned over and whispered in my ear. After the absolution I asked him, "Do you feel better now?"

"Father," he said with a grin, "that was better than a reserve chute."

As the plane taxied across the runway, the men fell silent. The plane picked up speed, and everyone's jaw muscles tightened, and, as if to show that it was deliberate, each man adjusted the two chin straps on his helmet. The air became cooler in the cabin, and when the plane had cleared the pine trees at the end of the runway, the jumpmaster eased the tension somewhat by walking down the aisle and helping the men loosen their safety belts. He lit a cigarette, and we followed suit. The plane circled over the packing sheds, and we saw hundreds of tiny men down there waiting for these planes to dump their human cargo and come back to take them up for the identical insane purpose. Fort Benning looked awfully small from the air; the baseball park resembled a billiard table, and the muddy Chattahoochee seemed tiny enough to step across. I spotted a Catholic chapel, and for a moment in spirit I knelt before the Blessed Sacrament.

"STAND UP!" shouted the jumpmaster. He was standing in the open door, and the prop blast wrinkled and whipped the skin of his face like a dish towel in the wind. My legs turned to jelly, and there were butterflies in my stomach. Why couldn't I have been satisfied in some other branch of the service like the . . .

"HOOK UP!" We hooked our snap fasteners onto the cable. Hand around the inside of the static line just below the snap . . . that's right. Dozens of instructions began to race through my head . . . "jump clear of the door . . . keep chin in close . . . don't forget to count . . . check the canopy . . . don't forget to count!" They told us that a man could fall all the way to the ground before he knew it, if he forgot to count. I must remember, "Don't forget to count!"

"CHECK YOUR EQUIPMENT!" Each man glanced at the chute of the man in front of him to be sure that it hadn't broken open prematurely.

The last man in the stick called out, "Ten O.K.!" as he slapped the leg of the man in front of him.

"Nine O.K."

"Eight O.K." and so on down to myself.

"One O.K., Sergeant," I said as the pilot throttled the engines down and the red light just over the door went on.

"STAND IN THE DOOR!" The jump master stepped aside, and I took his place in the door. The men were pressing against each other. The plane was rocking and losing some altitude. The green light went on.

"ARE YOU READY?"

The men broke the tension with a roar, "ALL READY!"

"LET'S GO!"

The jumpmaster slapped my leg, and out I went. My exit must have been poor, for the prop blast spun me like a top. Head over heels I went, aware of nothing but my absolute helplessness. I forgot to count. The only rule that I observed was keeping my chin pressed into my chest. It was a good thing I remembered that, for, just as the chute opened with a loud smack jerking me almost into unconsciousness, I felt the sharp sting of the suspension lines strike my face. In a fraction of a second the opening of the chute slowed me down from almost ninety miles an hour to zero. Suddenly everything was quiet and peaceful. This quiet and peace of being alone, suspended between heaven and earth by a beautiful canopy of silk, was a pleasant sensation. The thrill was nothing at all like what I had expected. The excitement, nervousness, and tension were gone, replaced by a feeling of great satisfaction and genuine enjoyment. The descent was scarcely perceptible, and every second of it was precious. I remember that I had that same feeling once before, as a little boy, when I rode an escalator down a flight in a Minneapolis department store.

As I neared the ground, the rate of descent seemed to increase greatly. I grasped my risers and made half a body turn to get the wind to my back. (This is done by grasping the risers above the head with arms crossed and then pulling down.) *Then I hit!* Something snapped in my leg, and a sharp pain ran up and down my body without seeming to localize. I managed to collapse the chute after it had dragged me for about a hundred feet. For a time, after disengaging myself from the harness, I lay there gasping for breath and thinking, "If this is a broken leg or a banged-up knee, it might give me a chance to back out of this foolish business gracefully. Jumping is a boys racket, not something for a thirty-year-old man."

I got up carefully and tested the leg. It seemed to respond normally. With a sigh I thought, "Well, I guess I'm just stuck with the paratroopers, and nobody to blame for it but myself." But this feeling was to change shortly to great pride in the organization and to genuine respect and esteem and even love for the men in it.

We carried our parachutes to the waiting trucks. The men were jubilant, all talking at once, each man describing with great animation every detail of his jump. They were bursting with pride.

"How'd you land? I hit like a sack."

"What an opening shock . . . looka here!" proudly displaying the rapidly discoloring riser marks on his shoulders.

"Any business for the meat wagon? Was anybody hurt?"

"Yeah, the guy who lit next to me pulled his legs up and landed on his tail; they carried him off on a stretcher."

I'd like to go right up and do it again!"

"How about it, Chaplain? How'd you land? That makes you a double skypilot, doesn't it?"

It was impossible not to share their good spirits. We sensed, too, that our mutual experience really made us brothers in the airborne family. Thereafter, though they would often fight among themselves, paratroopers having trouble with the civilians, with the law, or with men of other units would just have to yell, "Geronimo," and from every tavern, park, and sidewalk within earshot would come running the men with the parachute wings on their breast. This loyalty caused the Army a great many headaches before it paid off in Normandy, Southern France, Leyte, Holland, Bastogne, Germany, and much later in Korea. Now, as we rode back to the sheds to shake the dirt and weeds out of the parachutes, the men broke into their song, "Gory, Gory, What a Helluva Way to Die," finishing strongly on the last phrase, They poured him from his boots."

By the end of the week we had made the five qualifying jumps, received a certificate to this effect, had the wings pinned above the left breast pocket by the school commandant. We then hastened to acquire the overbearing mannerisms and obnoxious characteristics of pre-combat paratroopers. Jump boots, the unique patch on the cap, and the wings were badges of such distinction that the jumper considered himself outside the law, above observing the customary courtesies toward civilians, and in a position to scorn all other branches of the service.

There is no difficulty in distinguishing the paratrooper who has seen combat from the one who has not. Combat was one day to mellow him and give him a wholesome respect for the foot infantry like the 28th Division, which, though reeling from smashing blows of five converging German divisions, still delayed the enemy long enough for the 101st Airborne to set up their impregnable defense at Bastogne. He never dreamed at Benning that he would one day be rescued by an armored division (the natural enemy of airborne) which had broken through the encircling German lines. He was even to learn that the air corps had its good points, as ammunition, gasoline, food, and other essential supplies were dropped just in time to prevent a great disaster for the airborne. That mission was a mighty expensive one for the C-54 men, for many planes went down in flames.

By this time the paratrooper had seen enough combat to really care what happened to the other fellow. He began to appreciate the necessity of team work with all branches of the service. He might even admit on occasion that the airborne could not win the war alone.

Yes, the jump-school graduate was a swaggering character, but give him time and he would develop into an efficient soldier with becoming poise and quiet self-assurance and a wholesome respect for the rights of others. One day, after the purgatory of combat, you might even think of him as gentle and kind—if he is not provoked to act otherwise.

CHAPTER 2

Training at Camp Mackall

MY ORDERS sent me to the 501st Parachute Regiment, at this time engaged in training at Camp Mackall, North Carolina; later the regiment was to become attached to the 101st Airborne Division. Camp Mackall was the first army camp in the United States to be named after a private, a soldier who had died as a result of a parachute jump during training. The camp was a bleak temporary installation with tarpaper shacks for barracks, but with a sizable runway for planes and a large desolate area suitable for parachute jumps and military training.

I was looking forward with real interest plus a certain degree of trepidation to meeting Colonel Johnson, the fabulous CO of the regiment. He had left a reputation at the jump school for being the toughest, roughest, and noisiest officer ever to "hit the silk." Lieutenant MacReynolds, a powerfully built ex-prizefighter and for the last six or eight years a career soldier, was the adjutant. This was June 7, 1943, and one year later to the day Macs very promising military career was cut short by a piece of a German 88 shell.

Major Julian Ewell, the executive officer, stepped out of his office when he heard us talking, and I introduced myself. I liked Ewell from the first moment I met him. He was a tall, almost gaunt, intelligent-looking individual, and behind his quiet dignity and courteous respect one could sense a depth of resourcefulness that in later days proved to be even greater than anyone guessed.

Colonel Johnson came in, and the atmosphere of the room was immediately charged with his forceful and domineering personality. He was dressed in a tailored jump suit and was carrying a long knife in his hand. This was overplaying his character a bit, I thought, but he explained that he practiced knife-throwing for an hour every day.

"Hi ya, fella," he said, "who are you?" Major Ewell introduced me. "Come into my office, Chaplain." The Colonel led the way. "Have a seat. Tell me, Chaplain, why did you join the paratroops?" MacReynolds had warned me that this would be his first question, but even so I was not quite ready for it. I could tell by the way he stuck out his jaw that the answer he wanted was a snarl and something about wanting to get at those dirty Nazis and at those lousy slant-eyed—! and that I wanted to be in the toughest outfit in the cockeyed Army and under the roughest, meanest, most hell-bent-for-leather CO in the business and that this outfit was it. I'm afraid that my real answer was quite a disappointment.

"Well, sir, they asked for volunteers at Chaplain School."

"You're a Catholic priest, aren't you?" he said. "I assume you know your religious business. . . . You fellas always do. I'm not a Catholic, but I think you can do a lot of good for my boys. They need a priest. I like your business of confession. I'm not a Protestant either, but I believe in God, and I believe in Jesus. You'll find I will back your religious program to the hilt. I expect you to back me, to be loyal to me. Got that? O.K.! If you have any problems—any problems at all—come in and see me. If any of my boys are getting a rotten deal, I want you to bring it to my attention. I want you to keep your fingers on the pulse of the regiment. You will know before anyone knows, before I know, if anything goes wrong with the morale, and I want you to come in as soon as you see something wrong and tell me. I want you to be with the men all the time, on their marches, on their night problems, in the field. Jump with them when they have to jump. This is what I expect of a chaplain. This is what I expect of you, if you are going to play on my team, fella. I'm the pappy of every mother's son in this regiment; I'm your pappy too. There it is . . . straight from the shoulder. Whadya say?"

"I'll do my best, sir," was my clever reply.

"MACREYNOLDS," he screamed, loudly enough to be heard in the next county.

"Yes, sir."

The author, all set for a practice jump.

"Take the chaplain over to meet Chaplain Engel. Then fix him up with quarters." I saluted, and the colonel responded with the most vigorous salute I had ever seen.

Chaplain Kenneth Engel, a Methodist, was a very pleasant fellow with a fine sense of humor and a warm way of greeting you that made you feel that he was sincerely glad to know you. He wore glasses and a moustache. He looked rather frail and seemed a bit awkward and not very soldierly in bearing; his shirttail was not tucked neatly in his belt, his tie was askew, and his insignia was on crooked and needed polishing. But any illusion of frailty was dispelled later when I saw him handle himself on the football field and on the baseball diamond. I soon discovered that he was solidly religious, had a keen mind, and possessed a great appreciation of the arts without being "arty." This was the beginning of a very happy association and a genuine friendship. Chaplain Engel always called me "Father," and I liked that. Priests are very reluctant to give up this title in the Army for the generic and less significant "chaplain."

Colonel Johnson had been very fortunate in his selection of officers for his "team." Major Kinnard was the S-3, that is to say, in charge of plans and training, the key job in any unit. He, like Major Ewell, his close friend and West Point classmate of 1939, was a product of great inherent leadership qualities, superb military training, and an unquestioning devotion to duty. All of this was brought to a zenith of perfection on the battlefields of Europe a year later. His abilities were not long in being recognized after the first test of combat. Major General Maxwell D. Taylor, later Commanding General of the 101st (and still later Chief of Staff of the Army) took Kinnard from the regiment after the Holland campaign and made him Division G-3, a full colonel at the age of twenty-seven. Harry Kinnard became a close friend. He and Ewell looked and acted like cold military machines, but the men of the regiment sensed in these two a deep concern for them and a genuine interest in their welfare. It is always an amazing thing to me that any group of soldiers can quickly discern genuine leadership qualities from counterfeit. Appointing authorities in higher commands are not always as shrewd or as infallible.

It is strange, as I think of it, that Colonel Johnson, so dynamic himself and with so much color—an extrovert of the extreme type—should have gathered so many men of reflective nature into his regiment, placing them in key positions. Perhaps this was Colonel Johnson's finest attribute, the ability to pick the right man for the right spot.

Majors Carrol and Ballard were fine soldiers. Ballard ultimately took over command of the regiment after Ewell was wounded at Bastogne. (Johnson had been killed in Holland.) Carrol was one of the first men to die in the invasion of France in the early morning of June 6.

Major Braden, executive officer of the third battalion, was one of the finest gentlemen I have ever known in the Army, and his strong support of the religious program of the regiment was a real help to Chaplain Engel and myself. Braden was not a well man, despite his six-foot-two, beautifully proportioned frame, and after a week of combat his ailment gained a victory over his tremendous will power, forcing him to be evacuated.

Bottomly, later to become a major and then a lieutenant colonel, and Allen, who followed a like pattern in promotions, were at first viewed by the men in garrison as the typical army disciplinarians of the regiment. Later in combat they were to win first the respect and then the genuine admiration of their men. Allen especially was a man of the highest integrity and was to acquire deep insights into human behavior and great compassion for its weaknesses. Bottomly was to remain a militarist, albeit a highly competent one.

Major Philip Gage was a tall Lincolnesque figure of a man and a fine soldier. He had somehow or other acquired a number of misconceptions regarding Catholic teachings. At first I was embarrassed by his direct questions about the Church, but in time we became good friends. For him religion was important, and he was honest and sincere enough to listen to my side. I have often found that the man with prejudices is a better man than the one who is totally indifferent to all religion and who brags about being broad-minded. Gage married a lovely Catholic girl, and he fulfilled his part of the contract to the letter by having his children baptized and educated in the religion of their mother. He lost an arm in Normandy, was captured by the Germans, and was liberated two months later when Patton's armored divisions raced across France. His disability forced his retirement against his will and against the will of all of us who respected his capabilities.

Major Francis Carrel of Indianapolis was the regimental surgeon. He was small in stature but mighty in many ways. A strict disciplinarian, an excellent surgeon, a man of strong faith in God and deep convictions about the inherent dignity of every human being, he chose his men and officers carefully. In choosing his men he preferred the qualities of common sense, moral integrity, and strength of character to the flashier talents or even to experience. He raised the despised "pill pushers" of garrison life to the level of being the most admired unit in the regiment during combat. Chaplain Engel and I will always be deeply grateful to "Doc" Carrel for insisting that we chaplains become fully qualified aid men. The tedious hours spent learning how to stop a sucking wound, how to apply a leg splint, how to find the vein for blood plasma, and how to effect numerous other emergency measures were to prove of immense value to us in later and graver days. Doc Carrel was wounded in Normandy but gave himself superficial treatment and continued to carry on when his evacuation would have been a staggering blow to the regiment as the wounded kept pouring into the aid station. Following the Normandy invasion and his hospitalization, Doc returned to the regiment and stuck with it for the remainder of the war.

Well, these were the field-grade (majors and above) officers of the regiment, the framework upon which Colonel Johnson was building his fighting unit; this was the coaching staff of his "team." Each of these men influenced the character of the regiment, and each contributed a great measure to the qualities they helped fuse into a first-class combat organization. To the casual observer the regiment was just a large edition of Colonel Johnson. It naturally reflected his color and some of his individual characteristics. But to those on the inside, the regiment was much more than that. Its own personality, formed by a thousand different factors, ultimately became the forceful and unique thing that captured the imagination of its personnel, giving them that much-spoken-of, most desired, and rarest quality in the service—a real esprit-de-corps.

Of the ten field-grade officers in the regiment, not one was a Catholic. At first I wondered whether this was by chance or by design and whether my presence in the regiment was simply a matter of filling a vacancy, or whether the staff really wanted someone to minister to the Catholic personnel. In the months that followed, however, I never detected a trace of discrimination, although, of course, we had our differences in matters of regimental policy affecting the religious and moral life of the men. But even in these instances Chaplain Engel's work was as much affected and his protests as loud as my own.

Camp Mackall had none of the conveniences of regular army posts. The chapel, like the rest of the barracks, was a squat, one-storied, tarpaper-covered building with one big pot-bellied stove to keep it warm in winter. A roughly constructed altar and benches constituted the furnishings of the chapel. Two very small offices, separated by plyboard and each furnished with a field table and a couple of straight-backed chairs, completed the building. Chaplain Engel and I stayed up all night the first Saturday trying to design a backdrop and canopy for the altar and in general to give some semblance of dignity to the chapel. The effect was fairly satisfactory under the circumstances.

Attendance at the two Masses that first Sunday was not satisfactory, however, although I realized that the regiment had been without a Catholic chaplain for a long time and many of the men did not know that a priest had arrived. I arranged with Major Kinnard to schedule me for a series of sex morality lectures to the men during their field problems. This gave me a chance to introduce myself, to get acquainted with the men, and to remind them of their religious obligations. Attendance at Mass picked up considerably.

An accident contributed to bringing me a great deal of notoriety and embarrassment after I had been with the regiment about a month. One day Captain Bottomly, a company commander in the second battalion, came into my office without knocking; he was flushed and angry. At the moment, I was giving religious instructions to a couple of soldiers. "Chaplain," Bottomly yelled, "what's the idea of calling up my First Sergeant and ordering him to release Private Coots to your custody? That fellow was restricted to his barracks; he was awaiting court martial. Between the company and the chapel he decided to take off; he is AWOL. You have no right to give orders to my First Sergeant."

I was totally confused by this diatribe. I had never heard of Private Coots, and I had made no such call to the First Sergeant. Apparently one of Coots buddies had used my name. Feeling that it would be better for Bottomly and me to discuss this out of earshot of the two soldiers, I got up and took Bottomly by the arm and led him out of the office. But as he turned around he caught his shoe in a loose floor board, lost his balance completely, fell against the screen doors which gave way to his weight, and tumbled down the stairs. He lay with torn trousers and bruised knee on the cinder path outside the chapel. I went down to help him up just as several soldiers were passing by. They looked at us in shocked surprise and saluted. I guessed immediately that they were drawing false inferences and were forming their own conclusions on the nature of this whole affair. Bottomly didn't help matters any by refusing my hand, and he stalked away more angry than ever. The men moved on quickly, but their low whistles confirmed my suspicions of their thoughts. In a few hours the story had reached every barracks: the chaplain had knocked Captain Bottomly through the chapel doors!

The next day Colonel Johnson sent for me. Surely he couldn't believe the story that had been the subject of so much merriment in the officers club the night before. Well, in any case, I thought, Bottomly and I can set him straight on the whole thing.

"Chaplain," Jumpy Johnson shouted as I came into his office, "what am I going to do with you?"

"Sir, I'm sure Captain Bottomly can explain this. It is all a mistaken notion everyone has. You see . . . ."

"Yeah, yeah, I know. He slipped on a loose board . . . that's better than I used as a kid anyway. I got all my black eyes by bumping into doorknobs. Now see here, Chaplain, you've got to get along with my officers, see? If anything comes up that you can't settle reasonably, you come over and see me, and the two of you can fight it out in the gym behind locked doors. But the winner will have to fight me afterwards, you understand? And there's no officer in this outfit I can't flatten in two minutes. O.K., so Bottomly slipped on a loose board. We'll let it go at that. That's all, Chaplain."

"Yes, sir." I saluted and started to leave.

"And Chaplain . . ."

"Sir?"

"I like to have a chaplain be able to handle his dukes." He gave me a wink and saluted in a "we have a secret" fashion. I didn't tell him I had never won a fight in my life.

Bruno was by far the toughest and hardest man I had come across in the regiment. He was in the "sweat box" when I first met him, for he was even too incorrigible to be allowed with the other prisoners. After this severe punishment he was returned to the stockade. When I visited there one day, I noticed that in his cell there was a rosary hanging from his bunk.

"I didn't know you were Catholic, Bruno," I said.

"Who says I am?"

"Well," I replied, "you have a rosary there on your bunk."

"Yeah? Oh, that. My kid sister sent it to me. She's Catholic." He seemed willing to talk, so I listened. He and his sister were orphans. She was now in an orphanage, seemed to like the sisters, and had asked to be baptized a Catholic. She was always writing him, he said, about her religion and sending him stuff like holy pictures, books, and now this rosary. "If she likes her religion, I'm glad. But that stuff ain't for me." I asked him if he wouldn't like to know how his sister used the rosary to pray. He was interested, and I continued to instruct him. But I was not able to finish, for Bruno was transferred to the 502nd Parachute Regiment.

I never saw Bruno again; he was killed in the first days of fighting in Normandy. Father Andrewjeski, O.F.M. Conv., the chaplain of the "five o deuce" told me about him. Bruno had completed his instructions, was baptized, and lived a pretty good Catholic life. "But," continued Father Andy, "I could never cure him of gambling. And he always won. I think he split the profits between his sister and the orphanage." I never forgot Bruno; he sneaked into heaven I think, like the good thief. He had many faults, but one virtue—a love for his little sister. The Blessed Virgin used that virtue, and a rosary, to lead Bruno to the feet of her divine Son.

One afternoon I was called over to the hospital to anoint a boy who didn't look as if he were going to recover from heat prostration. He did recover later. His name was Manuel Ortiz, the same name as the boxing champion, and I was later to anoint him again in Holland for a wound from which he did not recover. As I was leaving the hospital, they were bringing in a young man who looked as though he had caught his hands in a cement mixer. Colonel Johnson was with him and told me to come along. "He's one of your boys, I think, Chaplain. Names Butkovich . . . the best demolition man I've got . . . cap went off in his hands." When we arrived at surgery, Johnson grasped the doctor by the shoulder. "Save that boys hands!" he demanded.

The doctor bent over to examine the patient. "I can save one of them," he said.

"Both of them!" Johnson flared. "Save both of them, or you'll wish you had!"

Whatever may have been the Colonels weaknesses and eccentricities, I was never to forget his passionate concern for his men. In Holland a year later this concern was to occupy even his last thoughts as he turned to his executive officer and groaned, "Julian, take care of my boys." Death had ridden in on a German mortar shell as the Colonel was examining his front lines along the dikes.

Sergeant Stanley Butkovich of Peoria, Illinois, has always attributed to Colonel Johnson the fact that he has two very useful though badly scarred hands. The poor doctor received no credit at all. Butkovich, a cousin of the famous Butkoviches of Illinois and Purdue, was one of the toughest and best-liked soldiers in the regiment. His faith and piety and fine example were worth a hundred sermons. A shell fragment went through his leg while he was still in the plane going into Normandy. He jumped in spite of this, gave himself an emergency dressing, did more than a creditable job as a demolition squad leader, and was decorated twice for his extraordinary efforts. If he should happen to read this, he would never forgive me had I used the word "heroism."

Colonel Johnson (we called him Jumpy in private) was still practicing his knife-throwing daily. He used a six-foot ply-board for a target. On one side he had Hitler's life-sized image and on the other side that of Tojo. He would practice for an hour straight and would completely lose himself in this game, snarling and growling as he threw his big bowie knife with a viciousness that sometimes sent it completely through the ply-board throat of Adolph. Then he would yell like a wild bull ape. Sometimes he missed badly; on two occasions the knife, rebounding from the board, cut him rather seriously, once on the hand and once on the leg. As mentioned before, the man had eccentricities, but he had color, lots of it, and the men idolized him.

Two weeks before we were to leave for maneuvers, Colonel Johnson gave one of his famous speeches to the regiment. The name

"Jumpy" was given him, not just because he would sometimes make five or six parachute jumps in a single day, but also because of the antics he went through when he made a speech.

"Who's the best?" he screamed.

"We're the best!" everyone of the men and officers yelled back at him.

"What are we here for?"

"To fight!" they roared.

"That's right . . . to fight!" Jumpy's eyes were flashing, and he stuck out his jaw in his own inimitable manner. "Those slant eyed—in the Pacific and those dirty Nazi devils just four thousand miles from here know thats what you guys are here for. They're on top now. It's been easy for them so far. Ya know what they're doing? They're poisoning the water in Naples; they're poisoning little kids and wimmin! That little skunk with the moustache knows you're coming; he knows you are out to get him, and he's scared of ya!" In a rising crescendo of emotional pitch he screamed, "In just a few more months I'm going over and get him! DO YOU HEAR ME? I'M GOING OVER AND GET HIM! ARE YOU WITH ME?"

Johnson had actually swayed the men until they were sharing his emotions; they were really visualizing themselves jumping on the Reichstag or on the Eagles Nest in Berchtesgaden.

With the men solidly behind him, the Colonel would then berate them for the high percentage of AWOLs, for venereal cases in the regiment, and so forth. Then he finished by telling them about the coming maneuvers and explained that it would be a test of whether they were ready to go overseas. The men were anxious to get overseas, and when Jumpy ended his speech with another strong appeal to their emotions, they went back to their barracks to write letters home to their families and to their girl friends about their great CO and to confide their imaginary Top Secret information: "The 501st is the outfit selected by the army brass to capture Hitler. . . . It is still a military secret, though, so don't tell anyone."

"Geronimo" was the regimental mascot, a cadaverous, bleary-eyed, beer-swilling, tobacco-chewing goat. It was the custom of parachute regiments to get a bit of publicity with pictures of their mascots floating down from the sky under a canopy of silk. The Airedale of the 506th had already made a half-dozen jumps. Colonel

Johnson didn't like the idea of another outfit getting more publicity than the 501st; besides, there would be no non-jumpers in his outfit. So, fit a harness, make a chute, call the photographers! Geronimo is going to jump!

But the airborne is a volunteer outfit, and Geronimo had not volunteered. The plane took eight passes at the field, and each pass found Geronimo fighting a winning battle against four men, each of whom had grasped a leg. They were unable to get him out of the plane. Every time they got him near the door, Geronimo turned into a dynamo of energy. Those scrawny legs going like pistons threatened the life and limb of everyone in the plane. Colonel Johnson was furious and gave orders to get rid of this unworthy and cowardly mascot.

Because Geronimo wouldn't jump or be pushed out of a plane, the Colonel got a bear cub for a mascot, but the thing was missing before we had it a month. Geronimo was reinstated, the band staged a beer party in his behalf, and the goat guzzled the frothy stuff to his hearts content. Later, when we were overseas, the unit that replaced us at Mackall reported that a large and vicious bear had emerged in early spring from its hibernation under one of the barracks.

One day a young man came to me with a very sad tale. His wife was leaving that evening for home in Michigan. He had been rather cross to her of late and would like to make it up to her by taking her out to dinner and perhaps to a show. Unfortunately, however, he was caught short. As a matter of fact he was flat broke after buying her train ticket. Would the chaplain be so kind as to lend him about ten dollars? I would. A couple of hours later I dropped into the non-coms club as was my custom, and here he was, obviosuly wrapped around about nine dollars and fifty cents worth of beer. He greeted me with the jovial familiarity of an inebriate. With one hand on my shoulder and the other still holding an empty beer bottle, his nose about half an inch from mine, he asked me if he hadn't borrowed some money from me. I assured him that he had. He said that he wanted to pay it back, and I told him that that made it unanimous, for I also wanted him to pay it back. He then dug into his pocket and drew out a roll of bills as large as my two fists together. He peeled through the bills until he could find such a low denomination as a ten-spot and gave it to me.

When the same young man dropped into my office a week or so later, I was ready for him. He was short again, and would I be so kind as to lend him . . . ? I asked if his wife had left for Michigan. He told me frankly that he wasn't, as a matter of fact, even married. I assured him in an unmistakable tone of finality that I would not lend him any more money. Then hesitatingly he drew out a five dollar bill. Would I mind exchanging it for a five-spot of my own? "Why?" I asked. "Is that one counterfeit?" It seems that a chaplains money in a crap game is better than a rabbits foot and puts just the right "hex" on the dice. (Lest anyone draw any unwarranted conclusions, I should like to state that I did not bargain for half the "take.")

About the middle of September we were ready to board the troop trains for the Tennessee maneuver area. We were to leave on a Sunday morning, standard operating procedure for the Army. (It seemed we always moved on a Sunday morning.) But I had announced, the Sunday before, that Mass on the day of departure would be at 0430 hours, and that meant that the Catholics would have to get up at least half an hour before the rest of the regiment. I couldn't have blamed them too much had they overslept the hour of so early a Mass, but I was really pleasantly surprised by the way they turned out that morning, a tousle-headed, sleepy-eyed, yawning bunch of boys from almost every state in the Union. With unlaced shoes and open fatigues they knelt in quiet adoration when the sanctuary bell told them that Christ had come down again from His throne in Heaven to be with them.

The religion of the GI is basic, fundamental, sincere, lacking many of the artificialities and conventions that civilians are sometimes prone to confuse with essentials. Until I had been in the Army for some time, I had mistaken their swaggering for arrogance, their weaknesses for maliciousness, their frankness for disrespect. Looking back now I cannot recall a single instance of flagrant intentional disrespect on the part of a soldier. I have come to know thousands, some of whom had never seen a priest before they got into the Army but had heard many a strange story about them. Many young chaplains are harsh in their judgment of soldiers for the first few months in the service. As time goes by, however, they learn to see beneath the smoke-screen of crudeness which men in groups throw up to hide the gentleness and goodness in their characters.

Next to combat, maneuvers offer the chaplain the best opportunity of studying, understanding, and drawing close to the men. I suppose our regiments personnel was like any others except that the glamour and adventure associated with jumping attract a younger group of men than the average infantry outfit. Why had they volunteered for the airborne? Of course the extra fifty dollars a month was an obvious attraction and, for some of the older men, the only attraction. But for many of the younger boys, some of whom were well under the proper enlistment age, the boots, the patch, and the wings meant girl-appeal when they went home on furlough. These boys had been high-school athletes, gridiron heroes of the local school and home town. This type was used to being singled out of the crowd as quite a somebody, and in the service he wanted a unique branch, a special outfit, something that would capture the imagination of his little brother and the other movie-going kids of the neighborhood.

Then there was the quiet type, the man who accepted the challenge of the airborne to convince himself or someone quite special that he was not a colorless, run-o-the-mill dependable doomed to a lifetime of mediocrity. This type of man frequently did extraordinary things in combat. He would initiate a spontaneous attack when the others were doubtful; he would volunteer for the most difficult assignments; he would die trying when he might have lived and not been censured for holding back. This was the stuff of which most of the war's real heroes were made. They had little of the *passion* of courage, but they had the *virtue* of courage; they had a good deal of the emotion of fear, but they were not cowards. Their bravery was of the highest kind; they had thought it all out before they ever heard a shot fired in anger, and their actions were willful, deliberate, premeditated.

The outfit also had a fair number of professional thugs and ex-criminals. I had at the time thought that these men were put there by the authorities to "blood" the men, to toughen them, to make them killers. But I later discovered that they had gotten in by falsifying their past. This group was a nuisance in garrison and almost useless in combat. They moaned about the food, were bitter toward all officers, inferred that some officers were going to get a slug in the back in combat and not from enemy fire; they were habitual

AWOLs and in combat were seldom seen, except when they had a chance to push around a few prisoners. They got the easiest and safest details, for they couldn't be trusted to do their job at the front.

Naturally it is a simple matter to look back and say that one man was a good soldier because he possessed such and such qualities, and that another man was a poor soldier because he didn't have those same qualities. But this is arguing in a vicious circle by identifying in retrospect the qualities with the success. The actions of men are not that easy to predict, even the actions of the simplest of them. In the test of battle the ex-floorwalker sometimes succeeds where the professional soldier may fail; the former prizefighter may run, leaving his buddy, a lad who never got away from his mothers apron strings, to hold the position.

It is impossible to foretell with one hundred per cent accuracy what any one man will do under the tension and stress of fire. There are too many undetermined factors and considerations to which the prophet has no access. Chief among these considerations, of course, is the free will. But it stands to reason that the habit of self-control and self-discipline must be already strongly entrenched in a man's character if he is expected to make the honorable choice between duty and self-preservation. Religion alone possesses motives powerful enough to make a man persevere in his efforts at self-control and self-discipline. In other words, religion is the indispensable support of those qualities of heart and mind so necessary for a good soldier. Good soldiers are necessary for a strong army. A strong army is necessary for the preservation of those God-given and inalienable rights which can be lost through weakness. It necessarily follows then that our American rights are dependent upon the strength of our religion.

But let's get back to Tennessee. Maneuvers have always bewildered me. I could never figure out the objective, or what the waving of various colored flags could prove about the accuracy of either side's fire, or what was gained by tagging a man as wounded, putting a splint on his leg, and sending him back to the rear only to have him show up in his company again within the hour.

We moved quickly at times, usually at night, and I never could be sure just where we were or where we were going. I almost flunked the map-reading course at Chaplain School, so all I needed to get completely lost was a good map and a compass. These excursions in the dark, however, were very handy for falling in with some fellow who hadn't been to the sacraments in a long time and getting him to go to confession. The attendance at Mass and the reception of the sacraments on maneuvers was much better than in garrison. There is something inspirational about saying Mass in the open using a jeep as an altar, and you feel a kinship with the priests of the primitive Church when you hear confessions while seated on a tree stump.

"Chicken Hill" was a spot that none of the old 501st troopers will ever forget. We were bivouacked for a few days on the side of a hill just above a small chicken farm. The ever-hungry GIs relieved the poor farmer of just about all of his three or four hundred chickens during the first few nights. Jumpy Johnson made one of his famous speeches then and deducted twelve cents from the pay of every officer and enlisted man to pay for the chickens.

I had missed dinner one day and decided to go foraging for myself. The wives of Tennessee farmers were wonderful cooks, and they would receive hungry soldiers into their houses to have a bit of breakfast of pork chops, fried potatoes and gravy, apple sauce, soda biscuits, and so on. When the soldier would ask how much it would be, the lady of the house would blushingly suggest, "Is twenty-five cents all right?" With this sort of meal in mind I approached a farm house, but first happened to look toward the barn. A couple of soldiers with their heads stuck around the end of the barn were motioning me to come. They had two nice chickens roasting above a slow fire. The chickens were about done and smelled wonderful.

"Is there anything wrong with taking just two little chickens from a guy that has so many?" they asked.

"Well," I pondered, "it isn't exactly right according to the laws of God or man; but now if you were to share with a hungry man of the cloth. . ." We ate them right down to the last neck, and chicken never tasted so good. When we finished, I suggested, of course, that we ought to pay for them. The boys felt that was right. They didn't mind paying for the chickens after eating them, for they had little chance to spend their money while on maneuvers anyway, but they wouldn't have liked paying for them before. Snitched chicken always tastes better. We each threw in a dollar, and one of the men went up to the house.

"How much for your chickens?" he asked the farmer.

"Reckon about a dollar apiece."

"Heres three dollars." He handed the farmer the money and started to walk away.

"Wait a minute, young feller, and I'll get you the chickens," the farmer called.

"That's O.K. We've et two of them already. You can eat the other one. Have a chicken dinner on us."

Colonel Johnson was not altogether pleased with the way the regiment was performing, although most of the staff and unit commanders felt that we were scoring well according to the umpires. One day as Chaplain Engel and I were talking to Major Kinnard at the regimental CP on the edge of "Chicken Hill," Colonel Johnson came up to a screeching halt in his jeep. He jumped out, and the rest of the staff saw that he was mad.

"Kinnard, where is my van?"

"I sent it forward, sir."

"Why?"

"Because I was anticipating your moving the CP forward, sir, as was outlined in last nights briefing."

"Hell, that was Ewell's idea, not mine." Jumpy was furious and threw his hat on the ground and kicked it, a perfect three-point goal right over Chaplain Engels head. "You guys better learn who runs this outfit. I do the thinking around here, all of it!" He grabbed his hat from his driver who had recovered it. "Chaplain, you come with me." He headed for his jeep; Chaplain Engel and I looked at each other. Each of us hoped the Colonel was talking to the other. We quickly compromised, and both of us jumped into the back end of his jeep. "GET OVER!" he screamed at his driver, and Jumpy took the wheel. We pulled out and left the CP literally in a cloud of dust. Jumpy kept talking while driving, more to himself than to us. We kept nodding agreement to what we could hear. "Imbeciles . . . stupid, incompetent staff . . . if it weren't so late in the game, I'd unload all of them . . . ."

The jeep was going as fast as it could go over the rocky Tennessee back road, so Chaplain Engel and I were hanging on to the sides and to each other as best we could. All of a sudden Jumpy, getting madder and madder, put on the brakes. I landed on top of the enlisted man and Chaplain Engel on top of the Colonel. Jumpy pushed him off disdainfully, leaped out of the jeep, ran across the road and the ditch, pulled out his bowie knife, and screamed, "You dirty—!" and threw the knife at the telephone pole . . . a perfect strike. Tojo had died the miserable death he deserved—again. Colonel Johnson, calmer now, recovered the knife with a satisfied sneer and got back into the jeep. Chaplain Engel and I sneaked a look at each other. I reached for my rosary, and Chaplain Engel quietly appealed to his Maker.

At first, time passed very rapidly on maneuvers. Each problem lasted five days. Saturday and Sunday afternoons the men were allowed in Tullahoma to take a shower, to see a movie, to watch the local Military Academy play football, to flirt with the local belles, and, in some cases, to harass the civilians and police. But after about six weeks we began to tire of maneuvers; we were tired of training. All of us wanted to get home for a few days and then get overseas to finish up this war business in a hurry. (It just couldn't last long after we got into it!)

When men begin to feel a sense of uselessness, as we were beginning to feel, having had no real part in the war, morale goes down, men become very difficult to control, and they seek relief from their boredom in drink or something worse. Then strong disciplinary measures become necessary, and finally morale really scrapes bottom. Jumpy's speeches began to fall flat. The men had matured; they began to resent the pep-rally tactics of the Colonel and were embarrassed by the jibes of other troopers levelled at the famous antics of the CO.

On one occasion when the Colonel sought to rouse the men emotionally, he got no response. When he screamed, "What are we here for?" instead of answering with the customary, "TO FIGHT!" the men roared back at him, "FURLOUGHS!" Colonel Johnson was desolate, desolate, and scared. He was afraid that if the brass in Washington failed to send the outfit overseas soon, the keen edge of this great weapon, honed by superb training and leadership, would be dulled by apathy and indifference.

Short furloughs had been granted as soon as we returned from Tennessee. Before some of the men were back, wires had to be sent ordering them to return at once to Camp Mackall. Word had finally come! We were to leave almost immediately! Then came the turmoil of packing; personal affairs had to be cleared up; everyone had a thousand and one things to do, some of which were Army duties, others each man's own private concern.

It had come down by the grapevine that New York was the port of embarkation designated for the 501st. When we boarded the troop trains and headed north, we were sure the "big town" was our goal. But the trains didn't even stop in New York, and literally hundreds of wives and sweethearts were left waiting at prearranged spots in that city for the men who didn't show up. Many of the men were furious as they watched the towering skyscrapers recede into the haze of the Manhattan twilight. It turned out that Boston was the port from which we departed upon the great adventure.

How long till we would see these blessed shores again, and how many of us, we wondered, as our ship left the famous Boston harbor behind and pushed its way into the inky waters of the Atlantic, would perhaps never live to breathe again the free air of America?

CHAPTER 3

Yanks in England

T HE RUGGED Scottish landscape seen through the fog from the ship's deck in early morning is really impressive; it is virile, invigorating, energizing. It is the sort of country bound to produce such literature as the *Waverly Novels* and the vigorous writings of such men as Stevenson and Burns. We hugged the coast for several hours, and every one of us was enjoying this part of the trip immensely.

The last ten days on the Atlantic had been miserable. The men had been packed in the typical military-transport triple-decker bunks. The weather was so bad and the sea so heavy that it was dangerous to allow anybody on deck most of the time. The bad weather was a blessing in disguise, however, for it made any attack from a German U-boat less likely. The holds were stifling, and just about everyone was sick to his stomach and had a cold. In spite of this, Mass in the lounge was well attended, and I heard confessions for two hours a day. Men, lined up for confession, could watch the crap games going on beside them while they waited. Quite a row ensued when one of the big winners in the game quit to go to confession.

We disembarked at Glasgow and were treated to a "spot of tea" by a very cheerful group of Scotch Red Cross lassies. They were bright-eyed, apple-cheeked, and friendly but with just enough poise and reserve to keep our men from getting fresh. They laughed when anyone asked for sugar for his tea. "You Americans are the ones. There's no sugar over ere. There's a war on; or 'avent you 'eard?" And of course our men came back with the cracks that these girls must have heard from the men of every troop ship that docked.

"Well, sweetness, how about putting your finger in my tea and stirring it then?"

Or a would-be mimic of the Scotch would say, "How about a stroll in the brau bricht moonlicht nicht tonicht, me darlin?" And the girls would laugh in a friendly way as if it were the first time they had ever heard these wonderfully clever remarks.

The trains we then boarded seemed obsolete, with their worn-out mohair seats, cracked windows unreplaced, and the unsociable (from the Americans' point of view) private compartment system. We were to learn to respect the British railroads, however; for the speed of the trains and their punctuality made travel there easy and pleasant.

Trucks carried us from a station just outside Newbury, Berkshire, through this pleasant little city of fifty thousand inhabitants and to the tented area that was to be our home until "D Day" and again for a while after we returned from Normandy until we jumped into Holland. The streets and sidewalks of Newbury were narrow, the shops were small, and the soldiers were greatly amused by the signs: "Cinema," "Chemist," "Pub," "Fruiterer." Little boys ran alongside the trucks calling out, "Any gum, chum?" "Got a penny?" The GI scarcely ever failed to toss something and usually felt worse than the child if he had nothing to give. Children of any nationality have a way of extracting from the roughest soldier whatever he has.

The local citizens seemed very friendly; they smiled and waved, and even the girls didn't seem to mind being whistled at any more than American girls did. All the Americans were overdoing the broad "a," and everybody was "old chap" or "old bean" and was "jolly well glad to be in deah old England, dontcha know."

Merry England was really merry for the men of the 501st that first night. They were happy, and they could hardly wait to get their wrinkled but clean ODs out of their barracks bags, walk the two miles to town, look around, maybe meet some girls and see a cinema, and best of all, see what the inside of a pub was like. They soon discovered that most of the girls were in uniform of one type or another, the pubs served only warm beer, and one of the cinemas showed only westerns of the "Tom Mix" era and the other, strictly British pictures of almost equally ancient vintage. It was different, however, they thought, and fun for a while. The excitement of these

Father Sampson celebrates field Mass.

"Chow" on maneuvers.

novelties was soon to wear off and would be replaced by an uneasiness. This uneasiness was caused by the fact that just twenty miles of English Channel separated us from the Germans, and we knew that we would be crossing that Channel before many months had passed.

Before we pitched into training in earnest, we were given a few days to orient ourselves, to shake the salt of the ocean from our boots, and to visit London. The city of Newbury had scarcely been touched by Hitler's bombers. But the first sight of London and the first experience of an air raid while there brought us face to face with the realism, the tragedy, and the horror of war. Here was not just a newspaper account. You could see the walls of a bombed building collapse; you could hear the ominous air-raid signal, the clang-clang of fire engines, the screaming ambulance sirens; you smelled and almost gagged on the stench of a building that had burned last week and was still sending up puffs of white smoke from drenched embers in its flooded basement. But the imperturbability of the British is beyond description. Following the air raid the people came out from the shelters by the thousands, and they went about their business or their entertainment in this blacked-out city. You would have thought that air-raids were a normal and natural part of living—as indeed they had become for this amazing breed.

It wasn't long, however, before Charing Cross, Piccadilly Circus, Oxford Circus, and numerous other focal points of the second largest city in the world became as familiar to us as Times Square, Riverside Drive, or Hells Kitchen in New York; the Mall in Washington; Canal Street in New Orleans; Market Street in San Francisco, or Main Street in Council Bluffs, Iowa. The GIs took England by storm. There were now a million American soldiers on that little island, and I suppose ten million tons of American equipment. It was said that the primary purpose of the barrage balloons over London was not just to keep German bombers from attacking at low level, but to keep England from sinking under the weight of American men and equipment.

Every American soldier had at least fifty dollars a month (in those days in England that was a great deal), and he was determined to spend it on anything that offered a little diversion. The English were startled by the wanton display of so much money for entertainment. The British serviceman quite understandably resented the advantage the American had over him when it came to getting a date. Street fights between the servicemen of the two countries were common.

Major General William Lee, Commanding General of the 101st Airborne Division, to which we were now attached, gave the regiment a talk that inaugurated the intensive training program. This talk was the finest Christian analysis I have ever heard of the purpose of an army, of the dignity of the soldier's profession, and of the high standard of deportment and of personal integrity rightly expected of every man who had been given the opportunity of wearing his country's uniform. These were sincere words from a deeply sincere man. To this man soldiering was not just a career—it was a vocation, a total dedication like the priesthood. He told us what lay ahead, and that sacrifice and obedience to an heroic degree would be required of us. Enlisted men and officers alike were profoundly moved, perhaps as much by the greatness of the man as by what he said. There were no shouts or cheers after this speech, but when it was over, every man returned to his duties a better soldier. Confused minds began to see a break in the clouds of doubt and uncertainty.

A couple of months after this talk, Bill Lee, as everyone referred to the general, had a heart attack and had to go to the hospital. Sheer exhaustion and physical disability could never have kept him in bed; he had to be confined there by orders of his superiors. I had contracted a touch of the flu at this same time and had a room directly across the hall from General Lee's room. I made bold one day to rap on his door. Obeying a pleasant, "Come in," I inquired how he was feeling. After that, each day he would tell the nurse to invite me in for a short visit. A monk could not have more cheerfully resigned himself to his ailment than this man, who loved the title "soldier" more than "general." Bill Lee died shortly after the end of the war, but there are thousands of men to whom he is still the "ideal soldier." He is known as the "Father of Airborne." There are at least three airborne generals who have become Chief of Staff of the Army, and they speak of Bill Lee in a tone of awe and in terms of the deepest respect.

Lee was replaced by a younger, more vigorous man, General Maxwell D. Taylor. Taylor was one of the most successful young generals of World War II and following the war was appointed to the very responsible position of Superintendent of the United States Military Academy at West Point. In 1955 he became Chief of Staff.

Less than a year before taking command of the 101st he had given real proof of the promise of his meteoric military career when he landed from a submarine and went in behind the German lines in Italy. There, under the very noses of the Nazis, he obtained from Marshal Badoglio a declaration of Italian non-belligerence.

Training in England was a real hardship for everyone. The weather from January, when we arrived there, until June was cold and drizzly. Our field problems were long and difficult. Jumping in England was extremely hazardous. In North Carolina the heat waves thrown up by the warm sand had made parachuting fairly easy, and the sand also cushioned the shock of the landing. But the atmosphere in England was very thin, making the descent faster; and the rocky soil, numerous fences, and the omnipresent hedgerows were added hazards that we were not accustomed to. Besides this, we jumped with more equipment and were more heavily weighted down than ever before. The injury casualties were very high, about eight per cent, whereas they had been less than two per cent in North Carolina. (Due to new techniques and better equipment they are down to a small fraction of one per cent now.) On one night jump I lit in a tree and cracked a couple of ribs against the trunk. From then on night jumping has held real terror for me.

After four or five mass jumps in England it was decided to risk no further casualties, for such highly trained and specialized troops were not easy to replace.

On one of our night problems the battalion to which I had attached myself was to jump, assemble, and then work its way toward the village of Lambourne. A road block was to be set up outside the town; we were to dig in, wait for a couple of hours, then attack and take Lambourne just before dawn. After the roadblock had been set up, being very tired, I lay down in a ditch beside the road, pulled my trench coat tight around me, and went to sleep. I don't know how long I had slept when I awoke feeling something cold and flat pressing under my chin. Fearful that it was a snake I opened my eyes slowly. It was a long knife blade so sharp that I was almost afraid to breathe. "Chaplain," hissed Colonel Johnson menacingly, "in combat you would have been a dead duck by now."

About seven miles north of Newbury was a lovely residential district called Coldash. The Franciscan Missionaries of Mary, a wonderful order of sisters, had an orphanage there. All the orphans were girls except two little boys who stuck to each other like Siamese twins. The Catholic chaplains located in this section of England met in Saint Gabriel's Home for Children once a month, and the meetings were to be among my most pleasant recollections of England. For a couple of hours we would have a conference to discuss any problems we might be having in our units. The sisters then served a dinner that made us forget for the time being that there had ever been a shortage of food in England. The sisters worked their own farm, however, and the healthy, rosy-cheeked orphans, many of whom were children of people killed in the bombings, were at least spared the most dreaded aspect of war— hunger and starvation. After dinner the children would put on a little show, and they really were clever. They sang mostly American songs and always closed with a rousing "Gawd bless Awmerricaw, lawnd of the frrrrree."

I had just finished visiting our sick men in the hospital one after-noon when a call came through requesting a priest. Two badly burned young men were being brought in an ambulance from the scene of an accident. It seemed that their gasoline truck had blown up, and they had both asked for a priest. When they arrived I could see at once that one of them had not long to live; the other was not in too serious a condition. I asked the seriously burned lad if he wanted to go to confession.

"No, Father," he said, "I went Saturday, and everything is O.K." He made an act of contrition, and I gave him absolution, then anointed him and said the prayers for the dying. As the doctor and nurses covered his body with oil, the boy kept saying over and over again well-practiced ejaculations, "My Jesus, have mercy on me. Mary, help me. Saint Joseph, pray for me." When the doctor left, one student nurse remained to drop a little water now and then on her patients parched tongue.

Son," I said, "you may die. We all have to die some day, and I only hope when my time comes that I will be as ready as you are now. Shall we say the acts of faith, hope, and charity together?" He said these prayers without hesitation or help from me, and, as he continued to repeat them, the nurse, a very young girl with probably little experience, began to cry. The dying boy noticed her crying, looked up at me, winked, and, with just a trace of a smile on his face, he closed his eyes and died.

Since the regiment was split up into two different areas several miles apart, I arranged to have the Catholics transported by truck each Sunday to Mass in Newbury. They liked to have Mass in a church for a change, and I was happy to have the opportunity of singing a High Mass each Sunday, a rare privilege for the average army chaplain. Canon Green, a venerable eighty-year-old gentleman, was the pastor, and he dearly loved to preach to American GIs—"our gawllant Amerrrican allies" as he called us.

My evenings were kept pretty well occupied by instructions. Many men were becoming very interested in the Church, not just because they had any premonition of disaster, but principally because when men live together for long periods of time, they get to speaking their inmost thoughts, their secret desires, their fears, their anxieties, their unanswered questions about religion, their sense of confusion about life's meaning and its basic problems. Here and there a Catholic man had given a fine example and had been articulate enough to some buddy of his to convey the idea that the Catholic Church had the right answers. Instructions were streamlined to three per week for a period of two months. The correspondence course of the Confraternity Home Study Service was a great help.

When I had finished the instructions and was morally sure that the catechumens were sincere and intended to live good, devout, Catholic lives, I would take them up to Saint Gabriel's for baptism. After the baptism, I celebrated Mass, and the newly baptized and their godfathers received Communion. There were usually six to ten in a baptism group, and the sisters always had a festive dinner for them after Mass. Then the kids would put on their show. Even if there were only two baptized, the performance had to take place. The children insisted on it, and the soldiers loved it. Confirmations were also held at St. Gabriel's for the American soldiers in the area by the bishop of the local diocese. He was a very kindly man and was always highly amused by the quips, jokes, and jargon of these American extroverts.

I would frequently take a group of men up to the orphanage on Sunday afternoons. It is difficult to say whether the soldiers enjoyed the kids more than the kids enjoyed the soldiers, but these excursions were mighty popular affairs. Each child adopted a couple of soldiers and promised to pray for them when they would be in battle. Later, when we were in Normandy and Holland, letters, some of them just a child's scrawling and drawing, from their little friends in Coldash brought grins of pleasure to the faces and a warm glow to the hearts of these hard-boiled paratroopers. There was more than one soldier buried with the letter of an orphan of Saint Gabriel's still in his breast pocket. And whether their soldier lived or died, I know that God heard and answered the prayers of these little ones in His own way.

"Mouse" Rapp, a medic, had had quite a career for a little fellow who had just turned twenty-one. He had quit high school in his sophomore year and had become an acrobat in a carnival. He then switched to a tumbling act on the Pantages circuit, became master of ceremonies in a Chicago burlesque, and finally gave that up to work in a pet hospital for a man who practically adopted him. Aside from being an excellent medic and later doing a wonderful job in combat, for he seemed to be fearless, his greatest contribution to the regiment was as a natural comic. Mouse was what is commonly known as a "screwball," and he did more for the outfit's morale than all the high-salaried and often smutty professional entertainers who were sent to us.

One evening Mouse and I were going to the cinema in Newbury and were queued up in line to buy our tickets. A very attractive English girl was standing directly in front of Mouse, and he kept making remarks to me about her cute hat. The girl had given him several icy but ineffective looks before she turned to me.

"Does that belong to you?" she asked with a contemptuous nod toward my companion. That was all that Mouse needed.

"Father," he said, "you wouldn't want to sit next to me in the movie. I munch popcorn and crack my knuckles during the exciting parts. But now, if this young lady would just let me buy her ticket and sit next to her, I'd be as quiet as a mouse, I betcha."

The girl's native reserve broke a bit, and she smiled. That smile altered those two lives. Today Henry Rapp and Mary, his lovely English wife, are living in Wayzeta, Minnesota. If your travels ever take you by that beautiful little suburb of Minneapolis, stop by at Deep Haven Kennels and ask to see the manager . . . everyone calls him Mouse. He and Mary will be glad to see you, and you will be glad you stopped to meet them; everyone likes Mouse and Mary.

Like the Colonel, Sergeant Valent was also called Jumpy. He was later to be captured at Bastogne, and when he refused to give the Germans any information, they knocked most of his teeth out; but he still refused to talk. He was a natural soldier and highly respected by all his men. But the chaplains always had to watch him, for at church call he would call out every man and threaten him (in language not usually associated with church services) if he didn't go to chapel. We always liked cooperation in getting men to services, but not quite so extreme as Valent offered. "These so-and-so characters need some religion," he would say. Jumpy is a first sergeant now, still in the airborne in Germany, and still has to be watched by the chaplains for coercing men to church.

The Benedictines had a tremendous monastery about fifteen miles north of Newbury and operated a splendid boys' school there. American chaplains were always welcome, and frequently we brought out groups of our men to enjoy the very pleasant atmosphere of the place, to watch the English boys play cricket, and, once in a while, to put on a demonstration baseball game for the monks and boys of the school.

The Americans couldn't understand the quiet, studious deportment of the cricket players in action and were more than amazed to see the two teams calmly lay down their equipment at four p.m. to go in for tea even though the score was tied at the time. No amount of explaining by the English boys during tea could justify such procedure in the minds of the Americans. By the same token the English boys and monks were completely bewildered by the steady line of chatter of the American players during the baseball game and were shocked beyond words by the way one side or the other always challenged the decision of the umpire on every close play. Especially were they startled by such Brooklynese expressions as "Trow da bum out," "Why doncha get some glasses," "We was robbed," and so forth. I suppose they may have been particularly shocked because I happened to be the unfortunate umpire.

Sunday, May 11, was Mother's Day, and we prepared to hold a Solemn Field Mass for all the soldiers stationed around Newbury. I asked the Abbot of the monastery if he would be kind enough to allow the boys choir to sing. He consented. The setting of the Mass in the beautiful park of Lambourne was ideal, and, besides more than twelve hundred American soldiers and airmen, about two hundred local English Catholics attended. Father Fitzgerald, C.S.C., preached the finest sermon on motherhood that I have ever heard. After the Mass I took the choir boys to the officers mess for a big chicken dinner. I was glad to see that they could be as loud and boisterous as American boys of the same age, and with appetites just as big.

Toward the end of May, England was getting tense. The big day couldn't be very far away. The war room at division headquarters was under double guard; airfields were beehives of activity; long convoys of trucks were heading for the southern ports of the isle. We had the most realistic dry run yet, traveling to the airfields in trains, loading the planes, and boarding them fully equipped. Rumors were flying around fast, and *Stars and Stripes* carried the story of a major general who had been demoted to lieutenant colonel because he had hazarded a guess in public as to when D-Day would be (it so happened he hit it right on the nose). But the sure sign, in the minds of the soldiers, that the real thing was not far away was the buddy-buddy attitude of the officers toward their men. Censorship of mail became stricter than ever, and the GIs' letters became longer and more serious. Mass was better attended, and some long-timers were getting back to the sacraments. The men had been well trained; they were in superb physical condition, and they had confidence in the regiment's leadership as well as in their own abilities. We were ready . . . as ready, we felt, as we ever would be.

PART II

The War Against Germany

Paratroopers of the 11th Airborne Division board a C-119 "Flying Boxcar."

CHAPTER 4

Invasion of Normandy

THERE could be no mistaking the meaning of the elaborate preparations this time. This wasn't a dry run. They don't pass out "live" grenades and ammunition for a dry run. About ten days before the invasion two battalions of the regiment were sent to Merryfield Airport, the third battalion to the airfield just outside of Reading, almost a hundred miles away. The men were not allowed to leave the tent area within the field, except to march in companies to the war rooms where everyone was briefed on the mission. The closest possible guard and secrecy were observed; there was a double check of all passes. The band, which, of course, was not going with us, outdid itself with its music to keep the morale up. There was no KP, nor were there any other onerous duties either; a service unit took care of that.

The men were in high spirits as they sat in the sun outside their tents sharpening their knives, writing letters home, or just swapping stories. The tenseness of the past several months was gone, and the men seemed actually glad that they were finally going to be a part of the big show. They were confident. They were the best! Colonel Johnson had told them they were for more than a year now; they had come to believe it.

As General Eisenhower passed among the men with his friendly grin and informal chats, it is difficult to say whether he gave them more confidence than they gave him as they grinned back through their charcoal-and-linseed make-up. He was the soldiers "right guy," and he refused to show in his face the terrific burden of the decision for which he accepted full responsibility; nor did he betray a certain apprehension he must have felt. One of his high staff officers, it was rumored, had stated that to land airborne troops behind the Atlantic Wall, in view of the uncertain weather predictions that might postpone the beach landings, was "pure murder." Nevertheless a single day's delay now might destroy every advantage of surprise. General Eisenhower calculated the risks and was ready to gamble. But he was gambling with the lives of these fine young men; he knew it, any they knew it, but it was O.K. with them. They were ready and willing to vindicate his judgment.

Arrangements were made for Chaplain Engel and myself to fly back and forth between the airports so that we could see all of our men before D-Day and H-Hour. I had each man write his name and put it in a box beside my tent when he went to confession so that I might be able to check up later to make sure all the Catholic men received the sacraments. Though the confessions took more than three full days, it was a great satisfaction to know that all the Catholics of the regiment had fortified themselves in the sacrament of Penance. It took almost an hour to distribute Communion at the two Masses on the eve of departure. I could later write with certainty to the parents of men who did not return from Normandy that their sons had been well prepared for death.

After General Taylor had given an inspirational talk, Colonel Johnson also addressed the men. It was a talk the Colonel had looked forward to since the war began, a talk that I am sure he had rehearsed for months. He used his time-honored tactics, and they were effective. He was the fighter, nothing else, and he pretended to be nothing else. The men responded; they knew their CO had guts, a quality they admire in an officer above tactical ability. At the emotional peak of his talk Jumpy reached for his knife strapped to his boot. He pulled and pulled at it, but he couldn't get it out of its sheath. Getting very red in the face, he finally reached for his trusty bowie knife that was strapped to his waist. He raised the bowie high above his head and screamed, "I swear to you that before the dawn of another day this knife will be stuck in the foulest Nazi belly in France! ARE YOU WITH ME?"

"WE'RE WITH YOU!"

"THEN LET'S GO GET EM! GOOD HUNTING!"

Colonel Johnson jumped down from the stand, and we went to put on our equipment and to make any last minute adjustments of parachute harnesses. We were much over-equipped, the fault, we suspected, of some logistics expert in the Pentagon who tested his theories by jumping off a footstool fully equipped. Let me give you an idea of how loaded we were. Every man, besides his weapon and extra ammunition belt, carried two parachutes (one weighing thirty-eight pounds, the other twenty-eight), an extra complete set of gas-impregnated uniform and boots, several first-aid-equipment pouches, canteen, four K-ration boxes, grenades, blood plasma or mortar rounds or machine-gun ammo, a Mae West life preserver, and personal toilet articles. Also, most men carried that crowning insult to the enemy—comic books and murder mysteries. I carried no weapon or ammunition, but I did have a couple of extra sets of blood plasma, a doctors field kit, and a complete Mass kit. Most of us with all our equipment weighed well over three hundred pounds, and air corps people had to help the men get into the planes. I recalled that I had blown a couple of panels from my chute in jump school with only my own hundred and eighty pounds exerting the pressure.

Eisenhower was standing alongside the road waving to each group as it passed. As we marched to the planes, I waited as the men went by, shaking as many hands as I could, and gave each a sincere "God bless you!" After we were lifted and pushed into the planes by the airmen, we struggled to our seats and tried in vain to fasten the seat belts. Most of us pulled off the extra equipment. When we were settled, I led our plane load of twenty-two men in prayer.

We took off right on time, and once the formations had formed, we went at top speed. Once over the Channel the lead man kicked all the discarded equipment (including twenty-two gas-impregnated uniforms) out of the plane. Somehow the loss to the tax payer didn't even bother us. I walked to the open door and looked down at the Channel; it was choppy and uninviting; the sky was overcast. That was good; we wouldn't be such easy targets when we hit the French coast in another ten minutes. Our protective fighter planes shot past us now and then. The men were generally quiet; some tried to sleep, others smoked steadily, and a few tried to be nonchalant by humming some modern songs. It was hard to believe that we were now only seconds away from the enemy and that within an hour some of us would be dead.

We got across without mishap, but as soon as we were over land, the ack-ack was terrific. The plane was hit many times, and

Butkovich had a fragment go through his leg, but he didn't tell anyone until after we had jumped. As we stood up and hooked up on orders from the officer jump master, the plane was rocking badly in a strong wind. The green light came on, and the jump master pushed our equipment bundles out. We went out as fast as we could, my assistant right behind me. Our jump was a surprise all right—for us. The Germans were waiting for us, and they sent such a barrage of bullets at us that it will always remain a mystery to me how any of us lived. The tracer bullets alone made it look like the Fourth of July. I collapsed part of my chute to come down faster. From there on I placed myself in the hands of my guardian angel.

I lit in the middle of a stream over my head and grabbed my knife to cut my bags from me (my Mass kit, doctors kit, etc.), but I could scarcely move to free myself. The canopy of my chute stayed open, and the strong wind blew me down stream about a hundred yards into shallow water. I lay there a few minutes exhausted and as securely pinned down by equipment as if I had been in a strait jacket. None of our men was near. It took about ten minutes to get out of my chute (it seemed an hour, for, judging from the fire, I thought that we had landed in the middle of a target range). I crawled back to the edge of the stream near the spot where I landed, and started diving for my Mass equipment. By pure luck I recovered it after the fifth or sixth dive.

The whole area was swamp with deep little streams running through it. As I started to get my bearings, I looked for the lights to assemble on. I learned later that we were several miles from where we were supposed to jump, and that the ack-ack of the Germans had forced the planes to disperse and dump us where they could. Later, I learned too that this had been most fortunate; for the path finders with the assembly lights had landed on the proper DZ, and many had been killed almost as soon as they landed. Luckily I spotted my assistant not very far away, still struggling to get out of his chute. We got together and made for the nearest hedgerow that would offer cover. We no sooner got there than a plane on fire came straight at us. It crashed about a hundred yards in front of us and threw flaming pieces over our heads. We prayed for the men who were in the plane and then watched and prayed for the men in two other planes that were crashing about a mile away. My assistant had lost his weapon in the stream, so we welcomed two of our men who came crawling along the hedgerow.

Our little group discussed what we ought to do and then started toward the place where we judged our troops might assemble. We moved slowly under concealment of hedgerows and were glad to see a half-dozen paratroopers running down along the ditch by the road. They were not of our regiment but told us where we might find the 501st, or a part of it. We went in the direction they pointed until we came under heavy enemy rifle fire. We ducked into a nearby farmhouse where we found about twenty-five troopers, all wounded or injured from their jump. It was just a three-room house, and the French farmer, his wife, and little girl were being of what help they could to the wounded. Chaplain McGee, a splendid Protestant chaplain from the 506th Parachute Regiment, was giving first aid as best he could. He had run out of sulfa drugs and compresses, and since my assistant and I had quite a bit of medical supplies, he was very happy to see us. We worked with the men for the better part of the day. Chaplain McGee was a former aid man in the enlisted ranks during peacetime before he went away to study for the ministry, so he directed our first aid work with the wounded.

About four in the afternoon a wounded soldier came in and told us that he and his buddy had been shot a hundred yards or so from the house. His buddy still lay where he fell. Chaplain McGee and I went to find him. He was already dead. We dragged him back, rolled him in a blanket, and put him in the shed. Then a mortar shell hit the back door of the house just as the French woman and her little girl were bringing in water from the well. Both were killed. As I knelt to anoint them, the farmer threw himself on their bodies and broke into agonizing sobs. When I put my hand on his shoulder, he jumped up, his hands and face smeared with the blood of his loved ones, and went yelling down the road shaking his fists in the direction of the Germans.

Some of our patients were getting worse, and Chaplain McGee said that they had to have a doctor. I decided to try to find our regimental aid station. My assistant stayed to offer what help he could to Chaplain McGee. After going about a half mile, I found a patrol of men. They told me where they thought the aid station might be. Since the area was under fire, I avoided the road and went by way of the swamp. The deep swamp was filthy and cold but afforded good cover. Addeville was the village the soldiers had told me to go to; with dusk closing in, I arrived there to find Major Allen in charge of about two hunderd men scattered throughout the village. They were having a real fight with a German unit a few hundred yards up the road. I went first to the aid station to tell Doc Carrel about Chaplain McGee s predicament.

"Kingston," he said to the assistant surgeon, "you take Cleary and follow the Father's directions to that group of wounded."

I then went to speak to Major Allen. He was on the 300 radio talking to Colonel Johnson. Allen motioned for me to stand by. Johnson was, as usual, talking loud enough even over the radio to be heard by everyone around.

"Were going on down to the locks," he said. "You'll have to withdraw from your position and come with us."

"I can't," said Allen. "Wed be overrun. And how long will you last at the locks if we don't hold off here?"

"ALLEN," he yelled, "DONT TALK TO ME LIKE THAT! DO AS I SAY!" Allen looked at me and winked, laughing noiselessly.

"Think it over, sir," he replied. Johnson's reply was one long string of oaths. Allen laughed quietly again and said, "Yes, sir. Right away, sir."

Allen then turned to me, "Father, were pulling out in about an hour. Tell Doc Carrel that the walking wounded and the aid men and you and he will go with us. When we move, we've got to go quickly, cause the krauts will close in on this place fast. I'd like to stay and hold, for its a good high position; but we don't have enough men to do it." What he was trying to say was that the non-walking wounded would have to be left behind. It was one of those decisions officers hate to make but for the safety of the whole unit they are sometimes forced to make. Allen was back on the radio calling in heavy support fire from the light cruiser eight miles away at sea. "Give me six more rounds on the same coordinates as the last."

Doc Carrel looked at me when I told him what Allen had said. "This is a bad time to leave them," he said. "Neither side is taking many prisoners now, and the Germans will consider them a liability."

"I don't think they will do anything to them. Their record as far as the wounded is concerned is pretty good," I said. "At any rate, I'm staying with them."

"Well. . . ." Doc Carrel, a real friend, started to say something, then just shrugged his shoulders. He looked around the big room and pointed out the most serious cases to me. "That man in the corner wont live—hand grenade went off in his pocket; his leg is gone, and he's ground up inside. Fenton on the bed should pull through if you can get a full unit of plasma in him. He has a big hole in the back, but no vital organs touched. There are two broken legs among this group—they have splints on. The man with the head wound. . . . I don't know how serious it is, but for the time being he can't see. Just change the dressing now and then. Do what you can for the others; they should pull through. There are fourteen non-walking wounded in these two rooms and the shed. Incidentally, there's a psycho in the shed. Better keep him away from the others."

Doc then called the aid men together. "One of you is going to stay here with these men and the chaplain." He had a number of straws in his hand. "Here, draw one. The short straw stays." A man by the name of Fisher drew the short one.

As soon as the last of our forces had left, I made a white flag from a sheet and hung it out the door. Darkness came quickly, and I expected the Germans to come within an hour. Fisher gave the man with the grenade wounds another unit of plasma while I changed the dressing of the man with the head wound. With the walking wounded gone we had more room in the main part of the house, so I moved all but two men into the main room. Every fifteen minutes I would go out and wave the white flag because I was afraid the Germans, suspecting a trap, would fire hand grenades and mortars into the house before approaching it.

All night long this went on. The boy with the grenade wound died in my arms about four a.m. clutching the crucifix I had taken down from the wall. It was a peaceful and holy death. All the boys joined in prayers for him. The medic Fisher and myself again changed all the bandages of the men. As I was cooking some hot chocolate, I looked out and saw Germans set up a machine gun in the front yard. I grabbed the white flag and went out. A German jumped at me and stuck a Schmizer grease gun in my stomach.

I could see by the badges on their breasts that these soldiers were Hitler's *Fallschirmjagers* (paratroopers). I tried to tell them that the house was full of wounded men, but two of them pushed me toward the road and prodded me with their weapons. When we had gone about a quarter of a mile, they stopped. One of them pushed me across the road ditch and against the hedgerow. He stepped back, and both soldiers pulled the bolts of their weapons. I said a quick act of contrition. (It later dawned on me that whenever I was in any great danger, instead of the act of contrition which I intended and tried to say, I always said the grace before meals. . . *Bless us, O Lord, for these and all Thy gifts, which of Thy bounty we are about to receive through Christ Our Lord.*)

Just then there were some shots fired a few feet over our heads. It was a German noncom firing to attract the attention of the men I was with. He came running down the road and stopped when he reached us. He was a fine-looking, tough soldier of about twenty-five. He spoke to my two captors and told me in broken English to come with him. I told him I was a Catholic priest and showed him my credentials. To my real amazement he snapped to attention, saluted, made a slight bow, and showed me a religious medal pinned inside his uniform. (A great many German soldiers wear medals or religious badges and carry rosaries and prayerbooks.) The noncom took me a little further down the road to a German officer who in turn called an intelligence man who spoke English. I explained that I was a chaplain and knew nothing of military value. I requested to be allowed to stay with my wounded men. The officer permitted this, and my noncom friend took me back. The *Fallschirmjagers* had ransacked the house of what food they could find, picked up a few hand grenades that our men had left in the yard, and filled their canteens with wine from the barrel in the shed.

The Catholic German noncom, in a very friendly way, told me to stay with my "comrades" (I was so glad of the universality of the Church). He said that a German doctor would come in a day or so. I had to show him the wounds of all the men and practically every square inch of the house—drawers, cupboards, attic, etc.—to be sure we weren't hiding any weapons. Then he left; but the *Fallschirm-jagers* dug in about the grounds and in the adjoining fields.

The wounded men had been very badly frightened. One German had put a gun to one man's head and pulled back the bolt; all the others had turned their heads away. Another had fired above their heads and into the ceiling. The men were weak from fear, as I was, but they were all quite calm. Fisher and I spent the next few hours changing bandages and giving plasma. We fixed a bit of hot chocolate and what few rations had escaped the Germans notice. They were constantly running around outside the house and apparently were planning to stay permanently.

The men gradually fell asleep, and about ten p.m. I did so too. Just about midnight, shells began to fall. A good part of the village seemed to be disintegrating under the heavy barrage. Fortunately most of the French people had deserted Addeville the day before. The artillery became intense, and the whole house literally bounced and shook for four hours. One of the men said it must be our own artillery trying to root the Germans out of this strategic high ground. One ceiling beam cracked and looked ready to give way. The plaster was dropping all over the place. Window glass sprayed the room. As eleven of the most seriously wounded were in the big room, I put three of them under the beds for protection. The two men with broken legs were in the kitchen. Meanwhile Fisher was in the barn holding down the boy who had gone out of his head and who was trying to run out to the Germans.

About 0230 hours three shells made direct hits on the house one after the other. Half the house collapsed on the two men in the kitchen. I heard one of them call out, "Father Sampson!" Just as I got to the door, the rest of the ceiling came down on the boy. I held his head in my arm and cleared away debris till I could touch his chest. His heart pumped very hard for about one minute and then stopped. I dug in the debris until I found the other soldier. He was dead. The roof of the kitchen and the entire wall were blown out although the wall had been at least two feet thick. The wall between the kitchen and the main room had been pushed in, and some of the stones had fallen on the other men but had not hurt any of them seriously. The entire house was so filled with dust that I could scarcely find my way from one man to another to see if each was all right. I went to the barn to inquire about Fisher and his patient. Fisher said that the soldier was either asleep or unconscious; he hadn't made a move during the entire shelling. Examining him we found nothing seriously wrong, but he didn't wake up despite the noise.

As the shelling continued, I had the men take turns in leading the others in the Lords Prayer. Of all the times and places for a religious argument! When one of the men finished with ". . . for Thine is the Kingdom, and the Power, and the Glory, now and forever," one of the Catholic men said that it didn't belong there. The Protestant men insisted that it did. The other Catholic men joined in to insist it didn't belong. I was grateful for the argument, for it distracted them somewhat from the danger of our situation. I told them each to say it in whatever way he had learned it. Scared as I was, this argument struck me so funny at the time that I almost became hysterical. I was happy to notice that in spite of their differences, praying together seemed to calm the men.

A flashlight had been blown out of the house and somehow turned on. It seemed to flood the remainder of the house in light and was sure to draw continued fire both from our artillery and from the enemy small arms. Just as I stepped out to turn it off, a German soldier brushed past me running for all he was worth, and as I reached to turn out the flashlight, I saw another German soldier in the creek a few feet away. He moved a bit and groaned, and when I lifted him up, he died. After giving him a quick absolution, I turned around to go back into the house. There, leaning against the house, with a light machine gun across his knee, was a German facing in my direction. I said what was supposed to be an act of contrition (grace before meals again, I'm afraid) and ran into the house. The next morning the German was still there in the same position. He was dead and apparently had been all the time.

How we survived that night I shall never know, except that the calm, fervent prayers of those wounded men didn't leave God any choice in the matter but to answer them. The artillery let up just before 0400 hours, and the small-arms fire increased. A tracer bullet came through the window, just grazed my leg, and set my pants on fire. As the first rays of light shone in the east, the tempo of the fire became intense and lasted for an hour or more. Then it suddenly decreased to almost nothing. Either the American attack on this position was successful and the Germans had withdrawn, I surmised, or our troops had failed to recapture our position. We would know very shortly. Every building in the village was a shambles. Our house had been riddled with rifle and machine-gun fire. Dead Germans lay in the fields and in the roads and in the ditches, and bloated cows and mules were lying on their backs with legs sticking grotesquely in the air. All this made me realize how fortunate we were to have survived the last eight hours.

One of the men saw a lieutenant sneaking up on our building with hand grenades and called out to him, "Americans in here." The lieutenant turned out to be Blackmon, an All-American end for Alabama, who had taken over command of Company B after Captain Bogart was killed. I ran out and stopped him, yelling for all I was worth. He said that he thought there were Germans in there.

The Germans who had remained and were not killed were captured. Blackmon told me that the body of "Hap" Houlihan, of Ventura, California, one of the finest, most wholesome, and most devout lads in the regiment, was lying on the road a few yards down the hill; he had been killed in the latest counterattack.

The wounded men were quickly evacuated to the division hospital. The hospital was set up in an enormous French chateau. A wall around the chateau and its adjoining buildings made it look like a fortress. Between two and three hundred wounded were lying on the lawn. There were about the same number in the main building.

The hospital chaplain, Father Durren, looked completely washed out. He had had scarcely any sleep since his hospital unit had come in with the second wave on the day after D-Day. I told him to go to bed, that I would take over. He did so but made me promise to wake him at 0200 hours. It was then seven p.m. Father Durren had tagged the men he had anointed and indicated on the medical tags of the other men those whose confessions he had heard. The wounded were coming in steadily—both American and German wounded. I had picked up enough German to be able to ask if they were Catholic or Protestant and to tell them that I was a priest. About sixty per cent of these Germans were Catholic, and they always made the Sign of the Cross when I took out the stole. They made acts of contrition and received Viaticum reverently as well-instructed and good Catholics. These, I later learned, were mostly from Bavaria. Many of them were in their early teens; some had not even begun to shave.

As I was going from one to another hearing confessions, anointing, and helping the Protestant and Jewish men to say a prayer and make an act of contrition, a touching incident occurred. I had anointed a German boy who was horribly wounded; his abdomen had been ripped open, and his intestines and other organs had bulged out and hung down. An American with a serious head wound lay on a stretcher about twenty feet away. A medic had tucked a folded blanket under the head of the American, but the blanket had slipped from his litter. He was groaning because of the painful position of his head. The German soldier had crawled off his litter and along the floor on his back to the side of the American, fixed the folded blanket under his head again, and crawled back to his own litter. The German soldier, only a youngster, died within the hour.

I remained at the hospital until noon the following day, sleeping from three till six a.m. I did not wake up Father Durren until seven a.m. as he had been completely exhausted, and during the morning hours the wounded were coming only in small numbers. Front-line duty is not nearly as tiring, I think, as hospital duty, especially when the wounded keep pouring in as they did those first few days.

Lieutenant Sheridan of headquarters company arrived at the hospital with a couple of wounded men and told me that the regiment was assembling at a nearby town. He drove me there in his jeep. I reported in and went to find a place to sleep, for I could scarcely move by this time. Butkovich and two or three other men from the demolition platoon dug a deep, comfortable foxhole for me and bedded it down with a parachute.

Just as I was about to lie down, a German medium bomber, coming over at about twelve hundred feet, throttled down its motors and dropped three small bombs. The regimental staff came running out of the buildings at the approach of the plane, and didn't stop for permission to use any foxholes. It gave the men quite a laugh to see the brass taking running dives for the nearest holes. The bombs landed right in the middle of the field we were in, but the only casualties were three cows. The only exposed person during this small raid was a French woman in the middle of the field busy milking one of the herd. I don't think she missed a stroke when the bombs fell, and she went right on milking after it was over . . . *c'est la guerre*. If the whole German Luftwaffe came over then, it couldn't have kept me from going to sleep. I slept twenty-four hours straight through.

Thursday, after a full days sleep, I went to headquarters to see how well we had accomplished our mission and found that we had done a one-hundred-per-cent job. The regiment had done so well, in fact, that another mission was to be added. However, at this time only 950 men could be accounted for out of our jumping list of 2,100. In the next few days a couple of hundred more men dribbled in, singly or in small groups.

One of our men told me that the mayor of the town would like to see me. He took me to him. The mayor's twelve-year-old son had been killed in the fighting in the town two days before. Two Germans had used the boy as a shield, each holding one of his arms as they crossed the road. American machine-gun fire killed all three. The mayor was bitter only against the Germans. The local priest was in a concentration camp for listening to a radio which he had not given up as was required by the Germans. The mayor wanted me to hold the funeral for the boy. I held the funeral the following morning, and a large number of my own men attended as well as the villagers. The family could not express their gratitude enough. I was never to see in the rest of France faith as strong as it was in Normandy; these simple peasant people were of deeply religious and fervent stock.

Friday evening the Germans bombed the division hospital, and did a very thorough job of it with just two giant bombs, at least two-thousand-pounders. The bombing was probably intended for the division headquarters, which was in another chateau just a few hundred yards away. One bomb hit the corner of the hospital and the other about fifty yards away. Fortunately nearly all the patients had been evacuated that afternoon. The seven American patients that remained were killed. Six medical aid men, one doctor, and five German wounded were also killed. Father Durren was lucky enough to escape serious injury. The bomb that landed in the field by the hospital dug a tremendous crater, about twenty feet deep and forty feet across. The bomb landed twenty feet or so from two men who were sleeping in a fox hole; they were not injured although they were entirely covered with earth after being tossed several feet into the air by the concussion.

Saturday morning I went to the place where the division cemetery had been established. None of the bodies had been buried yet, but there were several hundred lying side by side waiting to be buried, some already wrapped in a parachute. I was shocked to find so many of my faithful boys among the dead. It didn't seem possible that these young men who had been so confident a week before, whose hands I

had shaken before we boarded the planes, who had confessed and
received Holy Communion on the eve of D-Day, who had wise-
cracked that "no Nazi bullet has my name on it"—it just didn't seem
possible that they were in eternity now. O'Callahan from Indianapolis had landed in a tree and had been riddled with bullets before he
had a chance to get out of his harness; Neumann from Minneapolis
had stopped a snipers bullet; Houlihan from Ventura had died in the
Addeville attack; Roberts from Detroit, Rodriguez from El Paso,
McMahon from Jacksonville, Lieutenant Bogart from Cleveland,
Colonel Carrol from Salt Lake City, Gleason from the Bronx . . .
they seemed somehow like younger brothers. All were in Gods merciful hands now. German prisoners were digging the graves for both
the American and the German dead. I read the burial ritual for all
and remained most of the afternoon for the actual burial.

Sunday I had Mass for the regiment in the village church of
Vierville. The church was quite small, a quaint old Norman building
several hundred years old. A few civilians had come early, for they
had not had Mass in over two years, and the Americans packed the
place, filling the sanctuary and the choir loft and even crowding up
on the altar steps. I am sure no Catholic who could possibly have
made it missed Mass on that day. We all felt that we had escaped
death only through Gods providential care. That afternoon I took
Sergeant Bordeleau, who spoke fluent French, with me to dinner at
the mayors home. The head of the French underground for that area
was a guest as well. He and the mayor explained to us how the
underground worked. Every German collaborator in his district, he
said, had been noted and would be taken care of.

Sunday evening I attached myself to our second battalion, under
command of Lt. Col. Ballard. We moved out toward Carentan to
attack the German positions on the high ground just south of the city.
The attack started at dawn. We had to cross a stream and an open
swamp that made our men easy targets for Jerry snipers and mortar
fire. Our wounded casualties were extreme during the first hour. I kept
very busy working with the aid men hauling wounded out of the
swamp. There is something about the unselfish task of an aid man that
makes him even more courageous in exposing himself to save a soldier
who lies helpless between the two opposing forces. The German aid
men were equally courageous, and I have often seen them come

directly into the face of fire to pull one of their own men back to safety. More often than not, soldiers on both sides would refuse to fire on any aid man with that sort of courage. This was one of the more humane aspects of the war against Germany. The fine example of the aid men made me more sure of myself, with the result that this was one of those rare occasions when I was not particularly afraid.

One big advantage we always had over the Germans was in tactical air support. Only rarely did German planes hinder our operations and movements. On those few occasions our air-liaison officer was quick to call in American fighters to drive them off. German tanks also had to stay well concealed, for our planes were constantly patrolling the skies looking for good German targets.

Colonel Ballard was successful in seizing the important position on high ground. The next day, however, German snipers and artillery made it hot for us. Having taken the heights south of Carentan, we started to dig in to hold the ground. The 88s zeroed in on us, and for an hour and a half we were under the heaviest barrage the regiment had experienced so far. Since German tanks had flanked us, we were in danger of being cut off. I worked during this time with a litter crew going after the wounded; the demands from all the companies for litters and help were more than we could supply.

The aid station that had been set up in a farm house here was being abandoned, for it offered too good a target for the German tanks that were closing in. Chaplain Engel and I had run back into it for sulfa drugs which had been left there. Suddenly a shell hit the building. Flying glass cut Chaplain Engel on the face, arms, and legs. He refused my offer of help, grabbed what medical equipment he could, and ran out of the building to continue his work with the wounded. I temporarily lost my sense of hearing from the concussion and was stone deaf for about forty minutes. My hearing gradually came back to normal.

In combat even fairly close calls get monotonous, and one gets careless and reckless. However, just when you think that you can take care of yourself in any emergency, something happens to remind you that you are still mortal.

It is a strange thing that morale is highest when the going is toughest. In the thick of things there seems actually to be a zest for battle that makes it as interesting as a big traditional football game.

When it is over, one is sometimes disgusted with himself to realize how eager he was to play in this rotten kind of game. Only occasionally would I feel any emotion at the sight of a body, although I always stopped to say a prayer for the dead soldier whether he was German or American. Once in a while the sight of a boy I knew especially well would choke me up; his expression in death would bear no resemblance to the normal happy-go-lucky manner that I remembered.

Confession and Communion are the greatest comfort to our men at the front, and non-Catholics observed with open envy our Catholics receiving the sacraments. Many non-Catholic men came to confession at the front, and not infrequently I discovered that they received Communion from me without my realizing who they were.

Of course a priest in combat hears confessions and celebrates Mass under every conceivable circumstance. One Sunday Colonel Johnson told me that he thought it would be safe to hold Mass in the reserve battalion under a grove of trees. As a large number gathered there, I started to say Mass, using my jeep as an altar. Some German artillery observer must have spotted us. The 88 shells began to fall all around us. At the elevation a shell threw debris all over the jeep and altar. When I turned around to tell the men to scatter, I discovered they had already decided that they could finish hearing Mass from their foxholes. I finished Mass in record time.

One afternoon Captain Rhett, commander of headquarters company of the second battalion, and I were sitting on a mound paralleling a hedgerow, discussing the general situation. We were out of range of small-arms fire, or so we thought. Two bullets whistled past our heads; there was no mistaking the intention behind them. Captain Rhett had dug a foxhole a few feet away. We both took a dive for it, but I got there first. The captain tried to edge in, but there just wasn't room at the moment. Two more bullets kicked up little sprays of dirt a few feet away. Rhett lay flat on his stomach using language very unbecoming an officer and a gentleman and especially offensive when directed at a gentleman of the cloth; nor did he take kindly to my censure.

A little later in the day Rhett saw a chance to get even. He asked me, in the presence of his men, Chaplain, we have to go on a little patrol; do you want to go along?" He knew perfectly well that I didn't want to go along, but I didn't dare say so. The men might think I was what they call "chicken."

"Why, sure," I said, with an enthusiasm I was far from feeling. "I'd be glad to go along."

We had not gone far when the platoon was fired on from both sides. We hit the ditches, myself right behind the captain. The enemy were few, but their fire was rather heavy. After an exchange of fire and some maneuvering on our part, Corporal Hoff, who spoke German, called out to the German patrol to surrender, for we had them in a tight spot. Three of them came in with their hands above their heads. Two Germans were dead, one was dying. Three or four others had gotten away.

After three weeks in combat we were told that we were going to Cherbourg to garrison the vicinity of that city for a couple of weeks. On the way up there we stopped at Sainte-Mère-Eglise where all those who had died in the invasion had been moved and reburied in three tremendous cemeteries. I said two Requiem Masses there, one for my men and one for Father Maternowski, O.F.M. Conv., the chaplain for the 508th Parachute Infantry Regiment, who was killed on D-Day while he was helping a group of men out of a glider that was under machine-gun fire.

Father Maternowski, a tough and energetic little Pole, had been a great priest who had been extremely well liked and respected by the men of his regiment. On more than one occasion he had volunteered to put the gloves on with officers who interfered with his work, tried to wise-crack about the Church, or made smart remarks about confession. To the best of my knowledge no one ever took him up on the invitation, but even those with whom he sometimes had difficulties respected him. His method of straightening things out was very effective, even though a bit unconventional. His men would never forget Father Matty and would thereafter be better men for having known a priest who had deliberately given his life for his men.

The French people of the little city of Sainte-Mère-Eglise had arranged that each family adopt a couple of graves. On Sundays and Holy Days they bedecked them with flowers, promising always to remember these soldiers in their prayers. This promise still holds good. American visitors to the cemetery are always moved by the sight of a French family placing fresh flowers on a grave or kneeling there offering their prayers for the soul of an adopted son or brother whom they had never seen in life.

On the way to Cherbourg we passed through a town where the Free French were having a riotous time shaving the heads of women collaborators and marching them through the streets. A French priest who had spent considerable time in a German concentration camp told me that the very ones leading the demonstration had themselves been very friendly and helpful to the Germans. In Paris and other large French cities, our forces were cheered and wined and dined by the "patriotic" populace. But our men who had been captured by the Germans and marched through to prison camps a couple of months before had been spat upon, kicked, and hooted at by people in these same cities.

The regiment was stationed a few miles from Cherbourg just outside the walls of a tremendous convent, a motherhouse, school, novitiate, and hospital of one of the numerous orders of French nuns. About twelve of the fourteen buildings had been completely flattened by our bombers, for the Germans had been using it as a corps headquarters. Not one of the fifty or sixty sisters who were still there had been scratched by the bombing. They had been deep in the cellar of the twelfth-century main building that was burned to the ground; the eight-hundred-year-old basement had four-foot walls that held firm. How the sisters escaped suffocation I can't explain.

I asked the sisters for permission to use what remained of their hospital for our sick and some recently wounded. They were happy to allow us and were as solicitous as they could be. They were the most wonderful group of women I have ever known. Their convent had been burned down some twenty years before and then rebuilt. Now they were stacking the still warm bricks in piles and getting ready to build again. Their magnificent chapel had caved in on two sides, and the roof was now piled up on the floor. The good nuns were clearing away the debris as best they could.

The marvelous (maybe I should say "miraculous") thing about this chapel is the life-sized crucifix hanging above the side altar. It was not even scratched, and although I studied the altar below it and the ceiling that had crashed down, I could not find any possible explanation for the crucifix escaping serious damage; for it hung at least three feet from the wall. Splendid life-sized statues of Saints Peter and Paul stood unharmed on each side of the crucifix. I may be credulous, but to me that crucifix was a miracle of providential protection, and so the nuns regarded it.

When I asked for permission to say Mass there, the nuns were delighted. I sent a runner to assemble the Catholics of the regiment. Many of my Protestant friends also attended. The sisters cleared the debris from the altar, but the tabernacle was smashed. Bricks, plaster, and beams under foot made it difficult to move about. I shall never forget that Mass; we had lost so many fine men, yet we had much to be thankful for. We had been moved by stronger and deeper emotions during the past month than ever before in our lives. Because this had been our first combat, perhaps we would never be so deeply moved again. Men became, I had been told, ultimately blasé even about the death of their dearest comrades. We had not yet arrived at such a state, and I prayed we never would.

The men were intense and attentive as I spoke to them. The image of the naked Galilean hanging from the cross has always inspired great love and fierce hate. Nero sought to make the cross a hateful image by putting Christians to death upon it, pouring pitch upon them, and lighting Rome with these flaming human crosses. Julian the Apostate said that he would make the world forget the Man on the cross, but in his final agony he had to acknowledge, Thou has conquered, Galilean. Communists forbid its presence because they fear its power against their evil designs. Hitler has tried to replace the image of our Blessed Lord on the cross with a stupid swastika. Invectives, false philosophies, violence, and every diabolical scheme have been used to tear the Christ from the cross and the crucifix from the church. Nevertheless, like the bombs that were dropped on this chapel, they have only succeeded in making the cross stand out more and more in bold relief. The image we love grows greater in our understanding because of the vehemence of the hate it occasions in wicked men. Each of us has that sacred image stamped upon his soul. Like this chapel, we are temples of God. And no matter how we are torn by the bombs of tragedy and trial and assault from without, the image of the Crucified remains if we want it to. Now at the foot of this cross let us renew our baptismal vows. Let us promise to shield forever His image in our hearts.

We left the convent the following day. The sisters gave literally hundreds of rosaries and medals to my men. A windfall gave me the opportunity of repaying the sisters for their kindness. Our supply officer, Lieutenant Jenkins, told me that he had dozens of every type of brush and broom and a supply of lime, soap, and many other things that we had no further use for. This gift to the sisters was received with such expressions of gratitude that both the Lieutenant and I were embarrassed. You would have thought that we had just endowed them with a brand new convent.

We remained at Cherbourg for about two weeks. I held my Masses in a beautiful little French church in a village nearby our bivouac. Here as elsewhere the French people were very much impressed by the large number of American men attending Mass and receiving the sacraments. Every French priest I met commented upon it with wonder and admiration. This particular church had been hit several times by artillery from both sides, but it was far from ruined. However, because the pastor's home was in complete ruins, he was living in the sacristy. I took up a collection each Sunday for him. Seven thousand francs were donated one Sunday and eight thousand the following Sunday. (This, before devaluation of the franc, amounted to well over three hundred dollars.) The poor priest, with tears in his eyes, tried desperately to tell our men how grateful he was, for this was more than his congregation had been able to contribute in a whole year. He was truly a man of God. I have never met a French priest who did not impress me as being a really spiritual man.

When the regiment was bivouacked near Utah beach waiting for the boats to take us back to England, a young soldier by the name of Fritz Nyland came to see me. He was very troubled in mind. The company commander of his brother, who was with the 508th Regiment, told Fritz that this brother had been killed and was buried in the Sainte-Mère-Eglise cemetery. We jumped in my jeep and drove the twenty miles back to that town. In checking the cemetery roster I couldn't find the boy's name.

"There's no William Nyland listed here, Fritz," I said encouragingly, "though there is a Roland Nyland listed."

"Father . . . that's my brother too. He was a lieutenant in the Ninetieth Division." The unhappy boy tried to choke back the tears. After saying a few prayers at the grave, we went to another cemetery just a few blocks away where we found the grave we were looking for originally. A third brother had just been killed in the Pacific.

As we were driving back to the bivouac area, Fritz kept saying over and over again, more to himself than to me, "What will poor Butch do now? What will poor Butch do now?"

"Who is Butch, son?" I asked.

"Butch? Oh, shes my mother." I looked at him and wondered if he were suffering from combat exhaustion and the terrible shock of this afternoon's discovery. He must have read my thoughts, for he explained, "We four boys always called mom Butch these last few years. That's because, when we wanted to listen to swing orchestras and jive bands on the radio, mom would always turn on Gangbusters or some other program about gangsters. . . . She liked those. Now I'm the only son left." Mrs. Nyland had received three tragic wires within a week. However, we managed to get Fritz sent back to the states, so Butch still has one son to comfort her.

I never thought that I would want to see England again, but it was almost like coming home. On the boat going back I spent nearly all my time cutting the men's hair. (Barbering had been my "obedience" or job all during the seminary.) The rival GI barbers claimed it wasn't fair; they couldn't compete with my bargain of a haircut and confession both.

Now came the most difficult job of all: writing to all the parents or wives of the men we had lost in Normandy. I tried desperately to make each letter as personal as possible. Since in most cases I knew the men quite well, I could speak about the last time I saw them and bring out some kindly trait that the family would recognize. Chaplain Engel did the same for the Protestant men. However, we were both only partially successful, and most of the letters sounded very much alike. After all, how many ways are there to tell a mother and father you're sorry their son is dead? I could assure the parents, nevertheless, that their boy had received the sacraments just before we went into Normandy, and this was their greatest comfort.

We were not in England long before we were preparing for another mission. About this time I began to receive answers from the parents and wives of our deceased men. These letters are among the greatest consolations I have received as a priest. I shall always cherish them. It was wonderful to see with what courage and fortitude and faith these people accepted the terrible sacrifice that was demanded of them.

CHAPTER 5

Jump into Holland

THE OLD tent city outside Newbury looked pretty good to us, especially with the band out to give us a rousing welcome. The local citizens were more friendly than before, for with the invasion of Normandy, the establishment of a permanent beachhead, and the opening of the long-awaited second front, the tide of the war had changed. The biggest hurdle to the destruction of the Nazi power had been leaped, Fortress Europa had been breached, and the destruction of Hitler's forces was now an ultimate certainty. Confidence began to show in the faces of the tired, war-weary British. Yet, they knew full well that a great deal of blood was yet to be shed on both sides and that more sweat and tears would be required before the final victory. But these sacrifices would be readily accepted by the civilians and soldiers of every Allied nation as the price for peace with honor.

Since seven-day furloughs were being granted, the men took off for London to tear the city apart. They were given some stiff competition by the German V-1 bombs, commonly referred to as "buzz bombs." German bombers had stopped coming over, for, besides needing their airpower to bolster their own defense on two fronts, they had unleashed a new long-range artillery weapon, the V-1, in a desperate attempt to turn back the tide. Hitler's cherished dream of defeating England by bombing its cities and civilians had failed. However, he still had a few aces up his sleeve, and the V-1 was the first to be played. This pilotless missile, travelling about two hundred miles an hour, sounded like a 1920 (I am old enough to remember)

Hupmobile. When the motor stopped roaring, you jumped into a shelter or fell flat, for in a few seconds the bomb would hit with tremendous blast and concussion effect. As the buzz bombs kept coming over day and night, there were seldom warnings given, and it was impossible to take adequate cover. The effect on the British was even more staggering than the blitz had been during the first two years of the war. One of these bombs fell in the middle of a street in London killing thirty-two Americans riding in a bus.

The Franciscan Sisters at Coldash had all the chaplains of the area up for a special home-coming dinner. As always, the dinner was grand, but the real surprise came during the middle of the meal. Dozens of silver airplanes covered the ceiling of the dining room. Silk threads that couldn't be seen were pulled by someone in the next room opening the bomb-bay doors of the planes, and dozens of little men with paper parachutes floated down, each with a "Welcome home!" sign on his chest.

The children wanted to know what happened to this man and that man; each asked about the men she had prayed for, and wondered when their adopted brothers were coming up to see them. Many of the children had received answers from their soldiers who somehow or other had found time in Normandy to write to their little "sisters." One little freckled-faced, red-headed tyke with a tooth out in front tugged at my trousers and asked if "Happy" Houlihan was all right. I swallowed hard and told her that "Hap" was dead. I could have bitten my tongue out when her lovable little face saddened and tears began to well up in her eyes. But then she perked right up again and said, "Oh, then he is with Jesus." Everything was all right. I picked her up and almost hugged the life out of her.

Two days of my furlough were spent in London relaxing at the Regent Hotel whenever the buzz bombs would grant a few hours respite. I saw the Lunts in a Robert Sherwood play about the war, someone else in "Arsenic and Old Lace," and Bing Crosby and Barry Fitzgerald in "Going My Way." Then a group of us went to hear Glen Miller's orchestra, and that was the highlight of our entertainment. That was, I believe, Glens last public appearance, for a few days later the plane in which he was flying to France was lost. I returned to Newbury and a four-day retreat at the monastery. The

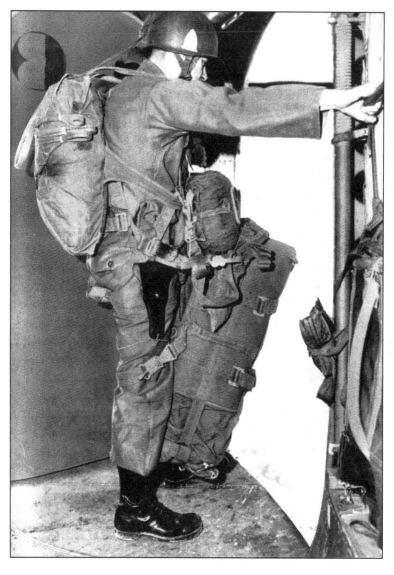

An 11th Airborner gets ready to jump.

Fathers there were most kind, and the peace and quiet of those days was just what I needed.

We were alerted again the first of September and were all ready to board the planes to jump behind the German lines at Le Mans, France, when word came down that the jump was cancelled. Patton's men were covering ground faster than they could plan another airborne operation. At a division review for Churchill, General Eisenhower thanked the men for what they had done in Normandy, decorated those who had distinguished themselves in a special manner, and stated that he looked to the 101st to justify his great confidence in future operations. In other words, our combat had just begun. Everyone swallowed hard on that one.

The regiment received several hundred replacements to take the places of those lost, killed, wounded, or missing. The battalion that had been stationed at Lambourne was at this time moved over to the regimental area; consequently more tents had to be put up, mess halls built, and so forth. As this was going on one day, the Countess on whose estate we were located made a tour of the grounds, accompanied by the keeper of the hounds and several of her dogs. She had just come from Colonel Johnson's office where she had told him that the next time an American soldier threw a hand grenade in her pond to get a fresh fish dinner, the soldier would get a caning from her personally. She was in a foul temper, and her dogs, baring their teeth, copied her mood well. She paused near a tall, lean, slow-drawling Texas lieutenant and myself. The lieutenant was supervising the men putting up tents.

"Lots of construction going on, isn't there, ma'am?" he said to the Countess, just trying to make conversation.

"Construction!" she said scornfully. "Don't be impertinent, young man. Destruction, don't you mean?"

"Well, ma'am," said the Texan, his face getting very red, "I guess you'll have to ask the men who died to save your damn estate the answer to that question." He started to walk away, then turned to me. "I'm sorry, Father, but I'm sore . . . damn sore."

September 16 we were briefed for our mission in Holland. I managed to get all the Catholics for Mass, but since time was so short, I had to give general absolution instead of hearing confessions. Everyone went to Holy Communion. As before the jump in

Normandy, I again shook hands with the men as they left the hangars to go to their respective planes; a large number of men knelt for a blessing.

We took off at eleven a.m. Escorted by P-47s we flew over the Channel, over Brittany and northern France, over Belgium, which was beautiful from the air, and then into Holland. There was not nearly as much flak sent up at us as in Normandy. At ten minutes of one we stood up and hooked up.

We jumped at one o'clock. Just after I left the door, I saw a large castle below with a wide moat encircling it. My chute opened well, but I had scarcely got my bearings again when I saw that I was swinging onto the top of another mans chute. I called out, *"Look out below!"* and tried to slip in the opposite direction, but it was too late. I landed almost in the middle of his chute and sank as if in quicksand. I lay down and tried to roll off. In the meantime my own chute collapsed and hung down, and now his chute was in danger of collapsing. I finally rolled off and both of our chutes blossomed out again just in time. . . . I was less than a hundred feet from the water. That was the closest I ever came to death in jumping, I think. We both lit squarely in the middle of the moat, but fortunately the water was only about four feet deep. Since we were not nearly as heavily loaded down as in Normandy, we were able to make the edge and help each other over the moat wall and the fence surrounding it. I had not heard a shot fired, and the day was so perfect that it seemed like a parade-ground jump. That illusion was dispelled a few hours later.

Quite a number of men had landed in trees, and there were many with broken arms and legs and back injuries. I located Doctor Kingston, who had jumped from my plane. He had landed in a tree and had hurt his back getting out. A drawbridge was over the moat, and the doctor suggested that we set up an aid station there immediately. Several aid men were about and began bringing the injured to the castle, which was now a museum. Torture racks, implements for mutilation, scourges, iron masks, and fearful pictures of these things in operation hung all about the many rooms. This was not the ideal place to inspire patients with confidence in an army doctor. The first patient had a broken arm and a dislocated wrist. I held the arm while a medic administered ether. The Doc pulled the bones into place. The boy woke up immediately with, "Gee, Father, are we

home already?" Then, looking about him, he began to realize where
he was and said, "Gosh, I had a swell dream about going home. How
many hours have I been here?"

Doc Kingston asked me to try to contact Colonel Kinnard, get
our location, and find out if the aid station should stay where it was.
The little Dutch town of Heezwik was only about a mile away. I
went there looking for Colonel Kinnard. More troopers were jumping in the area at this time, and the Dutch people were running out
to the men as they landed and offering them sandwiches and milk;
they would then cut the chute off the trooper, roll up the silk, and
carry it back home. Probably every Dutch house in that vicinity
eventually had parachute-silk curtains.

The people of the village were all out in the streets waving, cheer-
ing, and offering cool fresh milk to the Yanks. One of the soldiers
told them that I was a priest, and you can't imagine the excitement.
Southern Holland is solidly Catholic, and what Catholics! They
went immediately and got the pastor, who literally pushed me up to
the rectory, sat me down to a big meal, and summoned the village
barber. (I had a beard. We always wore them into combat—supposed to make you look tough, I guess.) First, however, I asked a
couple of soldiers to locate Colonel Kinnard and come back and let
me know where he was. Then I ate the fine dinner, was shaved, and
went outside where a whole monastery of Norbertines was waiting
to greet me. I had to shake everyone's hand. They all spoke English—all at once. This didn't seem much like real combat, or if it was,
I felt that I could take a lot more of the same kind.

The two GIs came back. They had located Colonel Kinnard, and
I went to tell him about Doc Kingston and to find out what our next
move would be. He told me that we were nearly eight miles from our
scheduled drop zone and that the battalion would have to hurry to
get there before nightfall and seize our objectives. He told me to
inform the Doc, then to procure some transportation from the civilians for the patients and aid men if possible, and to follow to Veghel.
I hurried back to the castle, told Kingston, and then went to procure
some vehicles if I could.

The Germans had taken all the motor vehicles from the Dutch,
but I was able to get two horse-drawn wagons and two Dutchmen to
drive them. When we came within about three hundred yards of the

castle, we saw Germans running all around the place. There was some firing going on. Three dead Americans were lying alongside of the road, and there was no sign of Captain Byrd, the headquarters commandant, who had been left there to form a road block. The castle was obviously now in the hands of the Germans, for the aid men had no weapons. We were lucky not to have been seen by the enemy, or, if seen, not considered worth attacking. My Dutch friends whipped the wagons around, and we hightailed it back to the village. I procured a scooter bike from one of the Dutch and set out for Veghel eight miles away to inform Colonel Kinnard. I located him there and gave him the story. He sent a platoon to try to retake the castle and rescue Doc Kingston, his aid men, and the patients. Unfortunately it was too late; they had all been removed by the Germans.

Things began to pop from all quarters. Our holiday jump turned into a nightmare for the next few hours. Then the Germans withdrew, but we knew that it was only to try to encircle us and that in a couple of days we would really be in for it. Our regimental aid station was set up in the magnificent and up-to-the-minute hospital in the town of Veghel operated by a splendid Dutch order of nuns. The priest chaplain of the hospital was very gracious. He got out all his pre-war tobacco and the radio which he had hidden from the Germans for four years. He had nightly sneaked into the basement to listen to BBC news. I couldn't convince him that a real battle was still to be fought, since the first two days were comparatively quiet.

"By the way, Father," the Dutch priest said, "how many Masses do you say a day?"

"One . . . when I can." It was a peculiar question for a priest to ask, since every priest is limited to one Mass per day except on Sundays or in an emergency. "Why do you ask?"

"You must use a great deal of wine at each Mass then," he replied, ignoring my question.

"Oh? No, I use very little, as a matter of fact." I was still puzzled.

"Well," he went on, "about twelve of your soldiers have come one at a time during the last two days asking for wine . . . said that you sent them, that you needed it for Mass."

"But I didn't send anybody. . . ." Then I caught on.

"I only gave the first three messengers the wine. Told the others I was out of wine after that," he said. We both had a good laugh.

But I began to wonder how many priests throughout Normandy and Holland (and probably England too) had been prevailed upon to part with their wine on the same pretext.

Lieutenant Ell, a fine Catholic officer from Wilkes Barre, told me an amusing incident he had heard about the Dutch underground. Two Dutch boys of about seventeen years of age had somehow received word of the coming Allied move into Holland. On the pretext that they knew where there was a big store of liquor, they had enticed German soldiers one at a time at night to the place of this hidden treasure. Once they got a soldier into the basement of the house, they hit him over the head, bound and gagged him, and put him into an escape-proof basement room. When the division came in, the boys turned their nineteen beaten, hungry, and embarrassed prisoners over to the Americans. I enjoyed the story, but that was the last time I saw Lieutenant Ell alive. He was killed near the Veghel cemetery the next day.

Our casualties were very small so far. The German artillery had been turned loose on the town of Veghel, and while the civilian casualties were heavy, few soldiers were hurt. Four nuns were killed when an 88 shell landed on the sisters' infirmary. Patients were taken to the basement of the hospital during the heavy barrage on the town. When I visited there, all were saying the rosary in unison.

Veghel was a lovely little city, and its church was really magnificent. It is impossible to describe how clean the Dutch are. Their homes are like doll houses and are very modern in style. They are far ahead of England or any place else in Europe. I would even say that the standard of living for the average person seemed to be above that of the United States. They scrubbed their sidewalks daily, and I would not have hesitated to eat off the brick street in front of the church.

The three Dutch doctors at the hospital were excellent men professionally and socially, and we became very good friends. The youngest of them, Doctor Leo Schrijvers, was to become one of the finest friends I had made since I left the States. Our regimental surgeon, Frank Carrel, later told me that Leo was one of the most skillful and talented young doctors he had ever seen. On one occasion an aid man had examined a patient waiting for surgery, listened for a heart beat and heard none, declared the soldier dead, and was having him removed when Doctor Schrijvers came up. The young doctor examined the patient again, quickly took a long hypodermic needle from his bag and plunged the needle directly into the soldiers heart. The heart began to beat again, and the young man survived.

One day as I was walking along the tracks at the edge of Veghel, I saw a platoon-sized group of men come through the woods up the dirt road. I sat down and waited for them, thinking that I would attach myself to them for the remainder of the day, for all was quiet in the city and most of the wounded had already been evacuated. When they were about two hundred yards away, I raised my field glasses and took a look. They were Germans. I took a nose-dive for the other side of the tracks and heard shots whine uncomfortably overhead. The really strange part of airborne operations is the constant presence of the enemy on all sides and the infiltration of each side into the others "lines." I hurried to tell the nearest unit CO about the German platoon. He immediately put one of his own platoons in that position.

Colonel Kinnard's first battalion was about to set out to take the key town of Schindel ten miles away. It was to be a surprise move, and we arrived at the town about one a.m. However, we did not surprise the Dutch underground, which was the best in all Europe. A Dutch priest, leader of the local underground, was waiting for us; the battalion staff went to his house, and he informed the Colonel that he had about ninety men armed and ready to help. He knew the number of the enemy in the vicinity and told exactly where they were. At this meeting was a boy of about sixteen dressed in a German uniform. He was Dutch but had enlisted in the German army to be more effective in the underground. Twelve years later I met this same young man, who is now a captain in the Dutch army, while visiting in Holland. He is presently attached to the American Military Assistance Group.

As a result of the information given, Colonel Kinnard seized the town without the loss of a single American life, and we had very few wounded. About sixty Germans were killed, twice that many wounded, and several hundred taken prisoner. We had to leave there in a hurry, however, to get the prisoners back to the division stockade, for German tanks were coming toward the town, and we had nothing to cope with tanks. I felt badly for the townspeople, who hated to see us leave; they had been so happy during their short liberation and were offering soldiers sandwiches and milk as they trooped out of town. When the tanks did get in, we were a couple of miles beyond and had set up road and tank blocks. Then we watched British Typhoons with rockets go to work on the tanks. A plane peeling off with those terrifying screaming rockets was an experience for the Germans that I did not envy.

We spent another week about Veghel, and the fighting became intense. In a regiment of two thousand men spread over a considerable area it is difficult for a chaplain to be present at the right places and at the right times when his men need him most. But Providence certainly guided my steps more than ever during these days, for few Catholic men died during this time without my being present to administer the last sacraments. I was carrying the Blessed Sacrament with me wherever I went. When I stopped in at a farm house being used as a battalion CP, a young soldier named Maloney, a battalion runner, wanted to go to confession and to receive Holy Communion. When we had taken care of this, the CO gave him a message to take to one of the companies. Just as he was about to leave, a stray bullet came through the door and went right through the boy's heart. His Communion of a few minutes before had become his Viaticum. Just then a soldier came in and said that a tree burst had hit one of the men a couple of hundred yards away. When I got there, I found that it was the regiment's other Maloney. He was dying. Extreme Unction and Viaticum fortified him for a very holy death. It was uncanny the way God was providing His greatest gifts and helps at life's crucial moment for His men through the medium of a very bewildered, scared, and unworthy priest.

We now moved up to Nijmegen; I rode a scooter-bike up there, since my jeep had not yet come in. On the way up I stopped off at Uden to see the famous church. The town had only about nine thousand inhabitants, but the church was almost as large as St. Patricks in New York and, I thought, just about as beautiful. The monks at the Crozier monastery invited my driver and me to dinner. One of the first priests I met had been a classmate of mine at The Catholic University of America in 1938. The monastery had been used as a German officers training school, and the last of them had just left a few days before. This was the first day the monks had reclaimed the main building, and Father Prior was supervising the removal of Hitler's and Goering's pictures from the dining hall before we sat down to eat. Father Founders and the present Father Generals pictures replaced those of the Nazi leaders. They seemed to look down from the walls with little smiles of complacency at having been restored to their rightful places of honor. The monks had all sorts of questions to ask about their missions in Minnesota and their high school and junior college in Onamia.

The first few days fighting north of Nijmegen was quite intense, and the casualties were heavy. The staff began to realize that the regiment was going to lose more men in this operation than it did in France. One battalion had clashed with an enemy unit at the dyke. The Germans are masters of the art of camouflage, but they never trouble to lower their voices. Every time a German would say anything, an American would toss a hand grenade over the dyke in that direction and then run, for a German grenade would come back over a few seconds later. This was probably the closest fighting in the war as the opposing sides were not more than thirty feet apart. The Germans, under cover of heavy fog at night, finally pulled back across the Rhine.

At this time while Colonel Johnson was inspecting the position of one of his companies along the dyke, several mortar shells began landing in the field. The other officers and enlisted men immediately hit the dirt as the book says and as they had learned to do in the hard school of experience. Jumpy just laughed at them and kidded them, little realizing that the next one to come in had his name on it. A fragment penetrated his back. He was immediately evacuated to the division hospital in Nijmegen, but he died enroute. He lived long enough to give instructions to Colonel Ewell, his executive officer, and his last words were, as mentioned earlier in this book, "Julian . . . take care of my boys."

Johnson had attended Mass in the bombed-out chapel of the convent in France that I have previously told about in this narrative. He had called me in that night and told me that he was thinking, and had been for some time, about coming into the Catholic Church. When we returned to England, he would like to have some things explained.

"It is the only church with enough guts to demand obedience and sacrifice [soldier virtues that he could understand]," he said, "and the only one capable of understanding and dealing mercifully with weak human nature. I like your business of confession." I remembered he had said the same thing about confession the first time I met him.

I thought that he had hit the nail right on the head, but I didn't want him to think that he was doing the Church a great favor by coming in. So I told him some of the obligations that would be his as a Catholic and finished with, "We have a lot of weak and bad Catholics . . . more than enough. But we are certainly in the market for anyone who wants to be a good one." I'm afraid that my lack of enthusiasm at that time hurt him, and I have always regretted my words. He was a man of tireless energy, unlimited ambition, and boundless enthusiasm, with a unique and irresistible, if somewhat trying, personality. Had a priest been with him before he died, I believe that he would have asked for baptism into the Church.

Colonel Julian Ewell took over the regiment, and he will always stand out in my mind as the near-perfect example of the officer and the gentleman. Whenever a company was going to be given a particularly difficult and dangerous mission, he would notify Chaplain Engel and myself so that we could hold our respective services. He had the keenest droll wit that I have ever known.

During his first week as CO, pressure was brought to bear from higher up because of the looting of livestock by the soldiers. Too many cows were ending up as steaks because they didn't know the password. The Dutch had complained to the military authorities. While Ewell was inspecting one of the battalions, it seemed that all the men were eating big two-inch steaks and pork chops; hams were hanging up in the trees to dry, and chicken feathers all over the place gave evidence of real variety in the menu. But Colonel Ballard was a resourceful fellow and had an excuse for everything. The cattle had been hit by 88 shells, the pigs had stepped on mines, and the chickens had just died, presumably from battle fatigue.

"Better to eat the things than to let them go to waste," Ballard pointed out. Finally, a pig came squealing and running past them, chased by four or five troopers, all firing at it.

"Look, Ballard," Ewell said, "I suppose you're going to tell me now that damn pig is attacking your men."

Somehow or other the news got through to us that Army had just beaten Notre Dame 59 to 0. Had the score been reversed I'm sure that it would have been censored out of our news channels, but I guess the top brass in Washington thought it would be good for the morale of the troops. It was—for the West Pointers—but it most certainly was not much of a morale booster for the Catholic chaplain of the regiment. I sent a note to the staff, asking that my mail be forwarded to me at the farthermost outpost. The beating Notre Dame took from the Army was nothing compared to the shellacking I was taking from the West Pointers. (Of course, as it was their first victory over Notre Dame in thirteen years, I could afford to be tolerant of their jibes.)

One Sunday I went up to the dyke to say Mass for the men on the main line of resistance (MLR). There was a nice little church beside the dyke, and the civilians, having been told by the soldiers that there was to be Mass, came in crowds. Just then the Germans started an intense barrage in that area. Of course, the battle-wise GIs took to their fox holes. The civilians, thinking that shells are only meant to kill soldiers, calmly filed along the top of the dyke and to church. Maybe it was their faith that saved them. Why a number of this group were not killed by 88s landing all about them I can't explain.

The Germans were occupying the high ground on the other side of the Rhine, and they could observe our movements quite well, for we had little cover on our side of the river. They apparently saw too many of us going into a farmhouse that was being used as a forward CP, and they opened up on it with their artillery. Of the twenty men in the house, one of them was known as the biggest liar in the regiment. He wanted to go home a hero—not by exposing himself to enemy fire, but by trying to get someone to put him in for an award on the basis of the stories of heroism he told about himself. To hear him talk, one would have thought that the whole German army had only one objective: eliminate him from the war and the victory would be theirs. During this heavy barrage most of us lay flat on the floor. Our would-be hero was lying with his legs spread apart. A shell came through the roof and buried itself between his legs. It was a dud.

After the shelling, he got up and was cursing and swearing. I said to him, "Why in heavens name Providence should be interested in saving your neck I can't imagine, but you ought to be thankful; a miracle saved your life."

"Yeah," he said, "but nobody will ever believe me now."

Talitha Cumi ("Maid, arise") was the name of a Protestant institution for wayward girls. It had been abandoned, and we were using it as a battalion headquarters. One evening after Mass there, a couple of my best boys stopped to talk with me for a while. One of them had just received a box of holy cards from his sister, a nun. He gave these to me to distribute among the men. The other was my regular server when I said Mass in this battalion. He had asked me to buy a crucifix for his mother when I was in Nijmegen. I gave him the crucifix, and he told me how much his mother would appreciate it. Just as I was about to pull out fifteen minutes later, the place was hit by three artillery shells. The two boys were instantly killed. War had never seemed more horrible and useless as I knelt to anoint them. The two of them had just received Holy Communion at Mass. The old cliché, *the good die young*, was no mere cliché in this instance.

Before we left Holland, we were told that we would have a regimental memorial ceremony at the cemetery. It is really shocking when you look upon row after row of white crosses, each one representing a young man you knew so well, so full of life before, so anxious to get home to his loved ones and they so anxious to see him again, and now. . . they lie here in Holland. Chaplain Engel said a short, appropriate prayer; Colonel Ewell called out the names of the deceased, and he spoke a few words of sincere appreciation for all they did; then I addressed the men assembled in formation in a complete square about the cemetery. Taps were blown, and the echo of taps was sounded from a distance.

The Colonel had had a wreath of flowers placed on each grave. After the ceremony he walked over to Colonel Johnson's grave and picked up a carnation from it. When he saw that I had observed him, he walked over to me and said, "I guess I'm a little soft, Father, but I thought his wife might like to have it."

Three days later we pulled out and were replaced by the British. We got out just in time, for that night the Germans dynamited the dykes and flooded the whole area. For us the Holland operation was finished.

CHAPTER 6

Defense of Bastogne

FROM Holland we drove in convoy through Belgium, by way of Louvain and Brussels, into France, and just beyond Rheims to Mourmelon, where we were to be quartered in an old French infantry camp. The Germans had been garrisoned there but had left in such a hurry that they had not destroyed anything. As a matter of fact, the Germans had made many improvements in the camp. The headquarters commander pointed out to Chaplain Engel and myself the buildings we were to use as both offices and billets. They were by far the most comfortable quarters we had had since leaving the States.

The first thing we noticed on entering the rooms was the art work on the walls. It had been done by a very talented artist, and with considerable skill, but was obscene beyond description. Chaplain Engel covered the art with blankets; he said his wife would know instinctively if he ever slept in a room where pictures of this sort were exposed to view. We agreed that such art would have to give way to our prudery, and the next day we would put a good thick layer of paint over it. We discovered that all the barracks of the men had been similarly decorated, but I'm afraid that most of the men were not as scrupulous on the subject as were Chaplain Engel and myself. The work had been done by the French, not the Germans, as was indicated by the signature at the base of each mural.

As we had arrived early Sunday morning several hours ahead of the rest of the convoys, Chaplain Engel suggested that we drive the eighteen miles back to Rheims in order that we might see the cathedral and that I might say Mass there. The Rheims cathedral is, I think, the most beautiful church I have ever seen. It is perfectly proportioned, lovely as a sonnet, and as delicate in its detail as fine lace. It is impossible to describe its ageless beauty. The five hundred and fifty carved figures on the exterior of the building seem to have been blended by the elements for eight hundred years right into the building stones, so that the effect is as though the entire structure is carved out of one gigantic piece of stone. Although the cathedral had been shelled badly during the first world war, it remains still a magnificent stone prayer, a lasting testimonial to the faith of the people who built it.

It was a privilege for me to say Mass that morning at the Blessed Sacrament altar. Chaplain Engel is a great student of ecclesiastical art and architecture and has an encyclopoedic knowledge of stained glass windows. Most of the windows that had been removed during the early stages of the war were now back in place, a sure sign of the French confidence that the war would not last much longer.

The regiment quickly settled down to training for the spring offensive the following March, for we had been told that we would not be used during the winter. We had lost too many men in France and Holland. Replacements weren't even in yet, and they had to be trained once they arrived. New equipment had to be procured. Many changes had to be made in the regiment. Yes, definitely we were told that we would be here for three or four months at least.

Since the Germans had built a fine, big theatre on the Post, the five priests in the 101st Airborne Division decided that we would have High Mass there every Sunday. The theatre held more than fifteen hundred, and we were able to fill it. I had to organize and conduct a choir, but since I knew so little about music, it didn't go too well. Happily, Lieutenant Roberts (he was Jewish) offered his services and took over the choir. In no time at all it was doing wonderful work and had expanded to ninety voices. The choir sounded so good that Colonel Ewell permitted it to take trips to the various hospitals in the vicinity to sing for the patients. The priests took turns in saying the main High Mass on Sundays and in preaching, while the other priests heard confessions all during the Mass.

Chaplain Engel and I were able to get to Paris a couple of times while stationed at Mourmelon. Even in wartime that city is like no

Geronimo!

other in the world. It is the most beautiful I have ever seen, with an endless number of famous places of interest. Its morals are candidly pagan. The French people are a paradox to the foreigner. However, I imagine that Americans are likewise a paradox to foreigners. Engel and I were fortunate enough to procure tickets for the ballet, and the Paris Opera House more than lived up to our expectations. The ballet was entertaining (my first), especially so when the ballerina, during one of her intricate twirls, fell. She rose, however, smiled prettily, and carried it off quite well.

When the replacements arrived, Colonel Ewell assembled them and spoke to them in a kindly way. As he welcomed them as full-fledged members of the regiment, he told them that the men they had replaced had set a very high standard of military service and that the new men were obligated to live up to that standard. His wonder-fully droll wit won the new men to his side immediately. Then the Colonel introduced each staff member in his own inimitably funny way. When he finally came to me, he said, "Men, this is Father Sampson. He will take care of you fish-eaters. In Alabama he lit in the Chattahoochee; in England he lit in a lake; in Normandy he lit in a creek; in Holland he lit in the canal. And I guess, if he ever jumps in the Sahara Desert, he will land in a puddle left by some cockeyed camel."

Chaplain Engel was present and almost fell off his seat from laughing—until the Colonel introduced him. "Now you left-footers, this is Chaplain Engel, the Protestant chaplain, and if I catch any of you saluting or wearing the uniform the way he does, I'll have you court-martialed." This time it was my turn to laugh. On our way back to our offices Chaplain Engel was unusually serious and quiet, and I was afraid that Ewell's crack might have hurt him. I knew the Colonel only intended to rib him, and I told Engel so.

"Father Sampson," he said soberly, "I have just been thinking. You know, I believe that the frequency of your immersions must be a providential sign that you should have been a Baptist."

Chaplain Engel and I had just finished writing letters to the families of our Holland casualties when we were awakened at two a.m. by Lieutenant Lawrence Critchell, the assistant adjutant. He told us that as Von Rundstedt was making a big break-through, we would be leaving immediately to plug the gap. We had been in

Mourmelon just a little over three weeks (and had been told we would be there at least three months). A large number of men were on pass, and the military police in Paris, Rheims, Mourmelon, and other cities were ordered to send all airborne men back to their base camp immediately. An officer was to be left behind to gather this group together and to follow us up to Bastogne.

Chaplain Engel and I were busy packing when the whole regimental band appeared. They were fighting mad. They had been the butt of constant jibes by the men of the regiment for having missed the operations in Normandy and Holland.

"Father," their spokesman said, "we have been ordered to stay behind again. We joined the paratroopers because we want to fight in this war."

"So?" I said, sensing that they expected me to give them a green light to disobey orders. "What can I do about that?"

"We thought you might speak to the Colonel."

"Speak to the Colonel?" I replied. "He'd throw me out of his office if I bothered him now. Besides, he's up at division headquarters, I'm sure, getting his instructions."

"Well, then, how about our jumping on some of the trucks when they pull out? This might be our last chance."

I shrugged my shoulders. I was on the spot and evaded the question; but at least I didn't say, "No!" They must have guessed that I personally thought the Colonel would be mighty glad to have a few extra men to bolster our thinned-out companies. Each company in the regiment found a couple of band members in line with them later at Bastogne, and from all I heard, they gave an excellent account of themselves. Several of them were wounded, but none that I know of were killed. Thus they regained in full measure the respect of the other men of the regiment.

We were leaving in such a hurry this time, and everyone was so busy throwing the few things we were able to take with us into bags, that there wasn't time to get the whole regiment together for Mass. Nor did I have time for confessions. I said Mass, and just before we pulled out, I went around to each company, called the Catholics together, gave general absolution, and distributed Holy Communion.

The several hundred new men in the regiment who had arrived only the week before had had no battle experience as yet. These men went into Bastogne very scared, poorly trained, and inadequately equipped. Nevertheless they were ready and willing. They quickly absorbed the spirit of the regiment, profited by the experience of the men alongside them, learned quickly, and, all in all, acquitted themselves well. Within a week they would be almost indistinguishable from the veterans. The older men, who had had their baptism of fire in Normandy, had matured a great deal. They had molded themselves into a smooth unit in Holland; now they were like the parts of a high-priced watch, working together smoothly and with absolute reliance and confidence in each other to do the job that was expected of them. The regiment was no longer just a collection of individuals; it was a single weapon of war. It had to be; it had to help stop in the next few days the last and most desperate attempt of the German army to reclaim the offensive. The Germans failed to do so only by the smallest of margins. Had they been successful, the war might have been extended by at least another year.

Chaplain Engel and I threw our combat equipment and bedrolls into my jeep (Chaplain Engels jeep was being overhauled), piled in, and took off for Bastogne, about a hundred and fifty miles away. The atmosphere around that town of about fifteen thousand was really confused. Roads were jammed with vehicles going both ways. A truck company commander leading his forty or fifty trucks westward had jammed the division's ten-mile-long convoy trying to get to Bastogne in a hurry. When General Higgins, our division deputy commander, ordered the captain to take his trucks off the road, he refused. General Higgins pulled his forty-five out and ordered the captain once more. This time he saw the wisdom of prompt obedience. Emergency called for emergency measures.

By sheer luck we found the regimental CP Colonel Ewell had his staff and battalion commanders there; he was pointing out on a map what little he had been told about the situation. When he finished, he looked around and said, "Any questions?" All the officers just looked at him with open mouths. Ewell broke into one of his rare laughs, "Cripes, what a mess, huh?" The tension relaxed. "Well, nuts! The situation is bound to clarify some in the morning. In the meantime the enemy are sure to be just about as confused as we are." With his frank appraisal and cool manner, Ewell had reminded these officers that they were under the finest leadership our country could provide for any regiment. Then he spotted Engel and myself. "Hi, Chaplains. How about putting a petition in to your Boss for clear weather tomorrow? Were going to need some air support. How about a cup of tea?" He poured some hot water into two cups, took out a much-used tea bag from his pocket, and dunked it a few times in each cup. A greater sacrifice for a buddy could be expected of no soldier.

The first day was not too bad, and our casualties were not very heavy. Ewell had been right; the Germans had apparently been so confused by the variey of reports from their patrols that they had paused just long enough for Ewell to get his battalions in position in time to be able to blunt the point of Rundstedts spear-thrust into Bastogne.

The regimental headquarters had moved into a Catholic junior seminary. We always seemed to headquarter in a church building. The rector of the seminary came to me with a problem.

"I have about thirty boys here," he said. "Do you think I should try to get them out of Bastogne or not?"

"I can't tell you, Father. I really don't know what would be best. There may be some fighting in the city later on. Do you have a deep basement where you can take the boys if it comes to that ? On the other hand, we know that we are just about surrounded and in a day or so may be entirely surrounded . . . we may be now, for all I know."

I wasn't much help to him.

I attached myself for the time being to a company just a mile or so west of the city. A soldier told me that there was a man a couple of hundred yards down the road in a culvert by the railroad tracks. He was wounded and had called out for a priest (a rare request under such circumstances, for a man just doesn't count on a priest being at hand everyplace). I asked the soldier to take me to him and grabbed an aid man to help me. A German tank had been knocked out on the road between us and the wounded man, but a German was still manning the machine gun on the tank. As we skirted his immediate area and started to climb through the fence, he let go at us. The soldier leading us had the upper bone in his arm shattered by a bullet. We all three took a dive to the ditch by the railroad track. The wounded soldier pointed out with his good arm where the man I was looking for was. The medic and I went to him. We were pinned down by crossfire. I lay down beside the wounded man, heard his confession, and anointed him. He uttered no word of complaint but expressed his thanks. He felt everything was going to be all right now. The aid man indicated with a shake of the head that the man didn't have a chance, but we carried him back to our position, and some other men took him to the aid station. I never heard whether he lived or not; he was not from our regiment.

Our regimental aid station was set up in the chapel of the seminary, and the wounded started coming in. The Germans had practically encircled the town, and enemy company and battalion-sized units were attacking from several directions. Their idea was to spread our defense so thin around the city that the main German force could hit us with all they had from the east. When they began to shell the city heavily with their big guns, we had nothing comparable to send back at them. Several days later they thought they had the 101st softened up enough to demand our surrender. They sent three officers in under a flag of truce with the terse ultimatum: "Surrender or be annihilated."

McAuliffe looked at the note and mumbled to his staff, "Nuts!" Then he turned to Colonel Kinnard, the youthful Division G-3. "What shall I say in answer to this stupid note?"

"I like the answer you just gave," Kinnard replied.

"What's that?"

"Nuts!"

"Good. NUTS it is." The General took a sheet of paper and printed the words in two-inch letters and returned it to the German officers, who were then blindfolded again and returned to their lines. It is said to have taken the German commander three hours to decipher the meaning of "nuts." Our general didn't know at the time that he was also labelling himself for life; he will always be remembered as "Nuts" McAuliffe. All this happened when I was no longer with the division but was a guest of the Germans for the duration.

Combat exhaustion is a peculiar thing and accounts for a large percentage of the casualties of a fighting outfit. Sometimes it would afflict men in very strange ways. One little fellow had given a wonderful account of himself in both Normandy and Holland. He was credited with knocking out a German tank with his bazooka, had volunteered for several very successful patrols, and had, on another occasion, helped wipe out a machine-gun nest. For these accomplishments he had been decorated twice. However, the lad just couldn't stand artillery. When the Germans were throwing in a few 88s at us, he lay in his foxhole shaking like a leaf and crying. Day by day he got worse, and even our own shells going out frightened him. He protested being evacuated, but his hysterical fear of artillery had become a bad morale factor, for fear and hysteria are contagious. There was nothing wrong with this boy's courage; he had plenty of it, more than most men; but combat exhaustion had made him useless to the regiment.

There were numerous other cases in which men had been subjected to as much fear and suffering as they were capable of enduring, then broke under the pressure of further demands too great for them to sustain. These men were as sick as those wounded by bullets or by fragments of enemy shells, and their evacuation was just as honorable. Yet, they were sometimes to suffer even further from the false accusations of their comrades, or from their own unfair suspicions regarding their courage.

On the twentieth of December, I was sitting around after dinner with a group of regimental headquarters men, Doc Waldman, one of the surgeons, and several of his aid men. As wounded had really been coming in fast, we were all quite tired from caring for them. We were just having a smoke and a short break when Mr. Sheen, the Communcations Warrant Officer, came in. "You should see what I have just seen," he said. "A group of troopers machine-gunned on the road about two miles north of here." I asked him where the place was . . . perhaps some wounded were left there. He couldn't explain it very well on the map, for there were four roads going north out of Bastogne.

My driver, Cpl. Adams, and I piled into the jeep and went to try to find the place. Since we couldn't find the bodies Sheen had spoken about, I decided to keep going a mile or so farther on to where our division medical company had been captured by the Germans the night before. A few German vehicles, armored cars, etc., had come up from a side road, shot up several American trucks bringing in supplies, and captured our whole medical company at the same time. Our own regimental supply trucks had been captured there too, along with several aid men. Since Doc Waldman told me that we were getting very short of supplies, I decided to salvage some of the stuff that the Germans had left behind. We loaded the jeep with two chests of much-needed equipment and were ready to head back to the regimental aid station.

However, a soldier on outpost guard told me that there had been quite a skirmish the previous night on the other side of the hill. He thought there might still be some wounded left there. Perhaps that was the place Sheen had referred to, I reasoned. We drove over the hill to see, and just over the crest of the hill we ran into Germans . . . hundreds of them. An armored car levelled its gun at us, and the Germans jumped out from behind trees yelling something. A light reconnaissance vehicle came up quickly.

"Stop the jeep, Adams," I said. "I'm sorry I got you into this mess."

"That's O.K., Father," he mumbled. We were captured.

PART III

A POW in Stalag II-A

Father Sampson as a POW.

CHAPTER 7

Journey to Stalag II-A

A GERMAN lieutenant got into my jeep and told me to keep driving down to the bottom of the hill, where there was a little village. The German soldiers there were having a time for themselves. They had broken into a small warehouse and were dragging the stuff out, smashing the canned goods against the wall, and looking through the other things to see if they wanted them. They had broken into a little school, had come out with musical instruments, and were blowing on the horns and beating the drums. These men were either suffering from combat exhaustion (which sometimes affects men in this fashion), or they were drunk, or they were under the influence of drugs of some type. The lieutenant took me aside and started questioning me, but I told him that name, rank, and serial number were all that I could tell him. I had my division patch on my shoulder, however, and "501" was clearly painted on the bumper of my jeep. He seemed like a decent fellow and didn't press me any further. Then he took Adams aside and spoke to him for a few minutes. The lieutenant left us for a bit, presumably to call his commander about our capture.

As soon as he went, the soldiers started after the stuff in my jeep. They threw out the two foot lockers of medical supplies and went through them, tossing sulfa drugs and penicillin into the ditch. I guessed that they might have real need of these things themselves before too many days had passed. Chaplain Engels Communion set was then tossed out, and a soldier took the chalice as a souvenir. I tried to rescue it without success. Then they got the box of cookies my Aunt Millie had sent me for Christmas; they dove into these and made short work of them. It had taken considerable self-control to save those cookies for Christmas, and I felt like kicking myself now for not having eaten them as soon as they had arrived.

A mule-faced, boorish soldier grabbed my arm and yanked my wristwatch off. I told him that I was a priest and an American captain and asked for it back. He just laughed. A couple of other soldiers began to argue with him, in my behalf I gathered, but without success. I began calling for the German officer as loudly as I could. The fellow started to go away, but I followed him, still calling for the lieutenant. Finally, with what I took for German profanity, he handed my watch back to me. (That was lesson number one in dealing with German soldiers. Yell at them, scream at them, get red in the face, distend your neck muscles, and be flushed with anger. The soft word never works. They seem to regard as weakness any order or demand that is not backed by the mailed fist.) The lieutenant returned and ordered my driver and me into an American half-track which they had apparently captured. We headed east. The next fifteen days were to be miserable ones. The first several hours were to be interesting, however. Three young German soldiers in the half-track seemed decent young men. As one of them could speak some English, he became their interpreter. They all spoke about their families, showing me pictures of their parents, brothers and sisters, and, of course, their sweethearts. All of them were Catholic and treated me with great respect. They wondered at a priest being in the army and said that although they had heard that their division had one chaplain (there are eighteen chaplains to a division in the American Army) none of them had seen him in two years of service.

Since I couldn't be sure that they were not after military information of some sort, I let them do the talking. They talked about everything during our five-hour trip. I was amazed at their ignorance of the real issues of the war. How thoroughly the propaganda about the Jews and "American-British imperialism" had been swallowed.

On our way back to their rear we passed miles and miles of German armored vehicles and tanks moving westward. They were making good use of many American vehicles which they had captured. This was the line, I later discovered, which was supposed to deliver the knockout punch at surrounded Bastogne.

At some little town in Luxembourg, Adams and I were let out to join a group of other captured Americans who were being marched to the rear. We stopped briefly to be interrogated by a German intelligence officer. This was the first day in more than a week on which the sun had come out.

"Where are your planes?" he asked.

"It hasn't been flying weather lately," I replied.

"But look! The sun is out. Perhaps you haven't heard the news. German all-weather planes have demolished the American and British airfields during the last two days. Yes, this is the turning point; you Americans without your Air Force will be finished, don't you think?"

"I don't know," I said, not wishing to argue.

"You will see, you will see." Could he actually believe that the American Air Force could be destroyed by two German raids? I wondered. At any rate he was trying hard to believe it.

After this short interrogation our small group of about thirty Americans were marched the rest of the day and into the night until two a.m. when we were herded into a filthy barn on the edge of a Luxembourg village. We remained there for about thirty hours. Despite my pounding on the door to demand food and water, the only response we got was an occasional laugh from the soldiers outside. I was the only officer in the group and knew that the men expected me to try to get their physical needs from the Germans. It was important that we maintain a degree of morale and discipline too, for lack of these things would give the German interrogators the opening they wanted.

About eleven p.m. the second night a German intelligence officer came to the door and called for me. He said that he hadn't known that there was an officer in our group (which I knew was a lie), and that I would have received better treatment if he had. He started his interrogation. When I told him that name, rank, and serial number were all I could give, as he well knew, he proceeded to tell me all about my outfit. My jeep had provided my regiment number. He spoke a bit about the history of the 101st Airborne Division, the part it played in Normandy and Holland, who our division commander was, and who our regimental CO was. (He was a few months behind on that; he didn't know that Colonel Johnson had been killed in Holland.)

After he had interrogated the rest of the men, he called me back in, saying he couldn't sleep and would like to talk with me. He offered me coffee and bread and cheese. I said that I should like some very much if he were offering it to all the men with me, that I considered it very unfair treatment of prisoners not to give them any food or water for nearly thirty-six hours. He called a German soldier and had one loaf of sliced black bread and a pail of water sent in to our men. He regretted that no supplies or provisions had come through yet for prisoners; we were too close to the front, and his own men had barely enough for themselves. He assured me that at our next stop we would be well fed, a lie that was to be repeated by other German officers many times and was to get very monotonous during the next two weeks.

For three hours until dawn the interrogator amazed me with the strangest monologue I have ever listened to. He had been a merchant in Hamburg, had a family, and delighted in showing me a hundred or more pictures of his wife and children, relatives, friends, and so on.

"See, here is my wife, Inge, and our children, Wolfgang and Maria, . . . this was taken on the Sugzpitze. That is the tallest mountain in Germany; wonderful skiing there, just wonderful. My Wolfgang is a fine skier for a little boy—only he isn't a little boy any more. He is fifteen and will be in the army next year. How I miss them!" The poor man was so homesick he was almost crying.

Then he spoke of the position of the Church in Germany—that it was the only stable and sensible organization in a world gone mad. The Church in Germany was very strong, much stronger than in France or even in Italy. He himself had been surprised at the German break-through but was convinced that it would peter out in a few weeks. He knew, as all sensible Germans knew, that Germany was beaten and had lost the war when she was driven out of Africa. America was more civilized than Germany, but Germany was more cultured than America. England was the real cause of the war, Russia the real menace to future civilization. Germans were home-loving, kindly, and unwarlike people, but the Nazi regime was ambitious, insanely so. Germany might have won the war had its stupid leaders been content with Austria, Hungary, Slovakia, Poland; or had they invaded England, which could have been done without great losses; or had Russia been left alone until England was defeated. Then a comparison of the various religions of the world. And so on and on until dawn. He seemed to be talking to himself rather than to me. He had gone on with all this without my asking any questions and without any apparent effort to draw me out. I didn't get it, unless I was simply being used as a soundboard for his emotional jag; he probably got some relief from vocalizing his frustrations and homesickness. He finished by telling me that he was sick of war, and that he could quite possibly be executed if the Gestapo knew what he had told me. I actually felt sorry for the poor guy.

In the morning we started to march again. No breakfast. No lunch. We stopped late that night at a rear-area supply depot and were each given a cold boiled potato and a small green apple. By this time we had joined about four hundred other prisoners and were split into two groups. That night we slept in a tiny church and were crowded enough to keep fairly warm. Again no breakfast the following morning. We marched until dark. No noon meal and no supper. This time we stayed in a large, dismantled factory and slept close together trying to keep warm, for the weather was bitterly cold.

The next day American planes came over, literally thousands of them. In tremendous waves they came from the west, from the south, from the north. They looked like great swarms of bees. I'd have given anything at that time to see the face of the interrogator who had said that the German all-weather planes had knocked out the American Air Force. The American prisoners tried to hide their elation from the guards. We passed a long German motorized column moving up to the front, and as we did so, some P-40s began to strafe the mechanized troops and vehicles. The weather had cleared perfectly. Following our guards we dashed into the woods and skirted the road for the next several miles. What a tremendous job those planes did! One vehicle after another went up in flames. The German casualties were so great that we began to fear German reprisal action against us.

We had walked from Belgium all the way across Luxembourg, and on Christmas Day we walked without breakfast or lunch to

Prum, Germany. We were herded (now more than eight hundred of us) into the large auditorium of a good-sized school where Hitler's and Goerings pictures covered the front wall. We were told that we were going to be fed, that the food was then being prepared. We expected that even the Nazis might remember that this was Christmas night. Our supper consisted of one half of a boiled turnip, a half slice of bread, and a cup of warm water. Nothing else.

The men were in a mood to riot. I suggested to the American colonel in charge of our group that I hold a short Christmas service. It was a black night and the city was being bombed constantly. The school we were in was in the most dangerous place in the city, right in the middle, and not far from the railroad station. A near miss would collapse the building. We sang *Silent Night, Holy Night* with the roar of planes overhead and bombs dropping near enough to make the building shiver. When one of the men started to read the gospel by the light of a small candle, a German officer came in and took this light away from him. In pitch dark without being able to see my congregation of eight hundred tired, hungry, and desperate soldiers, I said a prayer and then spoke to them for about fifteen or twenty minutes. The idea of the sermon was that Christ is always where He is least expected to be, and that He was just as surely among us that night as He was in the manger in the smallest and least-known village of Judea nineteen hundred years ago. Though we might be thousands of miles from home, in enemy hands, cold and hungry, we had that which makes Christmas Christmas, and He was stretching forth His infant hand to each of us to give us courage and help as we knelt to adore Him.

The next day we were given one slice of bread as we started on our way. No dinner. No supper. We marched about twenty miles to the town of Gerolstein where there was a group of about seven hundred Americans who had arrived one hour ahead of us. All fifteen hundred of us were pushed into an enormous bombed-out factory building. Just before we went in, American bombers came over. We prayed that they would keep on going, but, just as we thought they had passed us up without dropping any unwelcome Christmas gifts, we heard the terrifying whistle of falling bombs. As we hit the ground, the most terrific blasts bounced us up in the air. They had hit about two hundred yards away just next to the other group of prisoners. Eight or nine of that group were killed and many badly wounded. About thirty Americans were killed in the group about a mile ahead of us.

Some of the bombs hit the local hospital in which were several Americans. All the wounded Americans were sent down to our building, and, although we were so packed in that we couldn't budge, let alone sit or lie down, we had to make room for almost a hundred wounded. None of us would ever forget the filth and misery of the place. The patience of these wounded was a great lesson to all of us. A lieutenant with his leg blown off just below the hip told us to take care of the other men first. He died quietly during the night, as did several of the other wounded. Although our aid men had no equipment left to take care of the wounded, the Germans ignored all requests for bandages and compresses. A number of the prisoners were sent to assist in putting out fires in the bombed city, and they were abused unmercifully by the soldiers and civilians.

We were given nothing to eat that night, or the next morning, or the next afternoon. We were allowed out one at a time to relieve ourselves. I was allowed out to bury our dead in a local improvised cemetery. The Germans always seemed more solicitous about the dead than about the living.

When I returned to the building after burying the dead, I saw a guard stop a prisoner who came out to relieve himself. I watched for a bit before going back in. The guard offered a slice of bread for a wrist watch. The American made the exchange. The German made the same offer to the next man; he had no watch, but only a Parker pen. He offered that to the guard for the bread; the guard took the pen and tore the slice of bread in two and gave the soldier half a slice for it.

That night the first group of prisoners were sent down to the depot, which was already being repaired from the damage of the previous night's bombing. The men were placed in boxcars and sealed in. It was still early evening, and a group of P-40s came over, strafed the railroad yards, and unwittingly killed eleven more of their own countrymen. Gerolstein will always remain in my mind as a town of misery for both Germans and Americans.

Bombs are the most terrifying of all the weapons of war, for there is nothing you can do during a raid but pray.

The next morning each man received a cup of soup, a fifth of a loaf of bread, and two inches of liverwurst. The guards told us that this was to be our ration for two days, but every man was so starved that he bolted the whole ration almost at once.

We walked for the next two days from dawn till dark without food. American fighter planes looking for targets would sometimes swoop down at us, but we stayed in formation and waved whatever we had. They would recognize us as Americans, tip their wings and wave, then look elsewhere for something to attack. Often, as we approached a town, it would be just getting a going-over by fighter planes and dive-bombers. We would have to wait at the edge of town until it was over. You can be sure we were not royally welcomed in these bombed villages. I had an air corps leather jacket on. A civilian spotting this ran up and cracked me in the rear with a shovel. It didn't hurt very much, and after seeing the wrecked house that he returned to, I could scarcely blame him. However, after that, I was careful to wear my trenchcoat over the jacket when we went through towns.

On our march through this part of Germany we saw dozens of V-1 buzz bombs take off from their camouflaged ramps on the other side of the hills that paralleled the road. With orange flame pouring out of the rear ends, they looked like giant birds with their tails on fire. Not infrequently we could see ten or twelve in the air at the same time. Watching these at least diverted our minds from our aching feet and our empty stomachs.

The first time we saw a V-2 launched from a distance of several hundred yards it frightened all of us. The guards were as scared as we were, for they hadn't seen these before either. The V-1 buzz bomb is to the V-2 as a 22 calibre shot is to a 155 mm shell. These huge monsters of destruction took off with such a terrific roar that we thought at first that a giant plane was crashing at full speed right on top of us. Then followed a very loud swoosh-sh-shing sound, and we looked up to see a ten-thousand-foot vapor serpent begin to dissolve slowly as the rocket, still visible many thousands of feet higher, gradually went out of sight. These rockets climbed more than sixty miles into the stratosphere before they began to descend with supersonic speed upon some unsuspecting section of England. The rockets were about the size of a C-47 plane. Observation platforms, always crowded with civilians, were placed a few hundred yards from the launching sites. It must have been a tremendous boost to their wavering morale to know that they possessed such a mighty weapon of war. It was a hard blow to our own morale, however, for we could visualize these things dealing death and destruction to our forces at Bastogne and all along the front.

On the second night out of Gerolstein we stopped at the little village of Boz. Here the townspeople went all out to feed us as best they could. Every housewife made potato soup and sandwiches and hot coffee (even ersatz coffee tasted good). These people were very kind, and when they found out that I was a priest, they tried to do even more. I couldn't quite understand why the people of Boz were so different; then one of the women informed us that the town's Catholic pastor had told all his parishioners to do what they could for any prisoners who passed through. I vowed to return to Boz someday, if I could, and thank the people and their priest for what they had done for us.

Many of the men were getting footsore and had difficulty keeping up. We marched till dark and were put in a warehouse; but it was so bitter cold that the guards decided to march us all night rather than have us try to sleep on the cement floor of that frame building. At three a.m. we arrived at Koblenz. A more devastated city I had never seen. Another bomb dropped on it would simply have been wasted; it could only have moved the debris from one place to another. This city of about three hundred thousand was absolutely and totally destroyed. We waited at the edge of the city until the usual morning air raid was over. Then, to our amazement, people by the thousands came out of holes and cellars to go about their business. We tried to make our way through the city, but fallen buildings blocked every street. Finally, holding each other's hand we had to walk carefully single-file across the bombed and wrecked bridge on the Rhine. We had now walked twenty-four hours straight and had had to drop many men off at village infirmaries.

Ten kilometers beyond Koblenz we received our first rations in almost three days. Each man got a fifth of a loaf of black bread, and six men shared a quart can of pressed meat. Most of us ate the food as soon as it was given to us. Then they pushed us on with no rest. It was sleeting and very cold. We were in wretched spirits. Most of the men were in bad physical shape by now; every step from there on was in misery.

At three in the afternoon we arrived absolutely exhausted at Bad Ems—well named, believe me. We felt that we could go no farther. But the townspeople would not have us; they refused to allow us to stay in the town stables, which had nothing in them but mighty inviting straw. They marched us into the park in the town square, and the people came out in droves to ridicule and laugh at us. I was proud to be a member of that tired, worn-out group of Yanks. One of the men called for a prayer. Every man bowed his head as I led the prayer for strength and courage for all of us, and we finished with the Our Father. The hospital there was also a corps headquarters— a violation of the Geneva rules. The German officers refused to speak or listen to our American colonel, and they sent a sergeant out to tell us to get moving. The colonel and one of the two doctors with us and two majors were through. They had to be helped to the local hospital. The rest of us moved on at the orders of our guards.

About twenty kilometers on to the next town, which turned out to be Limburg, and we were definitely finished. We could go no farther. They told us that there was a prison camp only three miles from town. This, we felt sure, must be our destination. Just then warning sirens sounded—the first warning. A few minutes later a different signal from the sirens indicated that the planes were definitely headed this way. Then came the repeated sirens, the signal to hit for the air raid shelters.

The guards took all of us down to one of these huge underground cement shelters. It had dozens of very large rooms deep and safe from anything but a block-buster. The Germans poured in by the hundreds; children and mothers with babes in arms, old folks and sick people, soldiers and ministers, police and prostitutes. There was no panic, and everything was done with fine order as though it had been a daily habit for years.

The look on these poor peoples faces was enough to soften even our own bitterness into something like sympathy and compassion. They regarded us with neither fear nor hatred; nor did it seem to occur to them to enjoy seeing us subjected to a bombing from our own planes. One of the pilots in our group told me that had he been able to really envision the misery suffered by the poor people of the towns he bombed, he would never have been able to do it. In a plane, he said, it all seemed so impersonal.

Then the American planes came over. Limburg was apparently not their target for that night. They passed over the city dropping only five or six bombs as a token that the city was not forgotten and would be taken care of later.

When we came out of the shelter we were told that the Limburg Stalag was absolutely filled up with prisoners; it could hold no more, and we must go on. Major Saunders, the ranking prisoner since the colonel was put in the hospital, told the chief guard that we were not capable of walking farther, that we must stop here, that we would be glad to sleep in the air raid shelters or in the park—anyplace. The chief guard went to see the local commandant for instructions. It was three hours before he returned. We were desolate because we were not taken to the Limburg prison camp, little realizing at that time how fortunate it was for us that they had no more room. Two days after this, New Years Day, 1945, the German newspapers and radio carried the story of the bombing of the Limburg Stalag. They took great delight in describing how one American plane, flying above the low fog that covered the town and nearby camp, dropped five bombs on the prison camp, killing more than sixty American officers. Nor was this just propaganda. It was verified by men transferred from Limburg to Neubrandenburg, our future prison home. The American press and radio likewise verified the story months later.

At last, after walking over a hundred and eighty-five miles in the last ten days, we were put in boxcars, sixty men to a French forty-and-eight car ("forty-and-eight" means that it can hold forty men or eight horses). And now, difficult as it is to believe, we were sealed in these cars for six and a half days without a single bite to eat or a drop of water to drink. This seems incredible, but there are more than four hundred witnesses to the fact. We took turns sitting in each others laps, for there was no room to sit down. Our hunger during those first three days seemed more than we could stand. All I could think of was my Aunt Millie's rolls and homemade bread and bacon and eggs at 821 West Sixth Street. The men couldn't seem to stop talking about food. Everyone became very irritable at times, but, generally speaking, the men took this hunger trial in stride. We would take turns reaching through a sort of port hole near the top of the car to scrape snow off the roof.

The train stopped once for several hours in the city of Geisen to repair the tracks that had been bombed the night before. Someone called to a woman walking by to bring us some water. We threw four helmets out to her to bring it in. She came back carrying the water and had a fourteen or fifteen-year-old boy helping her. She had just reached us when the chief guard saw her. He ran up, dumped our water on the ground, and gave the woman a push. The boy went down to the other end of the car to hoist up the water quickly, but he was not quick enough. By this time another guard came up. The two of them pushed the boy against a brick retaining wall and gave him a beating. This sounds hackneyed and like a second-rate Hollywood version of Nazi tactics. Had someone told this to me a couple years before, I would have laughed at such propaganda.

New Years Day I held what passed for a service in our crowded car, and every man present made resolutions which I believe will be more lasting and carry more weight than the usual New Years resolutions. As for myself, every Christmas and New Year since then has meant so much more to me than it ever did before. After the third day I didn't feel quite so hungry, and the last few days didn't bother me at all. This was the case with the other men too. It seems that you can actually get used to going without food.

We had no idea where we were going. We had passed through Berlin and were heading north. Many of us had the same thoughts, I discovered later; but we didn't dare mention them to each other. We had begun to suspect that the Germans were intentionally starving us to death and that we would not be brought out of the boxcars alive. But on the sixth day in the evening, during a driving blizzard, we were let out of the boxcars and told that we had arrived at our destination: Neubrandenburg, Mecklenburg. Of the four hundred who had boarded at Limburg only seven had died en route. I had expected more. I said the final absolution for the dead, who were stiff as boards. We were all terribly weak, of course, and it was all we could do to walk the four miles to Stalag II-A, our home for the duration of the war. On the way we ate fistfuls of snow. It tasted better than ice cream.

Immediately upon arriving at the Stalag we were sent to take showers and to be deloused. The shower brought our spirits up immediately. Looking at my own body, I could scarcely believe that it was mine. Normally heavy men looked skinny. Thin men looked like skeletons. We had to laugh at each other, for we certainly were a sorry-looking lot. To have heard the laughing and kidding going on in that shower room you would have thought that we were a bunch of college men enjoying a shower after a vigorous day of skiing. To some civilians it may seem heartless to laugh so soon after the death of some of our comrades, but believe me, under such circumstances humor can sometimes be the only refuge from madness.

All the officers heads were shaved, to humiliate us, I assume, or to make us more conspicuous if we escaped. The enlisted men did not have their heads shaved. All the men had perked up considerably. That is something that will always mystify the Germans—the American sense of humor. American soldiers are a paradox; they gripe and complain about a very little thing in garrison life where things are comparatively comfortable. Yet when the going gets rough and they really suffer, they take it without a moan. It seems like a strange thing, but it is a fact that the more difficult and trying the circumstances are, the higher the morale is.

Eating, that almost forgotten experience, was next. They brought in buckets of soup, cabbage soup with a few turnips in it and lots and lots of little worms. We were given nothing to eat out of. A few men had canteen cups, others used helmets, and those with neither of these, in desperation for fear they would be left out, used a shoe. Our stomachs were not able to hold it down long, but it felt warm and good as long as it stayed with us. I will never forget the sight of one scrawny, naked soldier standing in the corner; he looked perfectly contented as he swilled his soup from a shoe. He looked up to see some men laughing at him and said, "The only kick I got is them worms ain't fat enough."

CHAPTER 8

Life in Prison Camp

STALAG II-A, we soon discovered, was a camp for enlisted men only, and we officers had been sent there by mistake. The German commandant of the camp told us that we would remain for two or three days and then would be marched to the officers camp about two hundred kilometers away. Sergeant Harley Lucas, the American "Man of Confidence" (the title given to the soldier that the prisoners selected to represent them to the German authorities), came to Captain Cecil B. Hawes, the doctor in our group, and to me to ask whether we would be willing to stay at this Stalag since there were between five and six thousand Americans in the camp without a doctor or chaplain. We were glad to accept, but the Germans were unwilling that any officer remain in an enlisted men's camp. Of course, the Geneva Convention Articles (which the Nazis pretended to observe) clearly prescribe that prisoners of war shall have the services of their own doctors and chaplains if such are available. The authorities of the camp couldn't see it that way.

Sergeant Lucas, this resourceful Man of Confidence, had recourse to other means to bring about the desired end. He contacted the Serbian doctor, who had been of tremendous help to the American sick and wounded. The doctor examined Doctor Hawes first and saw that he had an infected foot from frostbite and could walk no farther; this was a fact, as the German commander could see. The Serb then examined me and diagnosed a case of double pneumonia; this was not a fact. Tired and weak as I was, however, I found it quite easy to act the part of the patient. After the other officers had been marched out of the camp three days later, I made a quick recovery. Despite certain misgivings of the German authorities, I was permitted to remain at the camp until the end of the war. The commandant even obliged me by granting an *ausweis* (pass) and freedom of all the various compounds within the camp. The Man of Confidence not only represented the prisoners' complaints to the German authorities but likewise acted as the commander of the prisoners and provided good order and discipline within the American compound. Sergeant Lucas handled this difficult task with as much devotion, tact, and efficiency, I believe, as any commissioned officer could have done. It was not an easy job, for men in confinement have a tendency to grow surly and hypercritical of everything their own chosen leader tries to do in their behalf. He was extremely fortunate in his selection of men to help him in the command of the thousands of Americans in the camp. His "barracks chiefs" and other men given authority by him had a way of getting things done without seeming to throw their weight around. They managed to obtain the maximum cooperation with a minimum of friction. I have seen many officers in the army do far worse.

Two American doctors who had been left at the camp at different times had been denied the permission to visit the lazaret (hospital) or to treat our more seriously sick and wounded there. They had to confine their work to the less seriously sick men in our own stockade infirmary. The doctors constant complaints in this regard led to their being sent away to another Stalag. Not until just before our liberation (when many privileges were being granted) was Captain Hawes allowed to treat Americans and British in the lazaret, which was about a half mile from the camp.

If any reader of these pages has even seen one of our prison camps for German PWs in the United States, let him not get the idea that he knows what a camp for American prisoners in Germany was like. The only similarity is the high fence, the coils of barbed wire, and the guard towers. Aside from these essentials of any PW camp, the difference is greater than between Park Avenue and the Bowery. I had seen the German PW camp at Camp Forest, Tennessee, and had expected about the same thing in Germany, without the same quality or quantity of food of course. What we found is common knowledge now, for newspapers and newsreels have not spared the publics sensibilities regarding this necessary bit of public education. The filth of the camp struck us at first as appalling, but we seemed to get more or less numb to it as time went by. Rivers of human waste were ignored, and the stench became so much a part of our life that we could almost say we didn't notice it. It still remains a mystery to me, however, how we escaped typhus and typhoid epidemics.

The camp had separate compounds for the Serbs, Dutch, Poles, French, Italians, Belgians, Russians, Americans, and British. In all there were about eighty thousand prisoners registered in the camp, but about half of these were out in working groups miles from the camp. They returned to camp only to bring in the sick and dead.

The weather was bitter cold and the suffering intense. The Americans had been in the camp only about six months and consequently were in far better shape than the other prisoners, some of whom had been there for over four years. The daily food ration per man consisted of a bowl of soup (so-called), a tenth of a loaf of black bread, and a cup of tea (made from tree bark, I think) which the men used for shaving water, for they couldn't drink it. Four days a week each man received a couple of potatoes. The soup was invariably either cabbage (with worms) or rotten turnips (with worms) or a combination of the two (with a double ration of worms). The men were, of course, very thin, and many of them became sick and died, usually from amoebic dysentery. Fortunately for all of us, Red Cross parcels came through after we were there a short time.

One of the first things I wanted to do was contact the priests in the camp. There were six French priests, two Dutch priests, and one Italian and one Polish priest. Each of them greeted me with sincere warmth. The Italian priest died very shortly after my arrival, and I was given his Mass equipment. Many of the French and Poles worked downtown in Neubrandenburg. For this they were compensated in reichsmarks, and with this money they bribed the guards to get wine and hosts from the local German priest. The French had also made a very devotional and artistic chapel out of one of their barracks. Scrounging for materials was quite an art in itself.

All the French priests had been enlisted men in the French army, as France allows no clergyman's immunity from enlisted service. Since they were enlisted men, they had to do manual labor for the Germans, such as repair roads, work on bomb shelters, and so forth. The oldest among them was a very wonderful man with the charm and kindliness of a St. Francis de Sales. His thick hair was long and white, as was his neatly trimmed beard. The Germans seemed to respect him, and he was given freedom to visit all the compounds in the camp. The rest of us priests considered ourselves his curates. I received tremendous help from his kindly advice and priestly example. We spent many enjoyable evenings together. Though no one was permitted to go out of the barracks after eight p.m., I would frequently sneak out to visit M. l'Abbé in his barracks. We would talk most of the night using a goulash of his bad English, my worse French, our questionable Latin, and pidgin German. Our desperate efforts to express ourselves so delighted the old priest one night that he let out a loud laugh. A guard passing by came to the window and turned his flashlight on us. The old priest reassured him.

A shipment of boxes labeled "Red Cross" and addressed to American Prisoners of War arrived at the camp one day. The men grouped about those huge cartons thinking that at last food had arrived. Weak and emaciated as they were, they anticipated a real treat of good American food. Their pathetic feelings were beyond imagination when the cartons were opened only to reveal their useless contents: football shoulder-pads, badminton racquets, and numerous other items for which we had neither the space nor the energy to waste in their use. Decks of cards, cribbage boards, dominoes, and checker sets, however, salvaged some of the Red Cross honor in this instance and helped the men to pass the dragging hours of prison life.

The disappointing shipment of athletic equipment was followed a week later by the arrival of Red Cross food parcels. The prestige of the Red Cross soared to unprecedented heights. From then on these parcels came in steady shipments, and morale got a big shot in the arm every time they were delivered. Each box contained three small cans of pressed meat, a can of salmon or tuna fish, a can of cheese, a can of powdered milk, two bars of real chocolate, a box of sugar squares, a can of soluble coffee, a box of raisins, a box of crackers, a can of oleo or butter, vitamin tablets, toilet paper, and most precious of all (especially for their bartering value), five packages of cigarettes. Each man was issued a parcel a week, and we shared our parcels with the British in the camp, allotting them one parcel per man each week.

We figured we could ride through the rest of the war O.K. now. Through our food parcels we became the aristocracy of the camp. Even the Germans were not eating as well as we were in some respects. Our men continued to lose weight despite the parcels, but generally their health and energy improved. Because our coffee, chocolate, and cigarettes were especially desired by the Germans, bartering and trading became the most intriguing and profitable occupation in the American compound.

German guards could scarcely restrain their enthusiasm for American cigarettes, and since the demand was so great on their part for our luxuries, which we now had in some abundance, it became expedient that we set up our own OPA price scale to prevent an inflation and a cheapening of our own goods. To maintain our cigarettes and coffee and chocolate at the highest, possible worth we computed and posted our trade value in this manner:

KRIEGIES:

Observe this price scale, and keep the value of cigarettes up!

For 1 two-lb. loaf of bread . . . . give no more than 10 cigarettes or
½ chocolate bar.

For 1 two-lb. sack of flour . . . . . give no more than 15 cigarettes.

For 1 doz. eggs . . . . give no more than 25 cigarettes or
1 chocolate bar.

For 1 good chicken . . . . give no more than 1 small can of
soluble coffee.

For 12 large onions . . . . give no more than 12 cigarettes or
½ chocolate bar.

For 1 one-lb. beefsteak . . . . give no more than 25 cigarettes or
1 chocolate bar.

For 1 good pair of gloves . . . . . . give no more than 15 cigarettes.

For 1 good pair of socks . . . . . . give no more than 15 cigarettes.

By and large the Americans stuck pretty close to the price scale, except when they could strike an even better bargain, which of course was not contrary to our OPA intentions. Despite the manner in which American soldiers squander their money when they have plenty, they are still the world's best traders and keenest bargain-makers when they have little to give in exchange. All this probably strikes the reader as very amusing, and, as I reflect upon it, it was funny to see the German guards smuggling various food items past their own guards to get in exchange the coveted American cigarettes, chocolate, or coffee. But believe me, the actual bartering was a serious matter between the Germans and the Americans. I doubt whether the wizards of Wall Street ever juggled millions of bushels of wheat with greater self-interested cunning than a *kriegie* wielded his mighty cigarette to his own advantage.

Since there were no Pure Food Laws within the camp, the GI never scrupled to mislabel or misrepresent his article. One night I heard a terrific wrangle going on outside the little room the men had built for me for privacy of confessions. I went out to see what it was all about. A German guard had come into the barracks and produced a fine hen from under his "great coat" (this is a huge garment guards wear that hangs all the way to the ground to keep them warm on cold night duty and is large enough for two men). He wanted one of our small cans of soluble coffee and fifteen cigarettes in exchange for his hen. The American felt he could do better. (Usually three or four Americans would buy something like this together and would pick the sharpest fellow to do the trading.) This particular American haggled and argued with the guard for nearly an hour until the exasperated German finally agreed to trade his hen for the coffee and to forget the cigarettes. The matter having been settled, the articles were exchanged. The American felt the chicken critically, mumbling that he was being cheated; the German sniffed the coffee suspiciously. They parted, each quite satisfied that he had made a good bargain.

About fifteen minutes later the German came back, angry, fuming, and spouting German much faster than my untrained ear could follow. I got an interpreter to ask him what the matter was. It seemed that the can of coffee he had received for his hen turned out to be in reality just a can of sand with a sprinkling of coffee on top. Realizing the impossibility of locating the swindler, the German had to content himself with a few anti-Semitic invectives against all Americans.

The religious program for the American and British compounds was progressing well. We set aside one corner of a barracks for a chapel sanctuary and employed the very considerable artistic talent in the camp to make this corner as beautiful and as devotional as our limited tools and materials permitted. We were able to bribe the guards for the lumber necessary to build an altar. Several scarlet blankets were obtained by the same means. The altar was built on a platform with three steps leading to it. The blankets were cut to make an antependium and a backdrop for the crucifix, which was carved out of a block of wood by an Italian prisoner. By our usual means, a bribe again, we obtained from a German guard paper and a complete set of pastel crayons. With these the Serbian artist did a magnificent job on the Stations of the Cross. With a half-dozen chocolate bars we got two more scarlet blankets with which we covered the crude Communion rail. The material left over was sufficient to make into a canopy for the altar. A Jewish soldier working in a group at the railroad yards found time at night to paint a beautiful Madonna and a picture of St. Joseph for the sides of the altar. A German guard who became interested in the project obtained wiring material, and a socket was placed behind the canopy. The candles were fake, made from shaving-soap sticks stuck together.

When the light was turned on, the effect was so satisfying that I doubt whether any priest ever looked upon his church with greater pleasure and joy than did I upon our humble prison sanctuary. It became a spiritual oasis for our homesick men as they visualized something of their home church in our crude improvisations. Many a young man during our long days, weeks, and months of imprisonment found relief there in a quiet prayer. Many found there a fulfillment of our Lord's promise, "Come unto Me . . . and I will refresh you."

In my small room adjoining our little chapel I was able to have the privacy necessary for confessions and consultations. Each day most of the Catholics attended Mass, although I was forced to limit Communions to Sunday only because of the difficulty of obtaining hosts. We had no large hosts at all. I used the small ones for Mass and quartered these on Sunday for communicants. Twice a week I held a non-denominational service for the Protestant men. A soldier who had been in a Lutheran seminary also conducted Protestant services with dignity on Sundays. His sermons were well thought out, sincerely delivered, and very well received. Religion was a constant subject of conversation, and many men with little or no religion in their background sought instructions. The credit for these conversions belongs to a number of Catholic men who not only knew their religion and could present it properly, but lived it as well. One young man in a nearby working camp instructed and baptized nine men although he had never been beyond the first year of high school himself. When I discovered this and checked up on his converts, I found that the instructions had been thorough and his followers were solid Catholics.

So strong was the German feeling toward Jews that, with two or three exceptions, they separated all the Jewish-American prisoners from the rest of us despite vigorous protests by Sergeant Lucas and myself. These men were sent out as working crews and were treated no worse than other working groups (which usually ate better than the men in the camp), but we feared possible reprisals against them as the war drew to a close. Even when the Red Cross officials protested to the German authorities, nothing was done about this segregation. The Germans carried their hatred to such a ridiculous extreme that no Red Cross articles with Jewish names on them were allowed to get into the camp. We had a beat-up old phonograph, but all the records sent to us had a Jewish name on them either as composer, orchestra leader, producer, or manufacturer. Even Irving Berlins "White Christmas" was smashed in the censors office. The only record to come through was "Into Each Life Some Rain Must Fall. . . ."

I often wished that someone would drop that record and break it, but nobody ever did. It was a pity the Germans hadn't smashed that one too. Most of us felt that we didn't need the Mills Brothers to tell us that some rain had fallen into our lives.

The entertainment in the camp was homespun but really quite good on the whole and varied enough to interest everyone. For violations of discipline, lack of cleanliness, and other infractions of order, the Man of Confidence imposed fines—forfeiture of some parcel item, from a cigarette to a can of coffee, depending upon the gravity of the offense. With these fines musical instruments and other entertainment materials were bought from the guards. (Incidentally, the chaplains fund—to pay for bribing the guards to get hosts and wine for Mass—was constantly augmented by the contribution of one cigarette exacted from any man I caught using profanity.) A hillbilly quartet was only too willing to entertain at any time of the day or night. They were indefatigable, and their repertoire was inexhaustible. Another man, "Chick" by name, had had considerable experience in vaudeville and burlesque, and the shows he organized and put on were very clever and were great morale-builders. The shows became quite crude and a bit ribald at times, and I had to needle Chick occasionally. He took it well and tried to cooperate, although, as he said, he couldn't control all the asides and adlibs.

One night Chick staged a minstrel in the barracks. The makeup and costumes were masterpieces of Yank ingenuity. Most of the jokes and songs were racy and crudely insulting digs at the Germans. It so happened that about twenty guards got wind of the show and came to see it. They sat there and laughed and laughed at every joke and song. The colored costumes with bright ties tickled their funny bones. The Americans were pretty apprehensive until they saw that the Germans didn't understand a word of the minstrels contrived accents, nor did they catch any of the insinuations. Then the American prisoners got a big wallop out of that . . . the Germans laughing at the show, and the Americans laughing at the Germans who didn't know that they were being ribbed. This situation in the audience became actually funnier than the performance itself. Doctor Hawes and I had been holding our sides from laughing, but we were more than a little relieved when the show was over. The Germans slapped the members of the cast on the back and muttered something about Americans being "good comrades." We were to get this "good comrades" routine quite regularly now that Allied forces from the east and from the west were rapidly converging on the position of our Stalag.

The best of the entertainers, however, was a string quartet. The violinist had played for years in the Boston Symphony . . . with a name like Elephtherios Elephtherokos (the name has beautiful alliteration when pronounced aloud) what else could he be but a musician, or possibly a wrestler? The bass viol player and the guitar player had studied their instruments for years and were excellent. The vocalist, a cadaverous Sinatra-appearing lad, had a soft dreamy voice and had sung for several name bands in the States. The total effect was quite professional.

"Zaza" was one of the most interesting characters in the camp. He had been brought to the camp when he was not yet four years old. His parents had been killed in a bombing early in the war. An Italian soldier had picked him up and taken him with him. As both of them had been picked up by the Germans and sent to Stalag II-A, Zaza had been reared in this abnormal environment. He had never known or played with other children, and his manners were very grown-up. The stocky little fellow looked like a midget Mussolini although he would get fighting mad and throw stones at anyone who called him "Mussolini." In this strange environment Zaza had matured way beyond his years; he fixed his own bunk, went to bed and got up when he chose, washed his clothes, and prepared his own food which he was able to scrounge from the Americans. He was given the freedom of the entire camp. He could speak fluent Italian, some Polish, German, and French and could get along fairly well in English.

"Would you like to come to the United States with me when the war is over?" I asked him one day.

"I think America be vera vera nice," he replied, rubbing imaginary whiskers on his chin, "but Italy want us there; many things to build in Italy when war is over."

I never ceased to be astounded by his mature outlook, but I fear his abnormal childhood will result in later emotional crisis. One day I went to the bathhouse to take a shower (a privilege the German commandant had granted me). The German in charge, however, said that there was no water. On my way back to the American compound I met Zaza, who had the same bathhouse privilege.

"Whasa mat?" he asked.

"The Heinie says no water," I answered.

Zaza laughed. "He is liar." He went into the bathhouse confidently. I waited to have a laugh at Zazas disappointment. Pretty soon Zaza stuck his head out of the window and called, "Come, didn't I say he is liar." We both had a good shower.

The saddest part of prison life was the lack of the bare essentials for medical care. Quite a number of Americans and British had arrived at the camp with frozen feet. Although the Serbian and the Polish doctors did everything they could and worked with heroic patience and skill, they were hopelessly handicapped by lack of supplies. Five men had to have both their legs amputated; eighteen had to have a foot or leg amputated. Many of these and other wounded were serious gangrene cases, and the lazaret was filled with pneumonia and dysentery patients. Many of these poor boys died.

The Polish doctor would sometimes actually cry when he was forced to use toilet paper from Red Cross parcels as compresses, and newspaper for bandages. The wounded and the sick were cared for by our medical aid men with the greatest solicitude and, I might add, with unashamed love. Nothing, I believe, refines men's characters so much, or makes men so Christ-like, patient, and self-sacrificing, as caring for the sick and the helpless. I was permitted to go to the lazaret every day. Despite the suffering and agony there, the atmosphere was cheerful and pleasant, as the relationship between doctors, aid men, and patients was a strong bond of trust and devotion. The Polish and the Serbian doctors will always remain in my mind as the finest Christian examples of a profession second only to the priesthood in the dignity and greatness of its mission.

We buried an average of two Americans and two British a week. All of the Catholics were anointed and received Viaticum (a French priest had provided me with an oil-stock). The Protestant men readily said acts of faith, hope, charity, and contrition with me and then the Lord's Prayer. I have no doubt that they were very well received by Him who also died a prisoner.

The Germans as usual were more solicitous toward the dead than they were toward the living. We were allowed to take eight pallbearers and an honorary group of twelve men to escort each body from the hospital to the cemetery. The pallbearers carried the body in its wooden-box coffin on their shoulders. As the procession passed the camp on its way to the cemetery on the hill, everyone in the camp turned toward the procession, stopped, and saluted the deceased, a small act that never failed to impress me deeply . . . forty thousand men of various nationalities standing at attention and saluting a comrade that had been "liberated" by death.

After the burial ritual I always felt obliged to say a few words to those in attendance, usually something like this: "Though we bury our comrade-in-arms here in six feet of foreign soil; though he lies thousands of miles from his home, unattended by his family and friends; though he be buried naked in this crude coffin; though his prisoner-of-war tag remains with him still nailed to a crude marker, these are superficial and relatively unimportant things. The important

thing is that in the supreme moment of his life he was given the
grace of a holy and Christian death. The important thing is that he
has been liberated by his Saviour's love from the prison of this life.
Today we represent his family, his country, and his Church. As his
family would do, we offer up our prayers for his soul. His country,
we remind ourselves, must ever be grateful for the price he paid for
our ultimate freedom. His Church recognizes here a sacrifice closely
linked to the sacrifice of the Crucified. To this ground we commit
his mortal body, but into God's merciful and loving care we commit
his immortal soul." Taps would be blown, and we would return to
the camp.

Of the twenty-one thousand Russians who had been registered in
the camp, eighteen thousand died, most of them by starvation. Every
day the pitiful sight of a wagonload of naked corpses on its way to
cemetery hill made us Americans mighty grateful for citizenship in a
"grasping capitalistic country that has no regard for the masses."
Russia has no affiliation with the Red Cross, and, believe me, the
Russians that survived needed no argument other than the sight of
our parcels to convince them that there was something mighty phony
about Uncle Joe and the government of the proletariat.

The hatred of the Germans for the Russians was just about
incredible. The Russian dead were buried in pits, five hundred to a
pit, and lime was shoveled in on top of them. On one occasion when
I was burying an American and two British soldiers, a Russian
corpse had mistakenly been placed alongside of the other three. All
four bodies were buried in coffins and separate graves. When the
Germans discovered the mistake the next day, they dug up the Russian and dumped his body into the large pit with the hundreds of
other Russian dead. Some Russians were buried while still breath-
ing, for if they were unconscious or in a coma, they were tossed onto
the wagon of corpses as it made its morning round. Doctor Hawes
had examined some of the bodies of the Russians, at the request of
the commandant, to verify what turned out to be authentic cases of
cannibalism. (Somehow or other the commandant thought that this
was evidence of the Russian prisoners degradation rather than of his
own; actually he had been responsible for such inhuman conduct.) It
was also a common thing for the Russians to keep their dead with
them for days so that the dead mans meager rations could continue

to be drawn from the kitchen. At roll call a dead man would be held upright by the men on each side of him in the close, tight formation.

Horrible as all these things sound, I have come to believe that there is nothing that a starving man will not do to stay alive. Who can say that these poor, starved-crazy men were in any way responsible for their actions? The above descriptions sound like wartime propaganda at its worst. Had I not witnessed these things myself I would seriously have doubted their actuality, no matter who told me. But in this instance there are thousands of living, reliable witnesses who can substantiate every word.

On one occasion a little fourteen-year-old Russian boy was caught stealing potatoes from the kitchen. A guard made the lad lie flat on the ground and stretch out his arms. The guard shot him through each hand. One of the American aid men cared for the boys wounds, and we collected some food for him. Two or three weeks later Sergeant Lucas managed to get the boy into our compound infirmary. When his wounds healed somewhat, he remained to help our own aid men. He carried bed pans, washed and shaved the sick, scrubbed the place regularly, and became devoted to the Americans. I have never seen a happier boy in my life than when some Red Cross clothing came in and we fitted him in an American uniform.

All guards were known as "goons" among the prisoners, but one guard was known as "The Geek." He was a tall, apish-looking character with long arms and enormous hands and was the most vicious and cruel man I have ever known. He was even despised by his fellow guards, who hated him but feared him more. On several occasions on the slightest provocation he had grabbed a Russian and personally put the poor wretch to death with his knife in horrible fashion. In March when he received orders to move out to the Russian front, there was general rejoicing in the camp, although many of the Russian prisoners had hoped that it might be their privilege at the end of the war to take care of him themselves.

Another offensive character was known as "Little Adolf," partly because of his Hitler-style moustache and partly because, though only a corporal in rank, he had tremendous authority in the camp. His position in the army was unimportant, but he was known to be a Nazi party official. His word in the camp was law, and even the commandant, who held the rank Oberstcolonel, was careful not to cross Little

Adolf. Most of the guards, who were just soldiers and not bad men on the whole, blamed Little Adolph for all the atrocities of the camp.

Not many Americans attempted escape, and those who did attempt it were unsuccessful. We were guarded closely (except toward the very end of the war), and no one was allowed out of the barracks at night, except to follow the direct path to the latrine. We had seen the German police dogs go after an occasional crazed Russian as he desperately tried to dig and squirm under the fence. The only chance our men had to try to escape was when they were put on some labor detail in town or on the roads and railroads. However, double guards and dogs made any attempt extremely hazardous. In spite of all these things about twenty men tried to escape, each one without success. Three of them were killed. We were several hundred miles in the interior of Germany, and the civilians were jittery and armed. They were daily expecting American or Russian airborne landings in this area. Besides, considering all the hazards of attempted escape, the war was rapidly coming to a close, and we had now enough to eat to sustain life. Freedom was bound to come to us by way of advancing Allied troops, and a successful escape could at best only hasten that freedom by a little.

About the first of March the Swiss Red Cross representatives arrived at the camp to hear our complaints against the German treatment and to make the proper adjustments. Naturally the Germans, upon the arrival of the Red Cross men, served the camp prisoners the first palatable soup we had seen and even gave every man a double ration of sugar, jam, and potatoes and two inches of bologna. The Swiss failed to help the prisoners very much, but one thing they did do that I appreciated was to obtain for me an outside *ausweis* that allowed me to leave the camp to visit American working groups within a radius of a hundred miles.

I availed myself of this new privilege to the utmost, and I kept a guard busy constantly escorting me on a bicycle about the country. The guard would invariably want to visit friends or relatives on these trips. In this way I became quite well acquainted with many German families. These families seemed to me to be very closely knit units (though the men of the families were away at war), and they possessed most of the virtues of hard-working Christian people. I am quite convinced that they were in great part ignorant of the atrocities perpetrated upon the conquered peoples. They did not condone the evils they saw in their government, but by nature the German people seem to have an exaggerated respect for authority, no matter how unworthy that authority may be. Fear, too, was obviously a deterrent from any expressions of dissatisfaction with those in power. The people treated me kindly and with respect and reverence. Each of them thought that I must know this or that relative in America, for the relative had prospered greatly.

The American working groups that I visited on these trips were making out much better than the men in the camp, for the German rations there were far better. They too had received Red Cross parcels and were able to barter not only with guards, but with civilians as well. One such group that I visited had a fine, tough sergeant as Man of Confidence. His name was Collins, and he was from Boston. When the chief guard refused to allow the men time off work to attend my Mass, Collins ordered a sitdown strike. The chief guard threatened him, but Collins just screamed threats back at him and told his men not to touch a single tool. The chief took out his pistol, but Collins didn't move. I tried to persuade Collins not to make an issue of this any further, but he told me politely to stay out of this. He knew his guards well, and after much yelling and screaming by both men, the chief guard allowed Collins to have his own way and gave the men an hour off. Collins told me after Mass that the chief guard just had to make a show of opposition to impress the rest of the guards; he actually wasn't such a bad guy.

Toward the end of March an American colonel by the name of James Alger had become very sick while being marched from the Stalag in Poland where many American officers were imprisoned. The guards brought him up to Stalag II-A, and he remained with us for nearly three weeks. He was a very clever man, and it didn't take him long to size up the guards and contact the one to be bribed. Through this guard he was able to have a radio smuggled in piece by piece. We had tried this before but had never been able to assemble a complete radio. He told us that BBC was broadcasting instructions every week to prisoners of war, and as the war drew to a close, it was essential that we comply with these orders.

The great problem was to find a suitable place to hide the radio, for the Gestapo each month made a thorough inspection of every barracks. They would pull up the floor boards, take the bunks apart, and probe the ground around and under the barracks. In short, they did their job thoroughly and well. Finally an idea dawned upon Colonel Alger that might offer security for the radio. After checking it with me (for I would be implicated), he had a man build a little pulpit for my chapel, and the soldier did a masterful job in fixing a little trap door on the top. He then covered the whole thing with a piece of the scarlet blanket material, and inserted into a hole a long spike that kept the trap door tight. By pulling out the nail, the door would fly open, and the radio could be put to use. The first time we tuned in on BBC a chill ran up and down my spine. It almost seemed like our liberation.

The idea was not long in being put to the test. The secret police came to the barracks one day and tore things apart in their usual fashion looking for escape equipment, weapons, and any other hidden things that were *verboten* . . . such as a radio. They looked behind the altar, and we tried to look casual as they passed the pulpit by.

Of course we had to use the radio with the utmost caution and not even let our own American fellow prisoners know that we had it. The reason for the secrecy with our own men was that the Germans had a "plant" among us; that is, a German who had been in America, who spoke perfect English, and about whom we would have no suspicion. A plant is a common means for the detaining power to pick up valuable information dropped by prisoners of war and also a very effective means of preventing escapes. We had our suspicions as to who the plant was, but we were never sure until the last couple of weeks of the war when he was so unfortunate one night as to talk in his sleep. Our camp intelligence NCO compiled enough factual information on this fellow to turn him over to our own forces as soon as we were liberated. The information from BBC came through perfectly, telling us what we were to do during the last few weeks of the war. This knowledge proved of tremendous value.

One Sunday morning shortly before our liberation a very embarrassing thing happened (and there arent many things in a prison camp that can embarrass anybody). It happened during Mass when I was just about to begin the sermon. After listening to the radio the night before, I had forgotten to put the spike back securely in the trap door, and as I rested my arm on the pulpit and quoted my sermon text: "Seek ye first the kingdom of God and His justice, and all these things shall be added unto you, the trap door flew open. The radio dropped out in front of the entire congregation. There was a long three or four seconds of silence, and then the place broke into a roar of laughter. It was with considerable embarrassment that I recovered the radio and stuffed it back into the pulpit. I then tried to compose myself and restore order. The constant snickering made it very difficult to concentrate on the sermon, and after about five painful minutes I gave it up as a bad job and went on with the Mass.

The worst part of the accident was the presence in the congregation of a few German guards. However, when they went to Communion, I felt pretty sure that they would say nothing. These particular guards had been very decent and quite helpful on many occasions. Just before our liberation, when most of the guards were taking off towards the west to escape the Russians and to surrender to the Americans, I gave each of these guards a note to the Americans who might capture them. The note stated that these Germans had been friendly and helpful to American prisoners of war. I haven't any idea whether the notes helped them or not.

Easter in Stalag II-A will always be remembered vividly and joyfully, I believe, by everyone who was there. The memory and lesson of that day will always remain with me until the day I die. Good Friday had been observed by Catholics and Protestants alike in the American compound with Stations of the Cross and an hour's meditation taken from the *Imitation of Christ*—the chapter on the Royal Road of the Holy Cross—a road of which these emaciated men of all nations had some personal knowledge. The French who worked downtown had managed to obtain from the German priest a set of dalmatics which they were successful in smuggling into the camp. We prepared, without the Germans' knowledge, to hold an outdoor Solemn High Mass. The guard crew had been reduced to a skeleton force by this time, for nearly every German under sixty had been sent to the front. Each nation was to be represented on the altar, and each nation had a little choir to sing part of the Mass, with the principal parts to be sung by all the choirs together.

We hoped and prayed for a good day, and it turned out perfect. About a half hour before the Mass, word was sent to the various compounds to assemble in the big field beside the kitchen. The

Germans were too bewildered to make much of a protest. Besides, the war was so close to being over that they were very anxious to be friendly. The saintly old French priest was the celebrant of the Mass. I was the deacon, the Dutch priest was the subdeacon, the Polish priest was the master of ceremonies, an Italian seminarian was the assistant master of ceremonies, the Belgian Man of Confidence was the thurifer. For acolytes we had a Serb, a Scotsman, an Englishman, and a Russian. (The French priest told me that this Russian was a saint.) Two French priests directed and coordinated the choirs. All of the Catholics and many of the non-Catholics atended. The number was well up in the thousands, the largest congregation I have ever seen, apart from a national Eucharistic Congress. The crowd entirely surrounded the altar, and what a sight it was! Many of the Germans were there too, not as guards, but as worshipers.

This was the Catholic Church. Here were Frenchmen kneeling next to Serbs, next to Poles; Americans worshiping beside Belgians, beside Italians; Scotsmen finding the bond of brotherhood in the Mass with the Dutch, with Germans, and with Russians. There was no argument here, no friction, no hatred, no intrigue or struggle for balance of power. Here was the Christ being elevated again and drawing all things to Himself. Here was a King whom all could love and obey and in that love and obedience find the happiness and freedom every man longs for. These were the thoughts of the brief sermon which was preached in four languages by the four ministers of the Mass: in French, in English, in Italian, and in Polish. Certainly no man who attended that Easter Mass will ever forget it. Hundreds upon hundreds of men went to Holy Communion at that Mass, and it took the four priests about half an hour to distribute Communion. I believe that every American Catholic received.

After the Mass the French priest had a little party for the priests and servers. It was then that he paid the finest compliment to American Catholics that I have ever heard. "You Americans," he said, "are the worlds greatest lovers of the Eucharist."

Shortly after this we heard the tragic news of President Roosevelts death. We held a solemn memorial ceremony to which every nationality in the camp sent its highest ranking representative. Later in the day a formation of all Americans and British in the camp was held at which the representatives of the various nationalities extended the sympathy of their countrymen to the Americans and extolled in brief talks the virtues of our past great leader. I said a prayer for divine help and guidance in behalf of his successor. Taps were blown, and the formation was dismissed. It was amazing to see the profound effect President Roosevelt's passing had upon the men.

We knew the day of liberation was almost at hand. Russian artillery in the east could be heard in the distance, and American artillery in the west. German civilians were evacuating Neubrandenburg, travelling on anything that had wheels. Confusion and terror among the civilians and the retreating German wounded was the order of the day. I thought that I had almost become emotionally numb to the sight of suffering and death, but the events of the next several days were to instill in me an even greater disgust and abhorrence for war.

CHAPTER 9

Liberation by the Russians

EACH NIGHT during the month of April Sergeant Lucas and I would slip out of our rooms after the men had gone to sleep and take the radio out of its hiding place in the pulpit. While a couple of trusted men kept watch at the door of the barracks, our Man of Confidence and I listened to the BBC instructions to Allied prisoners of war. Our instructions were few but specific and were broadcast in code. Colonel Alger had taught us this code before he was moved on after recovering from his ailment. An English sergeant from the G-2 section of the British airborne also listened with us. He knew the code better than we did and was able to decipher it almost as fast as it was given.

The orders were clear. We were not to make any premature attempt at mass break or escape, for it would be foolish to lose lives now with assured freedom so close at hand. If the German guards fled, the ranking officer or noncommissioned officer was to take charge of the discipline and order of the group. "PW" was to be painted in large white block letters on top of each barracks, as were the Russian symbols for prisoners of war; this was to prevent our attacking planes from mistaking the camp for an enemy garrison. A large "PW" was to be marked out with stones or anything recognizable from the air in the largest open space in the prison camp. Any prisoner violence against German guards or civilians was strictly forbidden. German soldiers turning themselves over to the Allied prisoners were to be held and given over to the force that liberated the camp. Every precaution was to be taken to avoid prisoner casualties of battles that might take place near and about the camp. Allied flags were to be flown above the camp as soon as the Germans were helpless to prevent it. Each night, as we listened to the radio, the Russian artillery's muffled "woompf woompf" in the distance became more and more distinct, coming closer and closer.

Russian planes flew over the city of Neubrandenburg and over the camp and dropped thousands of leaflets designed to terrify the German civilians, which they did very effectively. One of the leaflets simply stated in German, "Rokosovski is at your gates!" As the reputation of Rokosovski's army was enough to panic the Germans, the roads were soon jammed with German wagons loaded with the most cherished of family possessions. The occupants were children and old people heading west hoping to escape the Russians and preferring anything to falling into their hands.

Many of the guards in the camp deserted and fled in the direction of the American lines. About a dozen guards, as well as the camp commander, turned themselves over to the American prisoners and were locked up in the stone blockhouse. The small garrison of the town dug in and prepared to defend it; they also grabbed every civilian capable of firing a rifle or digging a ditch and quickly enlisted him into the defense force. We ourselves were busy digging trenches to take cover in as soon as the Russians would begin to shell the town. The events of the next few days were to be among the most terrible I have ever seen.

About midnight of April 28 the Russian tanks started coming in; the roar of these tanks coming from all sides was terrific. The opposition which the brave and determined Germans were able to put up was almost totally ineffectual against so much heavy equipment. As a matter of fact, the Russian infantry, riding on the tanks (about fifteen or twenty to a tank) and firing indiscriminately, killed almost as many of their own men as they did the Germans. Some of the tanks bypassing and surrounding the town rolled on to the camp, pushing down the barbed-wire fences and guard towers of the camp. These Russian soldiers seemed to be wild men; with "squeeze-boxes" and banjos strapped to their backs, they fired their rifles and tommyguns in every direction. They looked more like the old Mexico revolutionaries out on a spree than the army of one of the great powers of the world. Most of these soldiers were oriental or Mongolian in appearance.

Within an hour after their arrival Neubrandenburg was a sea of flames which rose higher and higher as the night passed. It burned all the next day, and there were very few buildings that were not razed to the ground. The Catholic church, strangely enough, was almost the only large building preserved.

The Germans had a large army hospital about a quarter of a mile from the prison camp, and it was packed with wounded. At the request of the guards I had gone there on several occasions during the preceding months to anoint dying Catholic German soldiers. This hospital was the first building set afire. I was unable to find out whether the wounded had been removed or not, but I have my personal doubts that they were. The heat from the burning city became intense and lighted the camp as brightly as daylight. The Americans kept calm and in perfect order during this time, due largely to the instructions by Sergeant Lucas and to his personal leadership qualities. The same could not be said for the French, Italians, and Serbs, who bolted the camp in mobs and went to loot what had not been burned to a crisp.

The Russian prisoners of war, of whom there were only three thousand remaining alive out of twenty-one thousand who had been registered in the camp, were, oddly enough, the only prisoners not particularly happy to be liberated. The Russian army doesn't recognize the right of any soldier to surrender; he should fight until killed. As soon as the Russian commander came into the camp, he went to the Russian compound and ordered each prisoner there to be tossed a rifle and to *get* himself up to the front at once. He asked the Russian prisoners which of their countrymen had worked for the Germans in any capacity. These were immediately shot as collaborators. The same was done to the Russian doctor. The German commandant of the camp was taken up the hill to the cemetery. After being forced to dig a hole, he was shot, and his body was dumped into the grave.

The next day a Russian general came to the camp. When asked for the ranking American, Sergeant Lucas brought him to my room. I offered the general a cigar, a couple of boxes of which had recently come through under the Red Cross label. The general thoroughly enjoyed the cigar and coffee I served him. After I had sent for an American soldier who spoke Russian, the conversation with the general became very interesting and enlightening. He said that the cigar was the best he had ever smoked and that the coffee was by far the best he had ever drunk. After trying one of his cigarettes I had no cause to distrust the compliment. He said that he would send "something good" to me. A Russian soldier brought that "something" the next day. It turned out to be a big crockery jug of vodka, one whiff of which was more than enough for me.

The general told me how sorry all Russians were that President Roosevelt had died, that they considered him a great friend of Russia. He spoke derisively of the British and had contempt for the French. He praised American equipment very highly and said that in his opinion the Russians could not have held out had it not been for American help in equipping the Russian army. This was obviously true, for almost every piece of equipment that we saw the Russians use was American. They used Sherman tanks for the most part; and our two-and-a-half-ton trucks, our jeeps, and our armored cars were all employed almost exclusively. They had their own rocket launchers. The Russian fighter planes that we saw in this area were all Bell Airacobras, a plane that American pilots considered obsolete and refused to fly because of the near-impossibility of bailing out in an emergency. During the course of our conversation the general drank at least ten cups of coffee and showed no signs of quitting until I had emptied the second pot in his cup.

A political commissar came to the camp, and he immediately called a meeting of the ranking officers of all the nationalities in the camp. He was a fine-looking young man, well mannered, and extremely intelligent—one of the best linguists I have ever heard. He told us that we would remain in the camp until contact was made with the American lines. He gave us our instructions in French, Italian, Polish, Dutch, and flawless English. He likewise said that our countries would be notified immediately that we had been liberated. The Americans (and only the Americans) might write one letter each to their families, and these would be flown to American lines. Food would be provided in abundance. Transportation would be available as soon as contact was made with the American lines in this sector of Germany. He said that he was leaving a Russian colonel in charge of the camp and that all our needs would be satisfied, but that no one was to leave the camp without a pass from the Russian commander. I asked the commissar for a pass in order to round up any Americans who were in working groups in or near Neubrandenburg. This he readily granted.

My old friend M. L'Abbé came over and asked me to go downtown with him. He wanted to see how the German priest and the people who had not fled were making out. I certainly admired the old man's courage; he apparently feared no one. The Russian commissar had warned us that the front line troops were not trained to regard civilians with consideration, and the old priest was wearing the cassock of a native priest. Many of these Russian soldiers were in the front lines to work out court-martial sentences and even under the best of circumstances were crude and rough. Expecting the worst, we were still shocked beyond words by what we saw. Just a few yards into the woods from the camp we came across a sight that engraved itself into our minds never to be erased. Several German girls and women had been raped and killed; some of them had been strung up by the feet and their throats slit. Some Americans had told me about this, but I had found it too difficult to believe. We paused to say a few prayers. When we arrived at what was once the beautiful little city of Neubrandenburg, I had the feeling that I was looking upon the end of the world and Judgment Day. I almost expected to see the Four Horsemen of the Apocalypse come galloping towards us.

Most of the buildings were still burning, and the streets were piled high with the debris of fallen walls. A large group of Germans, men, women, and children, were clearing the main street under guard of a Russian girl. Other Russian girls were directing the traffic of the tanks and armored vehicles moving through the city. Bodies in the streets were ignored unless they were in the way and obstructed traffic. In places the stench of burnt flesh was horrible. The old priest said nothing, but he would sigh deeply now and then when we met some new horror. As he lifted his cassock to climb over the debris and as he stopped by each body to say a prayer, he seemed to me at the time as a sort of symbol of the Church in a devastated world.

We finally arrived at the church rectory and went in. The house had been partly destroyed by fire and was completely wrecked inside.

The priest's two sisters, both nuns, and his mother and father had come to him for protection. The priest and his father were sitting on the steps, obviously in a state of extreme shock. The women were huddled together on a couch. One of the sisters spoke to the French priest and told him that the three women had been violated by a group of Russian soldiers while their brother and father had been forced to watch. The French priest asked them if there was anything he could do, though I doubted whether there was anything anyone was able to do. They shook their heads. I judged that they were on the verge of losing their minds; they were certainly beyond tears and beyond receiving any expressions of sympathy. A rosary hung loosely from the fingers of the old woman. As she sat there with her eyes closed, I couldn't be sure that she was alive.

We took a different route back to the camp, and we spoke very little on the way. As we were coming up the hill, we passed a wagon that had been overturned; it was one of those in which a German family had tried to get away from the Russians. The family had been killed, as was evidenced by the fresh dirt covering a part of the ditch by the wagon. I would say that there were five or six buried there. Someone had at least given them the last of the corporal works of mercy . . . burial. A shepherd dog was lying by the wagon, and though we tried to coax him to get up and come with us, he only looked up at us as dogs do when they have been beaten.

Looters had already gone through the family possessions. They hadn't bothered to take a little doll that lay among the scattered things, nor had they taken the old family Bible, which the French priest picked up and looked into. The Bible had several First Communion and Confirmation pictures pasted in, and there were many names under the headings of baptisms, marriages, and deaths. My friend really looked his years now. He had always been so cheerful and pleasant, with a young man's optimistic outlook on life; now the long walk of the day and the horrible things we had seen made him look worn, old, and tired of life. I was very glad when we got back to the camp, for I was afraid that the old man was ill.

Every Russian soldier receives a ration of vodka every day, and some of them had been able to find some liquor too. Accordingly the majority of them were pretty drunk most of the time. While in this condition some of them had taken groups of Americans into the woods and had stripped them of all their valuables. Especially did they prize the American wrist watches, which most of our men had managed to conceal by wearing them around their ankles. Then they forced Americans to dig their latrines. Finally, several Russian soldiers came into our barracks where we had our sick. They forced our men to drink vodka with them and demanded all their cigarettes. What I feared more than anything else was that some American might bust a Russian on the nose and that these "allies," undisciplined as they were, might turn a machine gun loose on us. We had come too long a way to lose men now. I went down to see the Russian colonel who was in charge of the camp but found that he was drunk too. We were beginning to feel much less secure under the Russians than we had under the Germans, and we were wondering what we could do about it.

On the 2nd of May an American colonel, who had been in a Belgian camp near Berlin, arrived at the camp and took command of the American compound. He was astounded at the treatment we were receiving from the Russians. Although he protested vigorously, it seemed that front-line troops in the Russian army just weren't expected to be disciplined troops, and the danger to our sick and wounded became critical.

On the 4th of May an American captain drove up to the camp in a jeep. He received a rousing welcome from the men, for they thought that he would be leading trucks in to take us back to the American lines. From there, we felt sure, we could almost see the Statue of Liberty. However, the captain was on a special mission and had an interpreter for Russian and German with him. The colonel asked the captain to take me back to the American lines with him so that I could explain our situation to someone who could do something about it. The colonel had strictly forbidden any American to leave the camp, for such were General Eisenhowers orders. Nevertheless, each day a couple of dozen men would light out on their own towards the American lines, which were about eighty miles away in a direct line but almost a hundred and fifty miles by road. The whole American compound was becoming quite surly over the delayed freedom; men were beginning to fight among themselves, and real trouble with the Russians seemed almost inevitable.

Once on the road, the captain told me what his real mission was. He had been sent in to pick up a German scientist before the Russians got him. The German was a man of considerable importance, and the captain was determined that nothing was going to stop him from doing what he was sent to do. The roads were congested and clogged with thousands upon thousands of liberated Poles, Serbs, Belgians, Dutch, French, and Italians struggling to get back home. Sometimes the procession moved only a couple of miles a day, and sometimes it would be hopelessly stalled for many hours. Every conceivable kind of contraption was used for transportation; a cow was hitched up to an old buggy; a group of German civilians were tied to the tongue of a wagon pulling a load of Serbs. Dead horses and dead humans lay uncovered along the road with no one bothering to cover them. The captain would sometimes leave the road and take to the fields, for the congested traffic was often impossible to cope with.

We arrived at Neustrelitz, about forty miles south of Neubrandenburg and the same distance north of Berlin. We went directly to the address of the German that the captain was after. The German lived in a first-floor apartment. After rapping at the door for some time, we finally let ourselves in through a window. We waited in the apartment for about four hours before our man finally showed up. The captain stood behind the door as the German inserted his key into the lock. When he stepped in, he felt a forty-five stuck in his back. The interpreter told the German to get into the American uniform that had been brought along for this purpose. As the German complied, he was told that he was going back to the American lines with us. He was greatly relieved at that and said that he would be glad to cooperate in every way; he had feared that we were Russians. I must confess that I was getting quite a schoolboy thrill out of my accidental participation in this adventure. Still, the whole thing impressed me as being even more "corny" than the usual Hollywood script.

The captain thought that we might more quickly reach the American lines by going south through Berlin. However, when we arrived at the outskirts of that city, it became clear to us that we would not *get* very far that way before our German friend would be interrogated by the Russian police who were stopping and questioning everyone. We turned around and headed northwest towards the Elbe river. Our first night we did not stop to sleep but caught what catnaps we could by taking turns driving. We stuck to the back roads as much as possible. The second night we stopped at an abandoned farm house, hiding the jeep in the barn. The German slept soundly all night, probably the first restful night he had had since the Russians took his little city. I was glad to see as we went through the towns that few if any had been as badly mauled and burned as had Neubrandenburg.

On the third day we met a group of ten American airmen who had been prisoners and were now trying to get to the American lines. They had been having a rough time of it and were mighty hungry. The captain had a case of C rations in the jeep. If this much maligned ration was never appreciated before, it certainly was then. They even ate the crackers (known as "dog biscuits") and the soggy spaghetti (known to the soldier as "fish bait").

The captain then stopped a large wagon which liberated Poles were using to get home in, and he hooked the wagon on to the back of the jeep. I protested taking the wagon from the Poles, but the captain said that he would have a better chance of getting the German scientist back to the American lines if he were mixed in with these air corps men, for as we approached the American lines, Russian interrogation officers got tougher and tougher, and passes were required. He also reminded me that I was just a passenger on this trip, that he was running this show, and that getting his man back was the most important consideration. I liked his frankness, which was firm but not disrespectful. With only four of us in the jeep, he said, each of us would likely be questioned; but with a wagonload of men probably only himself and whoever was driving would be questioned. I felt very sorry for the Poles, but they were not as disheartened as I had expected they would be; apparently nothing could spoil their joy at their liberation.

We spent three days covering the last seventy miles of Russian-occupied territory. Every ten miles or so we were stopped by the suspicious Russian police. The captain and myself would always go together to see the local commandant to get a pass. This procedure usually involved drinking several vodka highballs with the commandant and discussing various aspects of the war. We were very liberal with our compliments to the Red army's role in this final victory, and they seemed as pleased with the flattery as children at Christmas. Our interpreter apparently employed just the right words to win the Russians confidence. They always praised the American army in return and followed this up with a toast of course. The British part in the war was generally treated with contempt by the Russians. We never dared to refuse to toast Uncle Joe, President Roosevelt, General Eisenhower, and numerous Russian general officers. Failure to respond to a toast is the gravest of social errors and an insult to the proposer. After the third or fourth such affair I wasn't quite sure whom I was toasting; my stomach felt like a ball of fire.

When we got within ten miles of Ludwigslust, we were stopped again. What a headache it was to get a pass from the commandant there! The captain, the interpreter, and I went up to see him about seven o'clock in the evening. The captain excused himself for some reason or other after an hour (he couldn't have been any sicker than I was). He left me with the interpreter to try to get the pass from the Russian major. The major had a couple of Russian girls with him, one of whom could speak a bit of English and seemed to be the one who made the decisions for him.

Liquor of all kinds was flowing freely, and the table was loaded with fried chicken, very well cooked but too greasy for my paralyzed stomach. The major was almost too drunk to sign his name to the pass which he was now willing to grant. But the girl kept telling him not to, for she said she didn't trust me. She gave me quite a going over in broken English and said that she knew I was not telling the truth. I never felt so inclined to strike a lady (I use the term in its broadest sense) in my life but restrained myself by concentrating on my agonizing stomach, which was being continuously abused by the perpetual toasts that the major kept proposing.

Finally, for no apparent reason, the girl gave the major a pencil and told him to sign the pass. My faith in the essential goodness of womankind was restored. She let me know, however, that I wasn't fooling her a bit. It was now after eleven p.m. Four hours had been spent with that weird couple and their chicken and liquor. That I felt definitely the worse for wear is the understatement of this entire book. I was afraid that the others might have gone on without me, presuming that I had been unable to get the pass. They were still waiting, however, and I saw the airmen wink at each other as I staggered toward the jeep.

We finally arrived at Ludwigslust and were stopped for the last time at the bridge over the canal which separated the Russian sector from the American. The Russian guard stopped us and demanded another pass to get to the American side. The American guard on the other side of the bridge saw our predicament; he walked to the middle of the bridge and called to his Russian counterpart to meet him there. They went into a big discussion, and while they were talking, the captain stepped on the gas and over we went to the American side. The Russian became quite excited and shouted for us to come back, but Uncle Joe himself on bended knee wouldn't have been able to accomplish that. Now we were really free!

The 82nd Airborne Division was occupying this sector, and we found that besides being one of the best fighting outfits in the world, they were also the most hospitable. Captain Larkin Tully, CO of Baker Company of the 82nd, took us right down to the mess hall and had the biggest steaks I had ever seen set before us. He also gave us the great news that this was VE day. *The war in Europe was over at last!*

The next day, after another king-sized steak dinner, we were sent to Ninth Army Headquarters at Hildesheim. There I was able to contact the Ninth Army G-2 and tell him the whole story of the situation at Stalag II-A. He said that General Eisenhower had had similar reports from other Stalags. He said that negotiations were under way to evacuate American prisoners of war immediately. The captain turned his German scientist over to the G-2, and we parted. The G-2 fixed me up with a clean uniform and offered me the facilities of his quarters to take a shower, shave, and shampoo. That evening I flew to Paris.

The plane that flew us to Paris had six liberated Frenchmen aboard. They could scarcely control their joy at going home after those five long years of imprisonment. At the first sight of the Eiffel Tower they let out a whoop and brought forth three bottles of wine from under their shirts. They insisted (though it didn't take too much insisting) that all of us drink a toast to Paris. I had often heard that Paris was loved like a mother by all Frenchmen, and I was quite moved to see these scrawny, emaciated, homesick men feast their tear-dimmed eyes upon their beloved city. I wondered if any other city in the world is as dear to her native sons.

Our landing was delayed for about half an hour by the crashing of an English plane on the runway sometime that morning. As we continued to fly over the city, the Frenchmen pointed out the

famous landmarks for us. When we finally came down, we inquired
about the plane that had crashed and was still smoking at the end of
one of the runways. We were told that the two pilots and most of
the thirty-two liberated British prisoners aboard had died in the
crash. The next day I said Mass for their intention although I had
looked forward to a Mass of thanksgiving for our own liberation.

In Paris I was given some pay and a seventy-two hour pass before
I would entrain for Le Havre. When I met a group of men from my
own outfit who were in Paris on furlough, we greeted one another
like long lost brothers. Their warm welcome, their healthy faces and
strong bodies, their enthusiasm over Paris, their clear eyes and sure
movements . . . I couldn't help contrasting these men who had come
through the war unscarred with the haggard, dull-eyed, cadaverous-
looking group I had left at Stalag II-A. Please, God, I thought, help
the G-2 and transportation section at Ninth Army to get them out
of Neubrandenburg fast.

"Gee, Father, we'd scarcely know you. You used to be kind of
fa—, well, er, chubby. You look like a scarecrow now."

"Yeah, and we all thought you were dead," said another. "How'd
you get captured? Hey, come to think about it, I believe Chaplain
Engel held some sort of memorial service for you. I couldn't make it,
but I understand he said a lot of nice things about you. Of course
that was when he thought you were dead." Everybody laughed.

"How is Chaplain Engel," I asked, "and Colonel Ewell, and
Doc Carrel? Just start anyplace and tell me about everybody you can
think of."

"Chaplain Engel is fine. Colonel Ewell was wounded, and
Colonel Ballard took over the regiment. Jansen was killed—you
know him, Father, platoon sergeant in Baker Company; and let's
see, Frazier, Lyons, and old Honeybucket were killed. We lost a lot
of men at Bastogne, Father. Lets see, you were captured before the
aid station was shelled . . ."

"Let me tell you about Colonel Ewell," interjected one of the men.
"He was wounded in the foot pretty bad, but I don't think they amputated. He had walked into the open to get a better view of a couple of
German tanks about six hundred yards away. One of the tanks let go
at him, and when he was asked why he hadn't stayed under cover, he
said, "Why, I've read those lousy Kraut artillery field manuals, and

they say that an artillery piece is never to fire at individual enemy personnel, but only when several of the enemy are together. I guess the Germans weren't playing according to the book."

And so on and on into the night we discussed the regiment and all the changes that had taken place in it. These men seemed to be enjoying themselves although I am quite sure they had planned a little wilder evening than we were spending. Though I wanted to go back with them to Rheims, my orders stated that I was to report to Camp Lucky Strike near Le Havre and would be shipped back to the States as soon as possible. This wasn't such a hard order, however, as I was distinctly and completely homesick. I sent a couple of notes back with these GIs to Colonel Ballard and to Chaplain Engel telling them to be sure to hold my place in the regiment open for me, for I fully intended to return to it. Doubtless the division would soon be sent to the Far East.

My short stay in Paris was very pleasant, and I had a fine room assigned to me in one of the best hotels in the city. Paris was on one gigantic victory jag. Snake lines formed in the streets and marched and sang and danced till the wee hours of the morning. The following afternoon started the same thing all over again. I enjoyed watching this, as well as visiting some of the great churches I had missed on my previous visit to Paris. My greatest pleasure, however, was simply walking as a free man among free men.

Camp Lucky Strike was quite a place, a tent city housing the thousands of prisoners of war who kept pouring in from all parts of Europe. They went all out there to fatten us up before we returned to the States. My normal weight of about a hundred and eighty-five pounds had shrunk to a slender one hundred thirty. We were given the opportunity to enjoy the luxury of a daily shower and were deloused. (I had grown quite accustomed to, if not fond of, my little parasitic friends.) New pinks and greens were issued. The meals were tremendous and were prepared better than any army food that I have ever had. We could have five meals a day if we could eat them, chicken and steak being the chief items on the menu, which invariably finished with a pie â-la-mode. Eggnogs were passed out between meals. I gained almost thirty pounds in the two weeks at Camp Lucky Strike. A couple of other priests who had been prisoners of war were at Lucky Strike, and we all had a great time together.

May 26 we sailed on a converted French liner. The sea was rough, but the voyage was pleasant. The whole boat seemed intoxicated with the joy of going home. I celebrated Mass every day, and the attendance was very good. Apparently most of the men were mighty grateful to the Power that brought them through. I doubt if many will ever forget their experiences or the Providence that made it possible for them to return to their families.

After landing at the port of New York and being given a thorough physical examination at Camp Kilmer, we were put in troop trains. All the men in my train were midwesterners. We were heading for Fort Snelling, Minnesota, for the final processing before beginning a thirty-day leave at home, then another thirty-day rest period at army recreation hotels in Hot Springs, Arkansas. An officer was placed in charge of each car to keep the men from going AWOL the first time they spotted an American bar.

Everything was going well until we arrived at Cumberland, Maryland. The food on the troop train was wonderful, and we were eating army style served out of marmite cans on paper plates. That was O.K., and we were enjoying it until a streamliner rolled up beside our dingy train. The men saw a large group of German PWs sitting down in the diner where table cloths and white-jacketed waiters added class to the Germans' meal. Our men were furious. The streamliner pulled out just in time to prevent some real damage to its chinaware.

The colonel in charge of the train called the car commanders together and told us that we would be in Cumberland for exactly two more hours. We could let the men go into town for a beer, but we would be responsible for getting every man back on the train before it left. As the men left my car, I warned each man personally of dire consequences if he wasn't back in time. When I stopped at the local Catholic rectory to see the priest, I was told that he was at the Knights of Columbus hall. I went there, had a couple of beers with the men, and was enjoying myself immensely. Suddenly I glanced at my watch. I couldn't believe it; I had only five minutes to catch my train. I dashed out of the club for the station and got there just as the train was pulling out. I ran after the train as fast as I could but couldn't quite make it. The men were hanging out the windows laughing at my embarrassing predicament and mimicking my last words to them, "Look soldier, you be back on time for this train . . . or else!" I bought a ticket on the streamliner that was going in the same direction about an hour later. The streamliner caught up with the troop train in about four hours. I switched back to my car on the troop train, and the men really poured the heat on me for the rest of the trip to St. Paul.

We were still on leave when we heard on the radio and read in the papers the story of the atom bombs dropped on Hiroshima and Nagasaki. This was followed by the unconditional surrender of the Japanese on the battleship Missouri. The war in both theatres was now over. The American soldier could try to take up life again where it left off. The soldier's first step in this process was to obtain his discharge, exchange the uniform for civilian clothes, and recover his personal identity. He would no longer be GI Joe of the United States Army, but Mr. Joe Brown of 810 Elm Street in his own home town.

I think that I shall always hesitate to believe or to disbelieve war stories, for I know that soldiers sometimes tell whoppers, but I also know that the incredible does happen. The past year and a half was already beginning to seem more like a dream than reality. In time, I supposed it would fade almost altogether. Just at this time I was confused and bewildered and staggered by the terrific price of World War II in human life and suffering. History alone will establish, as only it can, whether the good that came out of it all will bear some proportion to the tremendous cost. Right then I was thinking of the peaceful and happy life of a parish assistant in some little Iowa town, busy with the school children, with Catholic Youth groups, with confessions, with daily Mass, and with the Sunday sermon. And that is what I returned to; but not for long.

PART IV

Peace and "Police Action"

Look Out Below!

CHAPTER 10

Civilian Interlude

W ELL, it did seem good to get back into the uniform of the Church. I had never realized before how comfortable and practical the black suit and Rom an collar were. Besides, I never could tie a decent four-in-hand. Taking off the army uniform and putting on the clerical garb seemed almost like a ceremony marking the end of one period of life and the beginning of another, something like taking the step forward during the reception of the sub-diaconate, *salva reverentia.*

Although all the Catholic chaplains I had talked to since returning from overseas were eager to get out of the service, not one regretted having served in the Army or Air Force or Navy. Everyone of them felt that combat experience especially had benefitted him a great deal. Combat truly was a perfect laboratory for a priest's study and work. There human nature was exposed for dissection and analysis. All the artificialities and superficialities of civilian life were cut away. There remained nothing but bedrock character, or sometimes, unfortunately, the almost total lack of character. Family position, social status, money, influence—these were mighty useless assets at the front.

The one factor that did follow the men wherever they went, the one thing that stood by them during the darkest hours and gave them the help and courage they needed, was the discipline and training they had received at home. These were the imperishable assets that did not disintegrate under the fire of temptation or the fire of enemy bullets. Yes, I reflected as I was leaving the Army, Christian home training is the greatest endowment parents can give to their children. Of course I had always believed this but had never had it so graphically illustrated in civilian life. Our religion with its wise emphasis upon inculcating the sense of duty and obligation in children gives them the moral stability that makes for ordered, happy lives, worthy members of Holy Mother Church, and useful citizens of our country.

About twelve hundred officers and enlisted men were being separated that day at Fort Sheridan. This was to be our last Sunday in the Army; or so most of us thought. The chapel was packed for three Masses. This would be the last time I would address soldiers as a chaplain; or so I thought. As I faced them for the sermon, I couldn't help but feel that I was going to miss my khaki-clad congregations. Soldiers are something of a paradox. Their faults and their sins are apparent; yet their virtues are many. They swagger and boast; yet they seem to have a depth of humility that reveals itself to a chaplain in so many ways. Their language is often coarse and crude, and their humor often disgusting; but their confessions are frank and their purpose of amendment sincere. The monotony and routine of army life seem to make them hard and sometimes even cruel to one another; but their sense of humor, their kindnesses, and their amazing bursts of generosity to each other more than make up for moments of meanness and pettiness. It is difficult to leave a group of men like that, men with whom you have lived for several years more intimately than with brothers. Catholic men have a tendency to glamorize their chaplain way beyond his merits. No amount of army regulations, circulars, and bulletins could get them to call their priest "Chaplain" instead of "Father." You can understand why I began to regret that this was to be my last sermon to the soldiers, and I had a hunch that I would miss them more and more as time went on. The thought that I tried to put over to them that day went something like this:

"When a man comes into the Army, he stands before a delegated authority. With his right hand raised, he swears to respect and obey all legitimate orders of lawful superiors and to protect and defend his country from all enemies foreign and domestic. Now you are about to be released from the Army and from many of the special obligations that were yours as soldiers. But in a very real sense army life is nothing new to Catholics. You have been in the service since the day you were baptized in the army of Jesus Christ. At your baptism, through your godparent you swore to obey all orders of Christ and His Church, and you vowed to protect and to defend the sanctuary of your immortal soul from all enemies foreign and domestic. As the waters of baptism were poured over your forehead, you were clothed in the spotless uniform of sanctifying grace; you were a rookie in Gods army, weak, untrained, incapable of combat yet, it was true. But your parents and the good sisters in school would teach you, Holy Communion and confession would strengthen you, and Confirmation would establish you as a fighting soldier of Christ.

"The enemy? Not the Axis of Germany, Italy, and Japan, but an enemy far more crafty, far more resourceful. Your enemy and God's is the Axis of the world, the flesh, and the devil: the world with all its tinsel and baubles, its false front, its sham and hypocrisy; the flesh with its poisoned delights, its insipid pleasures, its sensuality and insobriety; the devil with his hatred and his greed, his envy, avarice, sloth, and, above all, his pride. This is the enemy that you are duty-bound to fight. This is the enemy that has never gotten over the crushing defeat it suffered in the first clash of arms with Jesus on the battlefield of Calvary.

"But proper weapons of warfare are necessary in order to win the war against the enemies of your soul. You might as soon expect to stop a Tiger tank with a pea-shooter or shoot down Japanese Zero planes with sling shots as to fight the world, the flesh, and the devil without the proper weapons. No matter how well disposed you may be or how strong a will you have or how determined you are; no matter how favorable your home life and environment are or what material advantages you may have; unless you use the weapons our Blessed Lord has given to you and use them according to his instructions, you are doomed to inevitable defeat. Jesus has given you these weapons you need, and as your Commander He guarantees that if you use them properly, you will win out. These weapons are daily prayer, the rosary, the Stations of the Cross, and, most effective of all, frequent confession and Holy Communion. These are your machine guns, your tanks, your heavy artillery, your dive-bombers; they have proved their effectiveness in every battle of life, as all the saints in Heaven and devout Catholics on earth will testify.

"Combat was a spiritual rest period for all of us. When you were lying in a muddy foxhole miserable and scared, prayer came easy, didn't it? When you were on an outpost at night, and every rustle of the wind in the bushes conjured up in your imagination an enemy only a few feet away, you weren't planning a drunken brawl for the next weekend. When 88s zeroed in on your sector and tree-bursts were throwing shrapnel in every direction, you had no difficulty in banishing impure thoughts and desires. The peace and quiet of home and the real values in life were what you longed for, weren't they? You got a lot of comfort out of your rosary when you had a chance to say part of a decade at the front, didn't you? I believe you made a number of promises to God then, didn't you? Have you forgotton those promises? God hasn't. Are you as sincere about them now as when you made them? God is. Yes, combat was a spiritual rest period; you felt close to God, and it was a mighty comforting feeling.

"But now you are going back home, and though this may sound strange to you, you are going to be in a *real* battle. The opportunity and the temptation to break every promise to God that you ever made is going to be thrust at you from every side. Your family will be overjoyed to have you home, and the old gang will welcome you back, and your pastor will be delighted to see you; don't fail to make a special call on him. But still, no matter how small your home town may be or how large, the world, the flesh, and the devil will be there welcoming you too, urging you to compromise, to shirk your duties as a soldier of Christ, to shed the uniform of sanctifying grace, to go over to the enemy. This is not a mere figure of speech. You must know by now that the real battles of life have always been fought, not on French soil, or German, or Italian, not in Europe, Asia, or Africa, but in the souls of men like yourself.

"There is one saboteur of your soul more dangerous than all others. It is discouragement. Discouragement can infiltrate and undermine Gods grace, if you let it. Discouragement alone can defeat a Catholic. You have before you the wonderful example of Jesus Christ, and you have behind you, perhaps, a lifetime of miserables failures. Urging you onward and upward are the teachings of the Church and the examples of the saints and of your own good parents; holding you back and dragging you downward are the consciousness of your own weakness and the sins of the past. Yesterdays resolutions gave promise of real progress; todays failures teach you that you are still a pretty weak human being.

"With Saint Paul you feel like crying out, 'The good that I would, I do not, and the evil that I would not, that I do. Unhappy man that I am, who shall deliver me from the body of this death?' And then Saint Paul's answer to his own question comes ringing down through the ages, as true now as it was then and always will be, true for you and for me and for every man, woman, and child on the face of the globe, 'Who shall deliver me from the body of this death? *The grace of God, which* is *in Christ Jesus, our Lord!*' And you get this grace, men, principally through the Holy Sacrifice of the Mass, and through the sacraments of Penance and Holy Eucharist. Stay close to these, and you will always be strong and true soldiers of Christ, worthy to share in His glory on the Day of Victory!"

After separation I drove to Chicago to get a black suit. I went to at least a dozen big clothing stores, and not one of them had a black suit for sale. Finally, a salesman explained that they were forbidden to sell them because the OPA found that they were being retailored into tuxedos, not allowed during the war. I got my old black suit out of mothballs and went to Des Moines to report to Bishop Bergan for assignment. I shall never forget his welcome when I first returned from Europe. He is one of those rare individuals who combine the dignity and authority of a responsible position with a kind, humble, and extremely witty personality. Monsignor Lyons, rector of the cathedral, invited me to stay there until the Bishop decided what my assignment was to be. Three days later the Bishop called me in and told me that I was being assigned as assistant to Father Duren in Westphalia.

"I am leaving for Atlantic now for Confirmations. Can I drop you off any place on the way?" he asked.

"Well, Bishop," I said, "I'm just going out to the college for a little while. You go right by there, if you don't mind."

"Sure, come along." As we went to his car out in back of the chancery office, the cathedral curates carried his bags out and put them in the trunk; then they went back up and were standing on the steps waving.

"Good-bye, Bishop! Have a good trip, Bishop!" they called.

"Good-bye, Fathers! I'll be back in three days," the Bishop responded. Then he turned to me and winked, "They sound real sad to see me go, don't they? Before my car is out of sight, they'll be turning handsprings in the parlor. They don't fool me a bit." And shaking a finger at me, he added, "So don't you try to fool me either!"

Westphalia is scarcely discernible on a state map, but it is a well-known little Iowa town. The entire community is established on a cooperative basis. There are five points to the program: Religion, Education, Recreation, Commerce, and Credit. Father Duren (same name as the chaplain in the hospital in Normandy) formulated the fundamental principle by which these things are coordinated. "Build the Kingdom of God great . . . and all these things shall be added unto you." It sounds very idealistic and, to many, impractical. But Father Duren has made it work. Many communities throughout the country have modelled their cooperative after the Westphalia idea.

The village and the surrounding country are solidly Catholic, and the Church is the center of everyone's life. On Sunday the entire community sings the Gregorian Mass, and almost everyone receives Holy Communion weekly. When a young couple gets married, the parish throws a big wedding dance in the evening. The profits from this pay for the wedding, and the couple are given a sizable check as a gift from the parishioners. On All Souls' Day everyone attended the three Masses and the procession to the cemetery. Their faith enters into every aspect of the daily life of these people, their joys and their sorrows, their work and their play, their rising and their retiring. It can be said of these people that they truly live their religion from the cradle to the grave.

Education is the second point of the program, and Westphalia has a fine school and a splendid group of Franciscan nuns as teachers. They are the happiest and jolliest group of sisters that I have ever seen; perhaps that is why they do such a superior job of teaching. There are adult study groups, which are surprisingly well attended.

Recreation is one of the main points of the program. There is scarcely an evening that does not have something going on in the school auditorium and gymnasium . . . basketball games, dramatics, debates, Four-H Club demonstrations, sewing or flower exhibits, school dances or old fashioned dances, and so on. Father Duren has built up a splendid school band too. Every child in school learns to play an instrument. I found it really amusing to watch some of the little children blowing on a horn for all they were worth, trying to beat time with a foot that didn't reach the floor, concentrating on the music sheet, and trying to keep up. The total effect, however, was very good. He had established a club house for the men, too, where they could meet their neighbors, talk about the price of corn over a glass of beer, or play a game of pool or cards.

The cooperative store is the big contribution under Commerce. It undersells by a good deal the prices charged in the nearby towns for the same items. It saves the farmers and townspeople the ten-mile trip to the nearest big town, saves them money on the goods they buy, and returns a dividend to them each year from the stores profits.

The Cooperative Credit and Loan Association formed by Father Duren enables the people to borrow at small interest and to repay at their convenience. The people themselves have invested most of the capital in this and of course draw interest on their investment. Westphalia is one little country town that did not lose its young men to the cities when they returned from the service. The people also suport the church generously and intelligently, in a way that gives them a personal interest in the beauty of the church, the school, and all the parish property. Each farmer, for example, gives to the church one acre of corn for every fifty he has under cultivation. They haul the corn in to the cribs behind the school, get together and shell it, sell it, and turn the check over to Father Duren. As might be surmised, Father Duren is quite a fellow, big as a house and most congenial, with unlimited enthusiasm for the Westphalia plan. Yes, Westphalia is quite a place. As you enter the village, there is a sign by the road reading, "Where the world is at its best—Westphalia." The boast might sound a bit "corny," but it is true nevertheless. At least, I believe it.

Pleasant as Westphalia was, I missed life in the Army; I missed most of all my soldier congregation. So, when I received a letter from the Military Ordinariate stating that so many priests had asked for discharge that the services were in critical shortage of Catholic chaplains, I began to itch to return to the Army. Cardinal Spellman asked for the youngest of us to come back in. I approached Bishop Bergan on the subject. He likewise had received a letter from His Eminence asking that he allow some of his young priests to return to the service. He readily granted me permission. In these past twelve years I have never regretted that decision. I like the Army, for I believe it offers the greatest apostolate for the Church in America.

CHAPTER 11

The Agony of Korea

THE YEARS 1946 to 1950 were interesting years for a chaplain in the Army, often difficult and trying, but not momentous. I mentioned in the last chapter that combat was a sort of spiritual rest period, for most men had been given a glimpse of eternity as death came with sudden insistence to comrades close by; each man, in his own way, had reached for the sustaining hand of God. But the war was over now, and the new generation of draftees resented peacetime duty. The indolent missed the corner drugstore and pool hall, and the ambitious felt that they were losing valuable time and college credits while in the Army. With startling swiftness the civilian population changed its attitude toward the very Army that had preserved its freedoms. The soldier was no longer glamorized and prayed for; he was scarcely even respected. Morale hit an all-time low.

My first assignment after returning to the service in 1946 was to the 82nd Airborne Division under the command of Major General James M. Gavin. Gavin, who was until recently the Chief of the Research and Development Section in Washington, gave the same inspiring and dynamic leadership to the 82nd as his famous predecessor, General Matthew B. Ridgway, had given. Gavin's keen

analytical mind knew that America was not out of danger by a long
shot, even though Germany and Japan were decisively beaten. He
knew that the hammer and sickle might be used, not only in honest
labor, but to strike one's neighbor and to stab him in the back.

My predecessor in the 505th Regiment of the 82nd Airborne
had left a pair of shoes far too big for me to properly fill. He was
Father Philip M. Hannan, who left the service after the war to study
Canon Law at The Catholic University of America, then became
Chancellor, and is now Auxiliary Bishop of Washington. Father
Hannan had written a history of the regiment's war action, but
someone at headquarters had carelessly mislaid the only copy. That
bit of carelessness was not only a disservice to the regiment but
deprived all of us of the pleasure of reading a wonderful war story.

In September of 1947 I was sent overseas to the 11th Airborne
Division which was stationed in northern Japan. This fine unit was
commanded by Major General Joseph M. Swing, who had led it
through the entire Pacific War. Their wartime jumps on Leyte and
Corregidor were two of the most daring and successful jumps,
though hazardous and costly, in the history of the airborne. When
the 11th had jumped in on Los Banos prison camp in the Philip-
pines to liberate the Americans there, a priest prisoner had watched
these paratroopers descending (like God's direct answer to their
prayers) and commented to his fellow prisoners, "They look like
angels from Heaven." The name stuck and the 11th Airborne Division is known to this day as the "Angels." This was to be my outfit
for seven of the next ten years. My affection for the men of this division was to become as great as that which I had had for the Screaming Eagles of the 101st. I liked the name Angels, although I must
concede that not all of them were "angels of light," and a few of
them even sprouted a pair of pointed bumps on their foreheads.

The two years of occupation duty in Japan were wonderfully
pleasant. We were stationed on the island of Hokkaido, near the city
of Sapporo. Hokkaido is Japan's northernmost island and the least
populated. The terrain and climate are not unlike those of Maine, and
the hunting and fishing opportunities were all that an outdoor sports-
man could ask. The streams were loaded with trout, and you could
almost hunt ducks with tennis racquets. Bear, wild boar, deer, and
caribou were thick but clever enough to challenge the hunter. The

military camp itself was brand new, built under the direction of General Swing, and was the finest army post I have ever seen. Platoon-sized barracks, an enormous field-house for indoor football, softball, tennis, or horseback riding, a tremendous gymnasium with a fine indoor swimming pool, two outdoor pools, a fifteen-hundred-seat theatre, an Olympic ski slope with two lodges, a magnificent golf course, several clubs for enlisted men and officers, a six-hundred-seat chapel that was the showplace of the camp: all these facilities made life for the soldier in Hokkaido pleasant. The only really unpleasant aspect of duty on Hokkaido was the fact that Russia had moved large numbers of troops and planes onto the islands just a few miles north of us, and their attitude had become decidedly unfriendly.

The Japanese are in their way a wonderful people. It may be that, had I fought in the Pacific rather than in the European Theatre during the war, I would not be so kindly disposed toward them. But despite their cruel capabilities they possess many natural virtues in a high degree, and those who become Christians do not do so by half measure. The heroic patience with which they bore the hunger and cold and suffering of the post-war era, the family virtues that make them such close-knit and devoted groups, the beauty of their customs and courtesies in the home—all these things would make writing about them a pleasure. But this is primarily a war book, so I shall quickly pass on to those events that led up to the outbreak of hostilities in Korea and the employment of the airborne in that conflict.

In the spring of 1949 the 7th Infantry Division, under the command of Major General William F. Dean, replaced the Angels of the 11th Airborne in Sapporo. A very unfortunate incident occurred at this time. A couple of drunken Angels had refused to obey a 7th Division MP and, instead of obeying, threw beer cans at him. The MP, in the excitement that followed, lost his head and shot the two drunken men. At this time our own division commander, Major General Miley, who had replaced General Swing only a few months before, had already gone back to the States to prepare for the 11th's arrival. General Dean was in the ticklish position of trying to keep the men of the two divisions from declaring war on each other over the incident of the shooting. He called me in to ask for suggestions and approved of those I made. Fortunately, nothing further came from the incident. General Dean was later to suffer the misfortune of being captured in the early days of the Korean War. He was honored by his country by being given the Congressional Medal of Honor, but it had to be presented to his wife, as the General was not yet released from prison.

Fort Campbell, Kentucky, was the new home of the Angels. At that time it was a far cry from offering the facilities that we had known in Sapporo. Morale was low; traffic accidents and serious incidents went up; the men refused to enter into the vigorous training program with sufficient enthusiasm to really profit from it. Every means was exerted by the division's excellent leaders to snap the men from their apathy. Even the prestige of paratrooper wings and jump boots had lost its fascination for the average civilian. "Business as usual" was the creed of the day. Military budgets were cut; Congressmen were hypercritical of army spending: It's down the drain; the war is over; let's start cutting the services; we've got to economize." And then it happened. North Korea invaded South Korea. Within twenty-four hours President Truman took the only stand he could take. American troops stationed in Japan were ordered to bolster the sagging South Korean forces. The Korean "police action" had begun.

In August of 1950 I received War Department orders assigning me to study at Notre Dame University for one year. As I was home on leave a wire from Washington arrived cancelling the Notre Dame assignment and instructing me to return to the 11th. Nearly all military schools suspended operation at this time, for the Korean action was turning out to be much more serious than had been anticipated. North Korea was throwing a real Sunday punch at the Americans and at the almost disorganized South Koreans. Mike Michaelis, formerly of the 101st, was making a real name for himself by plugging the holes in the lines with his small regimental combat team. He became known as the "Firechief," for wherever the fighting was hottest, Mike would get in his aggressive and well-trained unit.

The 187th Airborne Infantry Regiment of the 11th was quickly formed into an RCT with attached units to enable it to fight unassisted by the division. We left Campbell by troop train for San Francisco and pulled out of the Golden Gate on the 6th of September, bound for Beppu, on the island of Kyushu, Japan. We made a fast crossing, for it was assumed that any danger of submarine attack was nonexistent. Four days were spent equipping us and loading the big C-118 "Flying Boxcars." We were not going to jump in but would be airlanded at the Seoul airport even though that airfield had not yet been secured entirely. The marines had given us the green light to "come on in," and when the marines give the green light, it means that they will hold the ground for you no matter what the cost.

It might not be amiss here to say a word about those marines. If a paratrooper is envious of anybody in the services, it might be the marines. This body of men possesses a discipline, a determination, a spirit of self-sacrifice, and an esprit-de-corps that "just wont quit"; and, believe me, they wont quit until the last marine is dead. I had never seen them in battle before, but if Inchon and the battle of Seoul at this time, and the Chosan Reservoir affair later on, are examples of marine fighting, then I would hate to be on the opposite side. I wonder what some people mean when they call marines "glamour boys" or "publicity hounds." They could never be attributed the glamour or given the publicity they have earned and deserve.

One day Major Jenkins, our G-4 (the same Jenkins that was the 501st regimental S-4 in Normandy and Holland) managed to tune in on a conversation between a marine company commander and his battalion CO. "Listen to this, Father," Jenkins said. I listened.

"Sir, I've lost a deck already," the company commander said ("deck" means about fifty men).

"So?" was the cryptic reply.

"Sir, there are gooks swarming all over this hill. We've got to have some help."

"You ain't going to get any help, not for a while anyhow. Davis and his men got into the city. Were pushing in behind him."

"Sir, we can't hold on without some help and quick." Despite the urgency of the information the company commander sounded just factual, almost casual.

"Listen, Dirk! You plant your big backside right in that gook mud where you are. When we get back, you better be there. Got that?"

"Yes, sir!" Nothing more. I'm sure when the battalion commander did get back, he found Dirk still there, maybe alive, maybe dead, but still there. I'm sure of that.

Jenkins looked at me. "That's the real war, huh? How Errol Flynn could lap up a part like that," he said.

On our first day in Seoul a Korean doctor by the name of Kim (at least seventy-five per cent of Koreans are named Kim) came to me and asked me to request General Bowen to take him on as interpreter. Kim had been cleared by our intelligence officer. The general said he didn't need another interpreter but that I could keep him if I had need of him. So Kim became my interpreter. He was a fairly young man for a doctor and really hated Communists, who had killed his parents in Pyongyang, the North Korean capital. He was a devout Catholic, but for a doctor he was much too eager to kill the enemy when he should have been thinking about caring for the wounded.

Our first real action was on the peninsula just northwest of Seoul. Colonel Harry Wilson's battalion plus a special-weapons company was to clear that area of the enemy. Organized resistance was small, but the guerrillas harassed our troopers at every turn of the road. They ambushed a group of headquarters men, killing four. The company commander and another man were killed by a defective grenade, and before we got back to Seoul, we lost three more men. Nine men lost seems like a comparatively small price for any action, I suppose, but when you know men well, statistics are meaningless and each life lost is a terribly heavy cost.

When marines had cleared the city of Seoul of all active resistance, the North Korean flags were quickly taken in by all the inhabitants and the South Korean flag hung outside each house. (The North Korean flag was carefully tucked away ready to replace the South Korean flag again should the battle for Seoul change once more.) These poor people just wanted to be friends with everyone; or better still, just left alone.

I called on the Bishop of Seoul, who had come back to his cathedral as soon as the Communists were gone. Together we went out to his seminary. A few seminarians started drifting back to clean up the place, which had been used as a North Korean barracks. The filth they left was almost indescribable. The holy pictures had been slashed to ribbons. Stalin's picture hung above the altar, and the life-sized crucifix it had replaced lay on the floor smashed and piled with human offal. Obscene pictures were crudely drawn on the walls. The Bishop didn't act shocked by what we saw but simply directed the cleaning of the place.

When we returned to the airfield, General Bowen ordered Chaplain Hope, the very excellent Protestant chaplain of the 187th, and myself to hold memorial services. Every man in the regiment attended one service or the other. It struck me that that is one of the greatest differences between the Christian and the pagan cultures—the importance of the individual, the great concern for nine dead men (in a country where death is as stoically accepted as a mosquito bite).

The tide of the war was changing rapidly now, and the North Koreans were falling back to prepare defense positions in the area of the 38th parallel. The airforce had spotted about two thousand American prisoners being marched north of Pyongyang. We were quickly briefed for an airborne drop with the double mission of rescuing those Americans from their captors and cutting off the retreating North Koreans who were fleeing from the heavy blows of the 1st Armored Cavalry Division. As we were to take off at dawn, that night I was hearing confessions in my tent. The men were lined up outside, and above the whisper of penitents I could hear a couple of Mexican boys arguing. One was trying to persuade the other to go to confession.

"Come on, Manuel, come to confession. Maybe you die tomorrow, who knows?"

"No, Miguel. I don' go to confession."

"Come on, come on, Manuel. The fadder wont bawl you out . . . he ain't got time. Look at all these guys he gotta listen to."

"No, I don go to confession. I think I get drunk tonight."

"O.K., O.K., you get drunk tonight. But come to confession and tell da fadder, and it is already forgiven."

Needless to say, the word of counsel in confessions that night was then and there changed to the necessity of a "purpose of amendment" for valid absolution.

We boarded our planes at four a.m. and were cold and wet from the steady drizzle that had started the day before. We flew directly out to sea so that we might turn back toward land two hundred miles north. We jumped shortly after dawn near the town of Sunchon. Yes, you guessed correctly. I lit in the water again, knee deep in a paddy field. Could Chaplain Engel have been right all these years? . . . *was* it a providential sign that I should have been a Baptist? At this stage I wouldn't have given Colonel Ewell any odds had we jumped in the Sahara Desert.

We soon learned that the prisoners we were trying to rescue had been moved north the night before; we failed in that part of the mission. Colonel Boyle's battalion jumped a few miles away at the town of Sukchon. A small group of seventy American prisoners there had been taken into a railroad tunnel and machine-gunned as the planes came into view. Six or seven of them were still living and were evacuated by helicopter. The helicopter was to prove itself worth its weight in gold in the Korean conflict, for if a seriously wounded man can get to a hospital quickly, his chances for recovery are at least doubled.

General Bowen ordered the battalion commanders to fan out in the three directions of possible escape routes, to locate enemy resistance pockets and destroy them. Then they were to regroup to catch in a large human net the enemy fleeing north from Pyongyang through which the 1st Cav was now driving them. This scheme worked well, and several thousand prisoners were squeezed between the Cav and the 187th. For this action General Bowen was decorated with the Distinguished Service Cross personally by General MacArthur. Our losses in this operation, however, were quite considerable.

Chaplain Hope was given the Silver Star for leading a group of men to recover the wounded and the dead from a platoon that had been ambushed in guerrilla-held territory.

Guerrilla activity increased considerably now. Tens of thousands of Koreans were moving south, all of them dressed in the white clothes of the native peasant. But among them were many Communists with weapons hidden beneath their clothes. It was impossible to screen all these people, and at night some of these daring Communists would sneak into a headquarters and shoot all the officers before being killed themselves. There seemed no way to stop this business. About this time a truck convoy arrived at our position with supplies of ammunition, food, etc. The trucks were driven by colored soldiers. The man in the lead truck heard some sporadic fire and called out to the colored noncom in charge.

"Hey, Corporal, where we goin dump this stuff? Lets bug out o here."

The noncom yelled back at him, "Don't you call me Corporal, man! Don't you know them Communists is shootin us leaders?"

The paratroopers roared.

It might be said that integration of colored and white troops began about this time, and it was found that under good leadership the colored soldier did as well as the white soldier beside him. The sense of humor and the pleasant temperament of the negro soldier were often fine morale factors too.

We returned to Pyongyang to garrison that former capital and to guard the twelve thousand prisoners that were gathered there. This was no small job, as guerilla activity was increasing day by day. I took my interpreter to the prison stockade to find out if there were many Catholics in the group; Chaplain Hope went to enquire about the Protestants. We found several hundred of each and made arrangements to come back on Sunday to hold services. I collected rosaries from my men, and on Sunday when I said Mass there, I was struck by the strange twist wars can make of things. These Christians had been forced into the Communist army; now here they were using the rosaries belonging to the men they had been shooting at only a few days ago. I spoke to them through Kim, my interpreter. A couple of men in the group had been parishioners of Father Pardy, a Maryknoll Missioner friend of mine, in Wonju.

Father Cleary, also a Maryknoll Missioner, who was helping the United Nations inspection team locate the scenes of Communist atrocities, came by asking us to help. "If you want to know anything that goes on in Korea, just ask the children," he said. "They are allowed everyplace and hear everything." Sure enough the children led us to the place where Christians and political prisoners were executed about five miles outside the town. These poor people had their hands tied behind their backs, were packed together as tightly as possible on their knees, and were shot in the head. Dirt had been dumped on top of them, but the rains had come and the dirt had settled, exposing hundreds of heads and shoulders above the ground. There were an estimated three thousand in one mass grave and about nine hundred in another. The United Nations Atrocity Committee took pictures. All over the city executed Christians and political prisoners were being brought out of abandoned wells and dug up out of ditches. No one will ever know how many men, women, and children were put to death for their faith.

The North Korean leader, Kim Il Sung, had previously taken over the Presbyterian college for his home. He had several thousand books from the Benedictine monastery in Wonsan, two hundred miles east of Pyongyang, brought to his home: he wanted a library. All these books on ascetical theology in Latin, French, German, English, and other languages filled his shelves. It made no difference what the subject matter, or that he couldn't read them; he just wanted an impressive-looking library!

The war was going very well for the United Nations forces, although our regiment was still being nibbled to death by guerrillas in the most aggravating fashion. Each day Chaplain Hope and I buried ten to twenty men, usually victims of unseen snipers in the city. Nevertheless, the North Korean army was beaten. Hundreds of their Russian-built tanks lay burned in ditches along the two main roads of Korea, thousands of their vehicles had been destroyed, and over two hundred thousand prisoners were in our stockades. They were finished as a fighting force; now only the mopping up of the guerrillas remained. At Thanksgiving Day dinner we were told that we would be out of Korea by Christmas.

Suddenly, the whole complexion of the war changed. It was discovered that at least two hundred thousand Chinese "volunteers" had crossed into Korea. General Walkers Eighth Army came to a screeching halt in its march to the Mongolian border. Then the main body of a million Chinese "volunteers" crossed over; and the Eighth began what is termed in newspaper language as a "strategic withdrawal." To the GI it was just a "bug out," and anyone who was there would verify that the GI had by far the more accurate term.

We were to allow the 1st Cav to pass through us and were then to follow them south. The Cav had gone through, and as we were pulling out at five a.m., it was discovered that a Chinese unit had sneaked around to the south of the city and closed the road. It looked for a short time as through we were trapped. Fortunately, another road was found, and the 187th just got out in time. That day and night of travel over the narrow and torn-up Korean roads across the mountains was miserable. All soldiers hate to retreat, but this was a devastating blow to the pride of the proud American paratroopers. Then Eighth Army commander, Lieutenant General Walker, was killed in a vehicle accident. What next? we wondered.

Lieutenant General Matthew B. Ridgway succeeded General Walker as commander of Eighth Army. If ever there was a man who was the embodiment of aggressive military leadership, it was this man. Strong-jawed, clear-eyed, and totally dedicated, he literally lifted up by its bootstraps his beaten, depressed, and "bug-out"-minded Eighth Army, turned it about face, and ordered it to attack. In one short week his tremendous personality and determination had reversed the trend of the war. It was a fantastic accomplishment. Morale immediately went up, a clear proof of the correlation between leadership and morale. More than any other leader I have ever known, Ridgway was a soldier's soldier and imposed his own aggressive and determined personality upon his subordinate commanders. Like Washington at Valley Forge, he was a man who met the supreme test in one of his country's darkest hours and won on sheer guts and leadership.

The bitterly cold winter had set in. With the return of the Communist army the people of North Korea—hundreds of thousands of them—left their homes in the north to seek refuge in South Korea. The sight of more than a million people trudging along and clogging all roads, with others packed in or on top of or on the sides of every train moving south, was unforgettable. Old people were carried on "A" frames on the backs of the younger. Women and children, the sick and the old had to face the sleet and the cold wind, hungry, freezing, and now homeless. My God! I thought, could this be the twentieth century? Had Genghis Khan imposed greater suffering on the weak and helpless than this? The dead were left by the side of the road, and after members of the family had shed a dutiful tear, they moved on. The Army set up soup kitchens along the way. This helped some, but it was like trying to fill the Grand Canyon by standing on the edge and tossing stones over the side. More than sixty thousand died along the roads or froze on the trains during this worst winter in twenty years. The exodus continued.

Christmas Masses were held in Suwon, and the men went to Holy Communion almost in a body. Again combat had proved to be a soul-searching experience for these young soldiers, and it had helped clear away the dross of false values. I don't know whether or not it is true that "there are *no* atheists in foxholes," but I do know that there are mighty few, if any, and that their arguments are unappealing and hollow-sounding in the classroom of the battle field. Since there were a number of other units attached to us, I had to say five Masses on Christmas Day to cover them all.

Several nationalities were attached to the 187th, and each of these had its particular national foods shipped over to us for distribution. Major Jenkins got caught in a veritable buzz saw when he mixed the rations up by accident and delivered the Philippine food to the Turks, the Indonesian food to the Greeks, and vice versa. The Turks were ready to carve up Major Jenkins when they discovered his mistake. These Turks were probably the most ferocious fighters on the side of the United Nations, and they liked especially the infighting where they could use their knives to advantage. Many of their soldiers carried strings of enemy ears as trophies of war. So far as I know, no Turks were ever taken prisoner.

As we moved north, each mile of fighting became more difficult. Since we were so badly outmanned in numbers, our new offensive was bound to slow down. Only the Air Force with its deadly napalm bombs of jellied gas kept the enemy from being able to overrun us. Since the war was in a stalemate, we concentrated on building up defensive positions before the anticipated spring offensive of the enemy. Ridgway consolidated our positions and then inaugurated an R and R program (Rest and Rehabilitation). In this program the men took turns in going back to Japan for six days of rest and relaxation. Battle fatigue was beginning to take a heavy toll of our men, and this R and R program was designed to give a shot in the arm to the men who had been in the lines for months with scarcely any relief. The R and R program paid tremendous dividends, for the men returned from Japan ready and willing to take up where they had left off.

Stealing equipment in combat, if not condoned, is at least accepted as being inevitable. Everyone took whatever he needed wherever he found it. I assume someone felt that way about my jeep, for it was stolen right from under my nose. The regiment was short of jeeps, and there were no extras for me after I had lost mine. Of course, I couldn't function properly without transportation. I couldn't even move. That afternoon I walked over to an English tank unit next to the 187th to say Mass for the British Catholics. After the prayers following Mass, I turned around and said, "Now, if any of you men can procure a jeep for me, from any source of your choice, I will give that man a jug of soluble coffee, a bottle of wine, and absolution." In twenty minutes a big rough-looking British sergeant drove up in a jeep; the owner's identification on the front bumper had already been painted out and a fresh "Chaplain" sign painted on.

"Here you are, Fawthaw. Now let me see; you said something about absolution, coffee, and what else . . . oh, yes, a bottle of wine. I 'ave a fearful cold . . . you know ow it is." The jeep was in far better shape than my old one, and I kept it the rest of my time in Korea.

Toward the end of February my turn came up for R and R in Japan. We took off from the Taigu airport after having the luxury of a shower and being given new uniforms and some money. When we landed in Tokyo, we were assigned to fine rooms in good hotels. The next six days were ours. I had looked forward to this rest, but on the second day I was taken to the Tokyo Army Hospital for surgery, and, though I didn't know it then, I would not be going back to Korea. I had served only seven months in Korea. Most of the others were there at least a year and many of them eighteen months before being relieved. For me the "police action" in Korea was over.

The room to which I was assigned after my operation was also occupied by a lieutenant who had been a Korean prisoner. He had to have the frost-bitten toes on both feet amputated. My other roommates were a colored lieutenant recovering from wounds received in Korea and a doctor from the Russian embassy, recuperating from some abdominal surgery. The conversation and arguments between the Russian and the colored lieutenant were a panic. The colored boy had a wonderful sense of humor and the Russian none at all. One day the colored officer was reading a detective magazine, and the Russian pointed at it.

"You Americans have so many criminals. They are every place in America. Our government doesn't allow crime in Russia," he said. "Yeah, I've heard," the lieutenant replied, "the government has taken over *everything* in Russia."

The Russian nodded agreement, and then got the inference, got red in the face, and said, "I do not think you mean anything good by that." The lieutenant guffawed with delight.

The room across the hall was occupied by a Turkish soldier with a long handle-bar moustache who was recovering from serious

wounds; he had been on the critical list for almost a week. One day
we heard the nurse scream, and several of the walking patients
dashed in. The nurse had just changed the Turks dressings and had
turned to leave. He had grabbed her from behind and was
smooching the back of her neck for all he was worth. Needless to
say, the Turk was taken off the critical list, and a male nurse changed
his dressing from then on.

Since my regiment was preparing for a second jump in Korea
while I was in the hospital, a young priest who had already seen considerable airborne service was assigned in my place. His name was
Father Joseph Dunne, who now serves as assistant chancellor in the
Military Ordinariate in New York. He was an enthusiastic and energetic little fellow who was very well liked by the GIs wherever he
served. When he heard that the 187th was ready to make another
combat jump, he immediately managed a switch to fill my vacancy.
For the time being I was assigned to the logistical unit in Tokyo with
the additional duty of taking care of Tokyo General Hospital Annex.

In this new job I was able to get away at least two evenings a
week to play a little tennis at the Tokyo Tennis Club. Beside the
many fine Japanese players there, people assigned to the various
embassies in Tokyo were also members. It was truly a cosmopolitan
group and an extremely cordial one. One day a big, strapping, ath-
letic-type young man asked me if I would like to play a set or two
with him. He spoke good English but with a decided accent. When
he introduced himself, I didn't quite get his name but took it for
Polish or Hungarian in origin. After a very pleasant hour of tennis
and a shower, he asked me if I would care to go out to a Japanese
restaurant to dinner with him. I told him I would enjoy it very much.
In the course of the dinner I discovered that he was neither Polish
nor Hungarian, but Russian. I was somewhat surprised, for the Russians in Tokyo don't mix with other nationalities, and especially not
with Americans. However, we made a date to play tennis again on
the following weekend.

My new friend had seemed very cordial and inoffensive, but I
thought that I had better report this association to the local CIC
officer. Shortly following my report I was taken out to the Tokyo
CIC headquarters and shown the brochure on Yuri Rostovorov, my
friend. It seems that he was the chief of the Russian secret police in

Japan and had been instrumental in transferring the Russian orders for the North Korean invasion of South Korea. He was also the organizer and coordinator and supervisor of the Japanese Communist spy system. I was afraid that I had got myself in Dutch with my military authorities, and I assured them that I wouldn't have any more contact with my Russian friend, that I had had no idea that he was such a sinister character. They told me to continue to play tennis with him and to report to the CIC everything that was said. I told these men that I was a priest, a chaplain, with plenty of work of my own to do, and that I was not interested in getting caught in a "cloak and dagger" operation. This was way outside my field, and I would surely ball it up" for them. Besides, the Chief of Chaplains didn't want any of his chaplains mixed up in such dealings. O.K., they said. If I would just continue playing tennis with anyone who offered, including Rostovorov if he suggested it; if I would go out to dinner if he asked me, they would take care of the rest. During the following month we played a dozen times or more and went to dinner on four or five occasions. The subject of politics and ideologies was scrupulously avoided by both of us. I assume that he knew that I knew who he was, but no mention was ever made of it. We simply enjoyed each others company as friends do.

It was about this time that the 187th made its assault jump on Munson-Ni. Shortly after the jump Father Dunne was seriously wounded when the ambulance he was riding in struck a road mine; Father Dunnes feet were really smashed up badly. Someone at the Tennis Club told me about Father Dunne, and I mentioned to Rostovorov that I was going to Tokyo Army Hospital to see a badly wounded friend of mine. He asked to go along. Since I saw no harm in his request, together we went to see Father Dunne. The young priest lay with feet raised in a cast and sling, saying his rosary. He had only come out of shock a short time before and was still a ghastly white. The nurse had told me that they almost lost him in shock. He was in terrific pain now but greeted me cordially, asked for my blessing and prayers. I introduced Rostovorov as from the Russian Embassy; Dunne smiled through his pain and shook the Russian's hand in a friendly fashion. I could see that my Communist friend was quite moved by Father Dunnes friendly gesture and by the priest's quiet composure in pain.

A little more than a year later the Washington department of the CIC arranged for a meeting between Rostovorov and myself. He had found his way into the democratic camp, and in the story he wrote for *Life* magazine on his conversion from Communism, he told about the deep impression Father Dunne's Christ-like suffering had made upon him.

One short anecdote before we leave Japan. A Japanese room boy had been assigned to take care of my quarters, to shine my brass, and to polish my boots. This was "standard operating procedure" in Japan; every American officer had a house boy. Mine was considerably more than a boy, however, for he was the father of two children, was a veteran of World War II, and had been gravely wounded in Okinawa. Despite his war record against the Americans he was a very devoted and helpful servant. One day I had four officers up at my apartment for a little snack after Sunday Mass. Whenever I had visitors, Itashi would dress in a spotless starched white coat and serve the refreshments with real oriental *éclat*. After coffee was served and we had sat around discussing the tight National League race, the Korean war, and other things, one of the officers excused himself and went into the bathroom. He came out a few minutes later holding his sides from laughter and pointed to the bathroom. We went in, and there was Itashi under the shower, singing a weird Japanese song and washing the dishes at the same time. It would be a shame in Japan to let all that good soap go to waste.

The last eight months of duty in Japan has taken up only two pages, but the next three years as a student at Notre Dame and as instructor at the Chaplain School at Fort Slocum, New York, will take up even less. Many of the friends I had made as an underclassman at Notre Dame years before were now instructors there. Amid the peace and quiet of this scholastic atmosphere (except on football Saturdays), I enjoyed the nostalgia of an old grad for one year. Only one incident marred the pleasure of those two terms. The fates decreed that I break my leg playing handball with three gentle and kindly priests who turned out to be not so gentle in hauling me off the court, nor too kindly in their ribbing.

Following the two years as instructor at Chaplain School, I returned once more to the airborne, where I felt more at home than any place else in or out of the Army. Major General Joseph P. Cleland was the commander of the XVIII Airborne Corps. His example both as a leader of men and as a devout daily communicant made him one of the most beloved men in the service. His lovely Spanish-born wife was a model of quiet dignity and piety. Though the General is now retired from the service, these two wonderfully strong yet gentle people hold open house for all soldiers who happen to be passing by Kemper Military Academy in Boonville, Missouri. The General is only the fifth president in the one-hundred-and-four-teen-year history of that fine school.

After only a half year with the 11th Airborne at Fort Campbell, the division was gyroscoped to Europe. We were on our way to Germany. The Angels of the 11th were replacing the 5th Infantry Division and would be known as "The Shield of Bavaria."

CHAPTER 12

Germany Revisited

A S WE disembarked at the Port of Brernerhaven in early March, we ran into the last big storm of the worst winter Germany had had in thirty years. This great port city still bore the scars of the terrific bombing it had taken ten years previously. Travelling the five hundred miles to Augsburg, Bavaria, by train gave us an opportunity to enjoy the beauty of the German countryside. As soon as the storm had abated at midday, the people were out in the fields preparing the land for planting. Everywhere new buildings were going up, and the intense activity in every town and city we went through showed that the Germans were recovering very fast. The collapse of their economy which followed the first world war was not being repeated after the second.

Augsburg, which was to be our home for the next three years, is a city of about two hundred thousand people, surrounded (the old city, that is) by a medieval wall and great protective gates which were vital to the defense of the city in the days of feudal states. It is one of the oldest cities in Germany, having been founded in 14 B.C. by Augustus Caesar, and it still retains many of the old Roman ruins. The fabulous Fuggers, probably the wealthiest German merchants in the Middle Ages, had built Augsburg into a thriving and beautiful city. It still retains much of its medieval charm in the early Renaissance style of its architecture, in the beauty of its fountain squares, and even in the leisurely manner and the colorful Bavarian costumes of its inhabitants. Fugger village in the heart of the city is said to be the oldest industrial welfare project in history. The head of the great Fugger firm built this housing project for his workers. Each worker paid only one and a half marks per month (approximately thirty-five cents in American money) for a small but quite adequate house to live in. In addition, each family was obligated to say an Our Father and a Hail Mary daily for the Fugger family. Local legend has it that the Fugger family, Protestant themselves, will continue to survive as long as these prayers are said. After almost five hundred years the same rate of rent is charged to workers who live there, and the prayers continue to be said by the residents. The village had been completely destroyed by bombs during the war but has been rebuilt by the Fugger family.

Though the city was gutted by bombs during the war, the shells of the buildings were reinforced and the original architectural style maintained. A tourist viewing the city today would scarcely recognize any war damage, unless he should visit the ruins of the almost totally destroyed Messerschmidt airplane factory.

Our division moved into the five large *kasernes* (barracks) that the German Wehrmacht had occupied in and about the city. Hitler had built well for his troops, and our barracks compared favorably with the best army posts in America. As soon as the division had closed in, serious and intensive training was inaugurated under the capable direction of Major General Derrill M. Daniel, the division commander.

The shake-down period for the division was a rather rough one in some respects. The average age of our troopers was only twenty, and many of them were only seventeen or eighteen. Their first experience with the heavy, potent German beer was more than they could handle. In many ways these boys seemed far less mature than those I had known in the 101st during World War II. These young men today were mere children during the last war, and their parents were often both working; they lacked some of the home discipline that should be inculcated under normal conditions. Many of them had to learn the hard way that their actions in the Army could not be dictated by the whim or caprice of the moment. Greater leadership was demanded on the part of the officers to control these men. Then, too, we were in a country where our prestige rested on the conduct of each and every soldier. The bad conduct of a single soldier reflected upon the entire division and upon our country as well. We had some serious incidents of crime, perpetrated by a tiny percentage of our men, but these men were either tried by court martial or declared psychologically unfit for military service and sent back to the States. Eventually, however, the division shaped up in good style and became a real credit to the airborne, worthy to be "The Shield of Bavaria."

I had come to Germany with some prejudices against these people, as had many other Americans, a natural carry-over from World War II. I remembered the viciousness of "The Geek" and "Little Adolf" of Stalag II-A. We remembered the slaughter of the innocent of Lidice and the burning of the people of Oradour. We had all seen the evidences of Dachau, Belsen, Buchenwald, and numerous other concentration camps. The Dutch and the French and the Belgians had described the massacre of hostages. Could I ever forget the eighteen thousand Russians that had been tossed like dogs into common graves after being starved to death in Neubrandenburg? We are all inclined, I suppose, to blame an entire nation for the actions of its most vicious element. But I was to learn in the next three years that Germany, like our own country, had its good people and its bad, as well as those whose lives are directed by the political expediency of the moment. Any analysis I might make of the character of the German people must in the very nature of things be somewhat superficial, for who can really know a people unless he is truly one of them and sees them not only from the outside but from the inside as well?

Without a doubt the Germans are among the most talented, energetic, and disciplined people in the world. Nearly every major city in Germany had been totally destroyed by our bombers; yet, in ten years these people had entirely rebuilt them along more beautiful lines than the original. Roads, factories, schools, churches, public buildings, hospitals, railroads, shops, and places of culture had risen in this short time from the ashes and debris of war to match their counterparts in the most progressive nations of the world. The home and family life were evidently strong and wholesome; religion was publicly and strongly supported; war reparations were being paid without default; Germany's international trade was leaving France, Italy, and even England far in the rear. Here was a people with a tremendous capacity for work. To watch even the laboring man working at repairing the street is to marvel at his energy and skill and pride in doing a good job. Most of the people that I came to know personally were kind, courteous, helpful, and eager to be friendly. They were also sensitive and easily hurt. How can these qualities be reconciled with the documented history and established facts of the Nazi atrocities ?

Whatever answer to the paradox is finally arrived at by the anthropologist and the philosopher of history, one thing is certain: the German people as a whole cannot be held totally responsible for the avalanche of suffering and bloodshed unleashed by the Nazi leaders in 1939. Neither, on the other hand, can they be held entirely blameless. Few Germans realized, when the Nazi regime was put in power, that it had any greater ambition than to extricate Germany from its economic doldrums, and this promise Hitler vindicated. Besides, the only really strong opposition Hitler had at the time was the Communist party. What choice did the people have between two dogs of the same breed? By the time the Nazi party had clearly exposed its world conquest ambitions, every means of communication, down to and including a conversation over a beer in the village *gasthaus,* was controlled in one manner or another by the dreadfully efficient Gestapo. The entire nation was literally incarcerated in the gigantic concentration camp that was Germany. Nevertheless, the German people must take some of the responsibility for accepting from the very beginning the Nazi anti-Semitic program, which all but exterminated the Jewish people in the territory the Nazis controlled.

One might seriously wonder, however, how the course of history might have been changed had the government of Chancellor Heinrich Bruning, 1930 to 1932, been given a better chance by the Allied powers to restore the self-respect of the German people and the economy of the nation. Of course the validity of this hypothesis can only be determined in time by the dispassionate research of impartial historians.

The various sections of Germany differ in temperament, dialect, customs, and traditions to an even greater degree than the various sections in America. Bavaria is by far the most friendly, fun-loving, and musical part of Germany. The quiet pastoral beauty of its hills, the breathtaking splendor of the Bavarian Alps, and its natural Catholic optimism all go to make Bavaria a tourist mecca and its amiable people perfect hosts.

The closest German friends I made were the Schmid and the Halbeck families and a young tennis opponent, Vernon Ruland. I met all these people at the Augsburg Tennis Club where I enjoyed many evenings of good sport. Since there are not more than a dozen golf courses in all of Germany (other than those the Americans have built), tennis is practically the only sport in which the business man and his family may indulge.

After an evening workout of doubles we would often go to a good German restaurant for dinner and then either to my apartment or to the home of one of these friends. It was from the discussions with these intelligent and honest people that I came to appreciate the dilemma that had been theirs before, during, and after the war. Herr Schmid had lost his large cement-mixer factory to Hitler's war needs; Doctor Halbeck had been drafted into the service and spent four years on the Russian front; Ruland had been too young to see service but had known the hunger and cold of the first years following the war. All were now prospering under the Adenauer government. They pleaded no case for Germany's part in the war, nor did they extenuate their own responsibilities for what had happened. They clarified many questions in my own mind and created another, namely: what would the average American have done in exactly their situation? What would I have done?

May I say in summing up my ideas on this subject that I am convinced that Germany is eager to be a good and strong ally of the United States, and that the people of both countries could learn much from each other to their mutual advantage. The peace of the world could well depend upon the strength of this bond of friendship. This is a practical fact, no matter how pedantic it may sound.

The five priests in the 11th Airborne Division lived together in two apartments, an ideal situation for Catholic chaplains. Fathers Cowhig (a former quarterback for Boston College's Sugar Bowl champions), Natale, Cronin, and Egan were among the most congenial priests I have ever known, and the constant banter and kidding kept life in Augsburg from ever becoming dull. The fine example and complete dedication of these younger priests was a source of inspiration to the troopers, to the officers and their families, and to myself.

With this full quota of priests in the division it was possible now and then for each of us to get away on a short leave to see Rome, Venice, Paris, Vienna, or some other interesting place. On my first leave in Germany I chose to revisit Holland and Bastogne. I drove directly to Nijmegen, walked around the area in which we had fought some twelve years before, and visited *Talitha Cumi*, the institution that we had used as a CP as mentioned in Chapter 5. Two of my favorite boys had been killed there. I then drove south to Veghel and over to Heezwick and to the castle where I had landed in the moat.

The castle is a national museum, and many of the precious things that had been buried during the German occupation were again on display. The instruments of torture were still there. As I was leaving the castle, I commented to the caretaker, "It looks pretty much the same as it did twelve years ago."

"This castle has been here for eleven hundred years," the caretaker said, scarcely concealing his scorn for my typically American comment. "It is hardly likely that it would change much in twelve years."

As I was leaving, I noticed a rusty old American helmet and pistol belt hanging high on the drawbridge. I asked the caretaker if I might climb up and take a look at them. He procured them for me with a pole. Inside the helmet, which had a jagged bullet hole through it, was the faintly discernible name "Captain Byrd." He had been our headquarters commandant and was killed only a few yards from that spot. The pistol belt bore the barely legible name of "Wm. Roark." This fine young man had been Chaplain Engels assistant and had been one of the wounded captured by the Germans in the castle. I learned later that he had died of his wounds. As I crossed the bridge over the moat, I took a last look. A hideous gargoyle leered back at me as he drooled into the moat below.

From a sister in the hospital in Veghel I was able to obtain Doctor Leo Schrijver's address and telephone number in Eindhoven.

He had been a bachelor when I had known him during the Holland operation, so I was a little surprised when a woman's voice answered the phone. In my very bad German I asked if Doctor Leo was there.

"Could this be Father Sampson?" came back the reply in clear, slightly accented English.

"Why yes! How in the world could you know?"

"Very simple," she replied, amused. "Leo has been waiting twelve years for this call. Come right on out to the house, Father!"

Two very pleasant days were spent with my friend and his wonderful family. Then I headed south for Bastogne. I wanted to see again the seminary that had been our regimental headquarters. I went a little out of my way to visit the American cemetery at Margraad. This was a far more difficult experience than I had expected, and after visiting the graves of the men from the 501st, I left the place saddened beyond words.

I arrived at Bastogne in the evening, and the seminary looked the same as it had during the war, except that one could see the repaired sections that filled in the former shell holes in the building. I arrived just in time for supper in the large new dining hall. The priest who had asked me what to do with the remaining thirty boys during the battle twelve years before was now the rector. He recognized me immediately. After supper, while we were enjoying a smoke and a glass of wine in his room, I asked him how the thirty seminarians had made out. The poor priest told me how he had allowed the janitor of the place to take the boys away from the city by the one road that they thought was still not cut off. The boys had been picked up by an SS group and each of them was shot in the head and dumped into the basement of a burned-out house. One boy, seeing what was happening to his companions, made a run for it, and although wounded, made good his escape. After the German army had been repulsed, the young man brought the local authorities to the scene of the atrocity. The bodies are buried in the courtyard of the seminary, and each evening after supper the seminarians stop by and say a prayer for their comrades. The priest was so overcome in telling the story, since he (unjustly) blamed himself for allowing them to leave the city, that I tried to change the subject.

I drove from Bastogne to the place where I had been captured and then along the route of our march as prisoners to the city of

Limburg, where we had been subjected on January 1, 1945, to the bombing of our own planes. It seemed that every foot of the road was familiar, for the experience had imbedded itself in my memory. At the village of Boz I stopped by the rectory to thank the priest who had asked his parishioners to feed prisoners going through. I was told that the old priest was now dead, so I requested his successor to thank his people at next Sundays Mass for the kindness they had shown a group of American prisoners during the war.

In October Major General Hugh P. Harris took command of the 11th Airborne Division. This energetic young general immediately made a tremendous impression on the officers and men. Highly regarded by his superiors as a brilliant tactician, he inspired his subordinates with the kind of loyalty that made each man produce to the very limits of his abilities. His strong face, trim and powerful physique, and aggressive, soldierly bearing immediately captured the attention of the men when he spoke to them in formation. Far more articulate than the average general officer, he outlined in detail the goals of the division and the standard of conduct and the training necessary to achieve these goals. In a little more than a year and a half he molded the 11th into one of the best-trained combat-ready units in the United States Army.

In April a peacetime tragedy occurred that killed two fine officers and injured three others seriously. Two helicopters crashed in midair and burned. I would not mention the incident in this narrative except that one of the officers, Captain William Dawson of New York, was beyond any question the most respected and beloved officer in the entire division. He was the commanding officer of the parachute maintenance company, the unit responsible for the packing of parachutes and the repair and maintenance of all "drop" equipment. I had never before seen enlisted personnel and officers as profoundly affected as in this case. He was the father of five children, and his lovely wife was expecting a sixth. He was the ideal husband and father and an intensely devout Catholic, but he still found the time to listen to the problems of every soldier in his company. Many a young soldier, lonely and embittered by the lack of any home ties, found in "Ace" Dawsons kindly counsel and help the substitute for a father's love he had never known. Troopers seldom cry, but no one was ashamed of the tears he shed at the Memorial Mass for Ace. The men of his company had an oil picture painted of Captain Dawson, and below the picture they had inscribed these words: "Behold a *man* in whom there was no guile."

The German civilians passing the Warner *Kaserne* in Munich paused on their way to work to watch the four formations, of three planes each, drone overhead at about twelve hundred feet. As these planes would soon be dumping their human cargo in the big open spaces across the road, the spectators risked being late for work to watch. Then they jumped; one, two, three, four (they always counted the jumpers as they leaped into space) . . . forty-three, forty-four. Yes, they said to each other, almost always forty-four in each plane. Every onlooker felt a little anxiety for each jumper until air filled the canopy of the falling man. Little German boys on their way to school (for school begins early in Germany) ran to the paratroopers as they landed, grabbed the canopy of the chutes to spill out the air, and then helped the troopers roll up the chutes. This frequently earned them a mark, and where in the world could a boy have so much fun and still be paid for it? they thought.

This day was a little different, the German people noticed. The troopers were not getting into trucks to return to their companies. They were all assembling at one corner of the field where they had piled their chutes on top of each other to make a sort of table. Now they were putting a white cloth on top of this parachute table. And what's that? they asked one another. Why, it looks like a crucifix from here. And that big man, he's putting on a long, white garment, and . . . yes, sure enough, its a priest, and he's going to say Mass. (Father Co whig, the Catholic chaplain of Warner *Kaserne,* was vesting.) Look! Now all the Americans are kneeling down, and all make the sign of the cross together as the Father begins the Mass. And some of our little German boys are kneeling too. Why is all this going on? they asked each other. Could it be some big American Feast Day? Lets see. The 29th of September . . . why, today is the Feast of St. Michael! Saint Michael must be the patron of the *Fallschirmjagers.*

They were right. Saint Michael the Archangel is the patron of the airborne. Gods angelic warrior symbolizes for the Catholic para-troopers the ideal of the winged soldier who strikes from above for the cause of God's justice. The Society of Saint Michael for American

Paratroopers was first organized at Fort Bragg, North Carolina, by Chaplain (Captain) Joseph A. Natale. This big, energetic young priest from Rochester, New York, is the best all-around chaplain the author of this book has ever known. Gifted with a Notre Dame tackles physique, an infectious laugh, a prodigious appetite and cast-iron stomach, a mule-drivers voice, the irrepressible enthusiasm of a young boy, and the fervor of an Umbrian friar, this priest of Italian descent is respected and loved by all troopers of the 11th Airborne— "my hoods" as he affectionately calls them. One young trooper told me, "Nobody, not even my First Sergeant, has ever chewed me out like Father Natale did. Whew! I deserved it, but it was something like the switchings my dad used to give me when I did something bad. It really hurt, but afterwards I felt it did me a lot of good."

When one of his men asked Father Natale to say a prayer for him as they were both getting into the plane for a jump, Natale quipped, "Look, Buster, once you get that chute on, its every man for himself. I've got my own praying to do." His sermons were famous for their application to the airborne. Few men would miss his character guidance lectures, for he would always pull something that left them in stitches. One day at one of these lectures he punched a wooden locker to emphasize a point; his fist went straight through the locker, and he pulled out a bleeding and broken hand. This chaplain was the soldiers' "right guy," for he would always back up his men if they were getting a raw deal; but if they were just trying to use him to avoid some duty or deserved punishment, they quickly learned that he could be tougher than any company commander.

One day Father Natale met a young man by the name of "Frenchy" who had been a Foreign Legionnaire but was then with the 10th Special Forces at Fort Bragg. "Frenchy" explained that the medal he was wearing was the official medal of the French Airborne Society of St. Michael. Investigating further, Father Natale found that the Canadians and the Belgians also had the society in their airborne units. He applied for ecclesiastical approval from Cardinal Spellman to establish the society for American paratroopers. When this was granted, he launched the society in every major airborne unit in the American Army. Then he went to England, and with the Padre of the British airborne he established the society at Aldershot. Colonel Coforio, commandant of the Italian Airborne

School, invited him down to Viterbo to organize the same group there. This international Catholic airborne society has grown to several thousand members including many of the ranking officers in these various countries. The spiritual requirements for members of this society are as demanding as the physical requirements for jumping. The members wear the medal of St. Michael around their neck with the same degree of pride that they wear the parachute wings on their chest.

THE RULES OF
SAINT MICHAELS AIRBORNE SOCIETY

1. I will worship God faithfully by regular attendance at Mass on Sundays and on Holy Days of Obligation.

I will increase my devotion to Jesus in the Blessed Sacrament by the reception of Holy Communion at least once a month.

I will make frequent visits to the Blessed Sacrament.

2. I will not be found wanting in my devotion to the Blessed Virgin Mary, "Queen of Angels" and "Mother of Paratroopers."

I will say three "Hail Mary's" a day for fellow troopers and will pray for my comrades before and after a jump.

3. I will do all in my power to promote devotion to St. Michael, Patron of Paratroopers.

I will recite daily the prayer to St. Michael:

St. Michael, the Archangel, defend us in battle, be our protection against the malice and snares of the devil. We humbly beseech God to command him, and do thou, O Prince of the Heavenly Host, by Thy Divine Power, thrust into hell Satan and all other evil spirits who roam through the world seeking the ruin of souls. Amen.

I will be mindful of my prayers of thanksgiving after a jump.

4. I will do all that is physically and morally possible to assist a fallen-away Catholic trooper to return to the practice of the faith.

5. I will bear myself both physically and morally as a Catholic paratrooper at all times in such a manner as to be a credit to my country, myself, my family, and my Church.

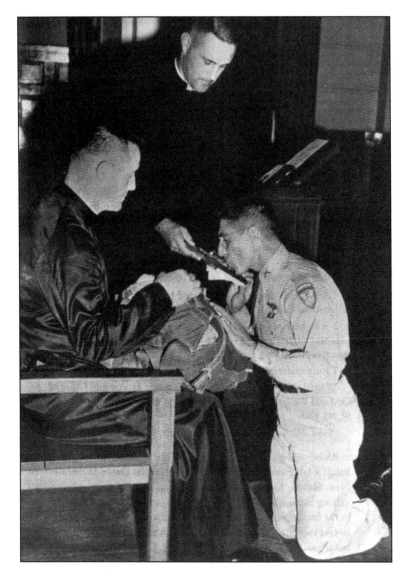

St. Michael Society Reception of first member, Captain Michael Cerrone. *Standing*: Chaplain (1st Lt.) Edward Cronin. Seated: Chaplain (Capt.) Edward Cowhig.

6. I fully understand that this is a PLEDGE and not a vow. What I do, I intend to do for the greater Honor and Glory of God and the good of my fellow troopers and the eternal salvation of my soul.

Saint Michael, patron of parachutists, protect us in battle.

Above the main altar in the Sheridan *Kaserne* in Augsburg hangs a large and brilliant painting by Gabriel Dante Luchetti of New Haven, Connecticut. The painting depicts Saint Michael driving Satan down to the lower regions, and parachutists are seen in the background dropping to assist Michael. Saint Michael seems to be expecting them, for he himself is wearing the famed "jump boots" with a "spit shine."

Twelve of my fifteen years in the Army had been spent in the airborne, and now I was being transferred to a "leg" outfit (this is the nickname paratroopers have given to all soldiers who do not jump . . . they are "legs"). Forty-six was deemed too old for this "young mans game," and besides, every chaplain needs a variety of types of experience if he expects to be effective with men of every branch of the service. But in the future whenever I see a soldier wearing the wings, the jump boots, and the airborne cap patch, I know I shall make a fool out of myself by greeting him like a long lost son. And if he says, "Look, leg, get lost," I will not be offended, for his arrogance and pride are as much a part of a paratrooper as his courage, his tenacity, his fidelity to duty, and, usually, his simple trusting faith in God.

Happy landing.

PART V

Salute to the Troopers

CHAPTER 13

The Commanders Speak

THE AIRBORNE trooper has established himself as one of the finest fighting men in the world. The unique personal characteristics that are demanded in this type of soldier are likewise demanded, and to an even higher degree, in the officers who command such troops. It is no mere coincidence that so many generals who have in recent years risen to the highest positions in the United States Army were also at one time or another airborne commanders. Men like Collins, Ryder, Ridgway, Taylor, McAuliffe, Lemnitzer, Gavin, Farrell, Hickey, Mathewson, Swing, Cleland, Adams, Harris, Sherburne, Daniels, Higgins, Smith, Miley, Michaelis, Westmoreland, Tucker, and others have given to the United States Army intelligent and aggressive leadership. All of them have commanded airborne units. All of them have contributed to the great airborne esprit-de-corps. Each of them has in turn been inspired by the splendid troops he has been privileged to command.

I have asked many of these officers to write a paragraph or two on any aspect of airborne they might choose. Most of them chose to write on the personality and the individual characteristics of the trooper himself. Others wrote on the training of the trooper, on the difficulties of his mission, on occupation duty, or on the airborne record in peace and in war. Others chose to bring out the simple faith and religious sincerity of the paratrooper. Some mention the chaplain's role in the airborne family, and others mention this book, which most of them have read. The reader will recognize in the following tributes to the trooper a humble acknowledgment by these generals that any success they have had on the field of battle is due to the sacrifices and the courage of the soldiers they commanded. I wish to again express my appreciation to these generals and colonels for their kind response to my request.

* * * * *

A Gallant Breed

"Look Out Below! is an inspiring story and will, I feel sure, provide spiritual exhilaration and stamina to a wide range of readers and, of course, to all that gallant breed of airborne troopers, whose battle records and peacetime achievements are themselves a rich source of inspiration and a set of high standards. Today, as much as, if not more than ever before in our national existence, we need to 'stand up' and 'hook up' to meet, with the paratroopers calm courage, whatever bumps we may have to absorb."

Matthew B. Ridgway
General, US Army (Retired)

An Honor to Command

"The 50lst Parachute Infantry has a record of achievement extending from the shores of Normandy to the mountain fastness of Berchtesgaden. From the moment when the regiment first met the enemy in the early dawn of June 6, 1944, until the close of hostilities, its soldiers enjoyed an unbroken succession of victories. Twice decorated with the Presidential Unit Citation, the regiment has been honored beyond the lot which fell to most of our fighting units. It is an honor to have belonged to such a unit; it is an honor to have commanded such a unit."

Maxwell D. Taylor
General, US Army Chief of Staff

A Flaming Spirit

"The magnificent combat exploits of American airborne units during World War II are evidence of the flaming spirit which motivates the airborne trooper. He is a proud individual, wiry and always physically fit, and filled with a strong sense of comradeship toward his fellows. In combat his actions are characterized by great dash, a bold but intelligent aggressiveness. He moves fast and hits hard.

"These inspiring soldierly qualities made possible the great airborne successes of Sicily, Normandy, Holland, Corregidor, Bastogne, and Wessel east of the Rhine. Our present troopers possess these same attributes in full measure and are prepared to meet the same stern tests if and when the country calls.

"*Look Out Below!* is a fascinating story, and I wish it every success. Certainly every trooper will want to read it."

Anthony C. McAuliffe
General, US Army (Retired)

Vigor, Courage, and Unparalleled Bravery   ·

"The 11th Airborne Division, which was activated in February 1943 at Camp Mackall, North Carolina, has the distinction of being the only United States airborne division to see action in the Pacific area during World War II. From its beginnings until its present assignment in Bavaria, Germany, the 11th holds an unequalled and unblemished record of distinguished service in war and peace. Its colors are marked by battle streamers denoting action in Manila, New Guinea, Leyte, and Luzon. One of its regiments, the 187th, added further glory to the good name of the 11th Airborne in its highly successful action in Korea.

"The 11th was the first to enter the Japanese mainland after World War II and remained there on occupation duty, fulfilling this assignment in its usual sterling fashion. Now stationed in Europe, the 11th has the honor of being the first United States airborne division to have served in the Far East, in the continental United States, and in the European area.

"The personnel of this division are proud to have won the satirical title of Angels because of their well-known vigor, courage, and unparalleled bravery in combat. This name they earned because of their rough, tough ability to absorb punishment and give back better than they received. Numerous awards have been made for valor and meritorious service, not excluding this country's highest awards— the Medal of Honor to its individual members and the Presidential Citation to its component units.

"It is a continued source of satisfaction to me to observe the progress and careers of the officers and men with whom I served in the 11th Airborne. Not the least of those fine soldiers are their padres, who also must be recognized for their devotion to duty. For this reason I welcome this book, *Look Out Below!* by Chaplain Sampson. Through his eyes I know that others will come to love and admire the paratrooper, the world's finest fighting man.

"Wherever the 11th Airborne may be assigned, and whatever may be its duty, our country may rest secure in the firm belief that this mighty division of Angels will give a good account of itself, wholly in keeping with the finest traditions of the United States armed forces and the spirit of the people of the free world. The greatest honor I have achieved is to have been the commander of this noble fighting team in war and in peace."

> Joseph M. Swing
> Lieutenant General, US Army (Retired)
> Commissioner of Immigration and Naturalization

Wellsprings Deep Within

"There is one aspect of a troopers make-up that has always fascinated me. The better they are, the more profound, apparently, are their sources of spiritual strength. They are responsive individuals, not a passive one among them, and they react quickly to situations in which they find themselves. Obviously they must be confident and self-reliant, and these qualities they have to a high degree. But fundamentally their sources of strength are, in my opinion, from the wellsprings deep within themselves. For they are, as a group, moved by a spirit of dedication and conviction—dedication to a belief in how things should be done, and motivated by a conviction that what must be done will be done. These make up the flock of the paratrooper padres.

"It follows that the padres themselves must be unusual men. They must not only be physically courageous, but inspiring in their spiritual leadership. Chaplain Sampson was one of these, and one of the very best, and his book *Look Out Below!* is well worth the reading."

James M. Gavin
Lieutenant General, US Army (Retired)

No Equal Among Fighting Men

"As commander of the 1st Allied Airborne Army during World War II, I say that the success we enjoyed belongs to the men that did the actual fighting. These soldiers were the ones who ate dirt, slept in the snow, and sweat blood; and they are the ones who have a story to tell.

"The airborne men are volunteers, and in my opinion they had no equal among fighting troops. It was in their nature to be tenacious, stubborn, proud, tough, and hard to put down. They had more vitality than the average man. They were unable to do anything by half-measures. What they sometimes lacked in military courtesy (I have not forgotten, though I have forgiven, the 501st man who stole my cap for a souvenir!), they made up for in military discipline at the front. They were well-trained troops. Their commanders were as tough as the men themselves, and it was no coincidence that of the three commanders of this particular regiment, one, Colonel Howard R. Johnson, was killed in action on the front lines of Holland, and the second, Colonel Julian J. Ewell, was seriously wounded in action at Bastogne.

"We must remember that some very brave, very daring, very willing young American soldiers fought their hearts out on a strange soil in order to go home in peace to a country they loved . . . and that many of them died trying."

Lewis H. Brereton
Lieutenant General, US Army
Wartime Commander, 1st Allied Airborne Army

The Champion of Fighting Men

"Although he is a relative newcomer to the long line of American fighting men, none has made a more glorious or colorful contribution than the paratrooper. This courageous warrior has firmly established his place in American military history by his daring exploits both in World War II and in the Korean conflict. The cockiness, confidence, pride, and all-around esprit-de-corps which are so characteristic of any airborne unit have made the trooper the envy of his fellow soldiers. He stands apart from all others because he himself knows that he is the champion of fighting men—and is prepared to drive himself to any extent necessary to prove it."

Lemuel Mathewson
Lieutenant General, US Army
Commander, Sixth Army

A Challenge to His Leader

"Command duty is the assignment to which every officer aspires. He who commands an airborne unit is particularly fortunate because of the type of soldier he is privileged to lead. The trooper is essentially a contradiction. He is basically an extrovert, one who has supreme confidence in his own ability to look after himself whatever the circumstance may be. He is aggressive and daring. His commander need not worry about the initiative of his subordinates. Instead, he may rest assured that in his outfit things will never go by default. The trooper is a doer. And yet, with all his fire and enthusiasm, his superb physical condition, he must be highly disciplined and, on occasions, definitely restrained. There is no levity in a stick of troopers ready to go out the door of the plane at the second the jump light turns green. This is serious business indeed, and there can be no deviation at all from prescribed procedures. The trooper is a challenge to his leader, regardless of the rank of this leader. It behooves him to afford excellent example whatever the circumstance may be. He can be certain that, if his own performance is good, his men will push him in a similar type performance. He can be equally sure that, if he is remiss, his men will exceed him in their own remissness. "Among the leaders who influence the trooper and have won his heartfelt admiration, I know of no one who is more consistently outstanding than is the paratrooper padre. The reason for this appreciation is not hard to come by. He can take it as well as the toughest of his charges, and he does not hesitate to prove the fact. He asks no favors in a fraternity where the initiation and the dues are a continuing series of hard knocks. He gives the out-and-out lie to the mistaken but sometimes held concept that a man of the cloth is somehow soft. He lives with his men. He knows them, and they know him. He comes to be a part of their operational scheme or picture. He is in a position to influence them far more than is the parish priest or the minister back home. The reason for this closeness can be spelled out very simply: There are no atheists in a jump stick!"

> Frank W. Farrell
> Lieutenant General, US Army
> Commander, V Corps

Angels in Peacetime

"The airborne concept and the trooper himself proved themselves beyond dispute in World War II as thoroughly reliable instruments of warfare. The paratrooper holds a unique position of respect when we speak of fighting qualities. Peacetime occupation of Japan, beginning in 1945, however, presented a new, and in some ways more difficult challenge to this soldier whose very nature clamored for activity. Could he bridle his wartime aversion and hatred for the Japanese? Could his intense activity and energy be channeled into peaceful and useful occupation duty? Would his conduct tend to reduce the Japanese fear of paratroopers? The airborne soldier met this challenge with the same success with which he had met the challenge of combat.

"The Angels of the 11th Airborne Division in Japan turned their energies from warfare to sports and were as eminently successful in the latter as they had been in the former. These same soldiers, who asked no quarter nor gave any in combat, became the principal support and help to Japanese orphanages and old people's homes. Hunting and fishing became their chief diversions. The fine qualities of heart and mind and initiative that had made them such excellent combat fighters were now serving their country in peaceful occupation duty. Intensive training continued, nevertheless, for Hokkaido was just a few miles from Russian-held islands and Vladivostok.

"The airborne soldier is the best in the world, airborne divisions constitute reliable insurance against aggression, and airborne chaplains are an integral part of this great team."

William Miley
Major General, US Army (Retired)

A Privilege To Command the Best

"It is the ambition of every officer to command a unit composed of young, intelligent, alert, loyal, patriotic, and aggressive soldiers. To command an airborne unit is to fulfill this desire and to be enriched by the association with such splendid examples of American youth.

"It is my firm belief that with our paratroopers jumping in peace and in war one great stimulus to courage is the sight of a chaplain in the stick.

"Father Sampson, who served as my Corps Chaplain at Fort Bragg, has proved himself a man of courage and has been a steady stimulus to the courage of untold numbers of troopers during the many years he has served in the airborne."

Joseph P. Cleland
Major General, US Army (Retired)
President, Kemper Military School

Airborne in the Atomic Era

"The history of our military service records few, if any, training feats which compare with the results obtained in the training of the United States Army airborne forces in a short space of time early in World War II. Right from the first test platoon in 1940, the airborne soldier proved his high caliber by establishing a reputation for soldierly qualities, both in and out of combat, during World War II, the Korean conflict, and since, that is second to none in the world.

"As we now forge into the atomic era, we are continuing to seek perfection in the quality of our airborne soldiers. They are carefully selected, given rigorous physical training and mental and moral indoctrination so that their qualities of initiative and quick independent action are brought to such a level that they can strike swiftly and confidently through the vast reaches of the atomic battlefield. Today more than ever our country's safety is dependent on men with qualities of the airborne trooper."

> Robert F. Sink
> Major General, US Army
> Commander, XVIII Airborne Corps

When the Chips Are Down

"Today's airborne divisions are designed to perform best when the chips are down. They are light and fast, wiry and hard. They are daring, courageous, versatile. They accept all challenges. Unrelentingly, they stick to the job until completed. They look with justifiable pride upon their records of achievement in two wars and in peacetime service at home and abroad.

"The average parachutist has the lithe, sinewy physique of a superbly conditioned athlete. He is intrepid, self-confident, and persevering; he finds it to his liking when the going is rough, and he asks no quarter and gives none. It is he, the trooper, who made the airborne divisions what they are. He supplies the character, builds the reputation, establishes the traditions, and insures the continued heritage of airborne service to our nation. He does this through his own leadership, the leadership of his NCOs and officers, and the influence resulting from the spiritual leadership of his chaplains.

"My thanks and congratulations go to Chaplain Sampson and all members of the Corps of Chaplains, whose loyal devotion to duty in bringing love and faith in God to our men have contributed so much to develop an airborne tradition within the United States Army."

> Hugh P. Harris
> Major General, US Army
> Commander, 11th Airborne Division

Airborne—An Exhilarating Experience

"The experience and good fortune of serving with airborne troops in World War II is still amazing to me; their spirit, condition, and equally sharp minds were always exhilarating, an inspiration, and their chaplains had to be exceptional people.

"The military life can offer no greater satisfaction to an officer than being assigned to command an airborne division. I count myself doubly blessed by having been privileged to be with this fine 101st Airborne Division in both war and peace."

> Thomas L. Sherburne
> Major General, US Army
> Commander, 101st Airborne Division

Religion in Prison Camp

"Adversity and suffering are, I believe, the test of the sincerity of ones religion and the depth of his faith. If this be true, then the prisoner-of-war camps in Japan and Germany during the years 1941 to 1945 were, so to speak, gigantic crucibles distilling and condensing the spiritual metal of our American youth. As a prisoner myself I saw these young men there who had been so accustomed to the ease and comforts of good homes, who had accepted the necessities and luxuries of life in the States as their natural birthright. How did they bear the physical suffering of gnawing and continuous hunger, of the bitter penetrating cold, of the enervating dysentery, of physical abuse? In a word, they bore them magnificently.

"But suffering of the spirit is always more difficult to bear than that of the body. The intense loneliness and home-sickness of the *Kriegsgefangener* (prisoner of war), the doubts and perplexities imposed upon his young mind by the insanity of war, his desolation of spirit brought on by war's travesty against his accepted and cherished principles, all these things put his religion and his faith to the test. In most instances the prisoner's faith in God emerged stronger than ever, and his religion more elemental, but more mature. He had, in the words of Paul, become a man having put away the things of a child.

"Father Sampsons misfortune in being captured turned out to be a blessing for the men he served in Stalag II-A and perhaps for himself as well, for a priest's greatest joy should be to serve where he is most needed, and surely God knew he was sorely needed there. It was my pleasure to know this young airborne chaplain in prison camp and to profit by his spiritual ministry. His book *Look Out Below!* is more than just another war story or a story of the airborne; it is an authentic witness to the fortitude and spiritual depth of the American soldier."

> James D. Alger
> Brigadier General, US Army
> Assistant Commander, 3rd Armored Division

Today's Lafayette

"The Special Forces Freedom Fighter is the most versatile soldier ever developed by the American Army. Deep behind enemy lines in wartime he helps enslaved peoples fight for their freedom.

"What kind of man is this Special Forces soldier?

"He is an experienced small-unit leader, or an expert with demolitions, or an outstanding radio or medical technician, or a competent instructor in infantry weapons. More often than not, he speaks a foreign language. He is mature; his age is nearer thirty than twenty. He like the outdoors. He can hike, swim, climb, fish, hunt, and trap. He is a man whose very survival may depend on living close to nature. His vigorous training changes many of his previous concepts of war. For example, he quickly learns the value of operations at night. He jumps, moves, trains, and fights at night. The most precious supplies dropped to him behind enemy lines are demolitions, not personal conveniences. The Special Forces training he receives in the mountains of Colorado, the swamps of North Carolina, the islands of the Caribbean, gives him that inner confidence which comes only with certain knowledge, strong physical capability, and keen alertness. He is a man not easily dismayed. He lives with the unexpected. Above all else he is sympathetic toward those peoples he is destined to assist. To them he is today's Lafayette in an American uniform.

"It seems superfluous to add that the dedicated Special Forces Freedom Fighter is a soldier of deep faith in his mission, in his country, and, above all, in his God."

> Edson D. Raff
> Colonel, US Army
> G-1, VII Corps

Airborne Comes of Age

"Holland in the early days was a storybook war for the 101st Airborne Division. The parachutists floated down to soft green fields (Father Sampson being the watery exception) amidst herds of startled cattle. A soft stillness reigned, broken only by church bells tolling in the distance. This hardly seemed a place for a war. The initial objectives were seized, in most cases, with ridiculous ease. The few German units dispersed to the winds as if struck with hammer blows. The fighting came in flare-ups with long lulls in between. This still seemed unlike war. The fighting was wide open with no front, flanks, or rear. The aggressive airborne troops had a field day fighting a war of maneuver against reasonable odds at first.

"As the Germans recovered from their initial surprise, the tempo of the fighting quickened, and there was no longer any doubt that the war was back in swing. Many brave men died in those quiet, pastoral scenes; yet, their sacrifices helped to temper the steel that turned the German blow at Bastogne.

"However, in later and grimmer days, when our troopers huddled in waterlogged foxholes on the Rhine, or lay, half-frozen, in the snow at Bastogne, Holland still seemed like a dream. As one tired and hungry soldier sardonically put it at Bastogne, 'If I am going to get killed, why didn't it happen in Holland where I could have died in comfort?'

"From a larger point of view, the airborne operations in Holland marked the coming-of-age of the American airborne effort.

In Sicily and Normandy, our airborne troops had to carry out their missions the hard way. Sheer guts and hard fighting were the ingredients that overcame deficiencies in doctrine, employment, and equipment.

"In Holland, however, the four years of hard work in organizing and training our airborne troops finally paid off. All at once, the intricate machine began to click. Everything worked. The 82nd and 101st Airborne Divisions accomplished all of their assigned tasks, and more, with distinction. From that time to this, the reputation of the airborne divisions in our Army as hard fighting and effective units, ready for any task, has been secure."

> Julian J. Ewell
> Colonel, US Army
> Commandant, United States Military Academy

The Contradictions of Bastogne

"Bastogne, the third campaign of the 101st, was a series of contradictions and surprises. First, we had no reason to expect such employment. Accepted doctrine indicated a respite after our seventy-two-day slugging match in Holland. We had every reason to expect some time to integrate replacements, to reorganize, to train, and to just plain relax a bit before being recommitted.

"The second major contradiction was that we were to be employed defensively instead of offensively—and against superior numbers of front-line enemy troops complete with armor. Such employment was in sharp contrast to accepted airborne doctrine. Airborne forces, we had been taught, would strike with surprise in the softer, less organized enemy rear areas and thereby gain and maintain the initiative. At Bastogne the enemy had chosen the ground and the time of attack and had plenty of armor which must be engaged.

· "The oddest contradiction of all was that, once employed in this unorthodox style, our division fought in more nearly the way we had been taught than in either of our actual airborne operations. We were in the enemy's rear (it was only incidental that he had us surrounded). We were complete in our order of battle and were fighting as a division in a way we had hoped for but not achieved in Normandy or Holland. We received superb air support from transports dropping supplies and from fighter bombers. Such air support was right out of the book.

"A final surprise lay in the little-appreciated fact that the toughest, most costly fighting at Bastogne was not before or while we were surrounded but in the aftermath while we were counterattacking to widen the corridor and gain maneuver room.

"Perhaps the high morale of the 101st under these circumstances should be accounted a contradiction or surprise. It did not seem so to us. We had come to expect such behavior. The surprise was that the dramatic nature of our stand caused our country, for the first time, to accord these men the respect they had so well earned in Normandy and Holland."

H. W. O. Kinnard
Colonel, US Army
Commander, 101st Airborne Division Artillery

Epilogue

The hard and difficult thing about war for those at the front were the long days that went by when none could raise his eyes beyond the next foxhole or above the next rise of muddy ground. Friends died and were taken away, and we were all too busy with the work at hand to think about them very long. A little later, during a lull in battle, we were able to assemble in formation at a military cemetery for services. The services were very sincere but short, for our duties called us back to the front almost immediately.

There are many things about war that we want to forget. We are anxious to forget the necessary sordidness and cruelties of battle. We want to forget the mud and the muck and the mire, the painful days and the endless nights. We want to forget the sickening sensation of fear. But there are many things that those who "were there" will want to remember. We want to remember the innate sense of humor of the American soldier, that reservoir of good nature that seems to be a by-product of his native courage and optimism, an incredible ability to joke and laugh under the most severe trials.

But there are other things I want to remember. I want to remember such men as Nathan Miller, a Jewish soldier, who was literally cut in two by machine-gun fire when he walked within fifty yards of a Tiger tank and knocked it out with his bazooka. I want to remember men like Philip Levitt, a Protestant trooper, who died saying the Lord's Prayer. I want to remember young men like "Hap" Houlihan, a devout Catholic, who stopped a snipers bullet in the attack on Addeville. Every chaplain wants to remember the men whom it was his privilege to be near in their last hour. All of us should remember, too, some three hundred thousand little white crosses that now dot foreign fields, each representing a priceless treasure of our country. Those simple little crosses have nothing on them but a name, a serial number, the unit, and the date of death. Some of them are unidentified but bear these engraved words, "Here lies in honored glory an American soldier known but to God."

We must never think of war casualties in terms of mere statistics. Every one of us must remember that each cross and each star of David represents more than the supreme sacrifice of a fine young man; they must also remind us of the tears of a mother and father and the empty place in a home that can never be filled even though his memory is perpetually cherished in the photograph on the family piano and the Purple Heart beside the photograph. The feeling I am sure you share with me is one of inadequacy. How, we ask ourselves, can the laying of wreaths, the parades, the heads bowed in reverence, indicate either their sacrifice or our sentiments?

Let us for a moment, in our mind's eye, draw aside the veil that separates us from these young men who gave their lives for our country. See them standing before us, row after row of them. There is the boy that used to deliver your paper, remember? And there is Tom Jones, who made such a name for himself in high school athletics. And there is Marvin Peters, who did so well supporting his mother after his father died. They look familiar: happy, energetic American youths, so full of the vigor of that age. What now do they expect of us? What can we do for them now that they are dead? Do they ask for praise? grandeur? eloquence? I think not. Do they ask to have their deeds eulogized? No, I think they would resent any attempt on our part to place halos about their heads.

But if they could look down upon our country today and see us working together for the ideals upon which our country was founded; if they could see us cooperating with one another in the spirit of understanding and Christian charity; if they could see us of every station in life, all working together, and ready and eager, each one of us, to make any personal sacrifice necessary; if those soldiers looking down could see that, then, figuratively speaking, they could polish up their boots and shine up their brass and, with shoulders back, each one could strut down the golden streets of Paradise (as we have often seen them strut down our streets), and he could nudge an old-timer up there and, pointing down at us, say with pardonable pride, "That's my country; those are my people; what I died for was worth dying for."

There is a dangerous tendency in all of us to accept the great principles embodied in our Constitution as inalienable rights about which we need do nothing. That right to life, for example, if it be inalienable, belongs to every person in the world, be he Chinese, Hungarian, Italian, Greek, or African. But millions of lives in these countries are in desperate need of the necessities to sustain life. If we really believe in the right to life, you and I must approve our country's sharing its resources. We must do more; there is a personal obligation. Each of us, as an individual, is his brother's keeper. We believe in the principle of liberty; then we are obliged to demand that right for peoples of other lands, even though our own wartime Allies may seem to refuse them that right. If we fail in this, our soldiers have fought in vain, for it was in defense of that right that this country went to war. The pursuit of happiness is our natural right, and we almost take it for granted. But this right is being attacked in the United States of America, the land of the *free*, as well as in foreign countries. Strangely enough, certain groups, such as the Ku Klux Klan, dare to rear ugly serpentine heads again and to sink deadly fangs of racial discrimination and religious bigotry into the war-weary public.

Our obligations and our debt of gratitude to the dead of World War I and of World War II and of Korea cannot be paid simply by accepting in theory the ideals for which they died and then continuing to live blindly selfish lives. The men in the service did not, perhaps, philosophize deeply about the cause of the war, but they did know that they were fighting for a way of life that they loved.

The sceptic and the scoffer may rant and rave about false causes of war, about money-mad war-mongers, about Imperialism of one country or another, and about any number of other things. I have no original answer to that. I can but point out our plain duty by appealing to one of the gentlest and kindest men who ever lived. Somehow, after more than ninety years, the words of Abraham Lincoln seem singularly appropriate today:

> It is for us, the living, rather to be dedicated here to the unfinished work which they who fought here have thus far so nobly advanced. It is rather for us to be here dedicated to the great task remaining before us; that from these honored dead we take increased devotion to that cause for which they gave the last full measure of devotion; that we here highly resolve that these dead shall not have died in vain; that this nation, under God, shall have a new birth of freedom; and that gov-

ernment of the people, by the people, for the people shall not perish from the earth.

Indeed it is proper that we be dedicated again, and that every aspect of American life be dedicated to the great tasks that still lie before us.

* * * * *

I am happy and grateful that the final words of this book should come from one who knows and understands so well the duties and responsibilities of the Army chaplains of all faiths and who has done so much to maintain and enhance the dignity and spiritual efficiency of the Chaplains Corps.

Accolade to the Army Chaplains

"The story of the airborne force really needs no further elaboration. The colorful history of its exploits and the intrepid valor of this great force are famous. It is rather my purpose in these few lines to offer an accolade to the chaplains and to the spiritual force which played such an important part in the success of the airborne operations.

"A soldier's value to the Army is proportionate to his spiritual stature. It is the chaplain who provides the spiritual aid and guidance which transcends all other qualities leading the soldier to victory.

The mission of the chaplain covers three general objectives: first, to provide for the spiritual welfare of all troops by conducting or making arrangements for religious services; second, to make men increasingly aware of the presence of God and the reality of moral law; and third, to contribute to the soldiers effectiveness by strengthening within him a living faith, thereby preparing him to render service to his nation and his fellow soldiers, both in war and in peace.

"The chaplain, by the nature of his work, is available to all ranks. His duties take him wherever he is needed—to his chapel, to hospitals, to the homes of bereaved ones, and to the front lines or to the jump area. He is always on call.

"Today the chaplain turns to the many problems of peacetime. New goals and purposes must be made articulate. The heroic aspects of wartime service must be subordinate to the less spectacular, but equally necessary, performance of peacetime duty. These aims are being achieved by chaplains whose unselfish devotion to their work has been traditional throughout the Army's history.

"Moral and spiritual strengths are recognized more than ever as being among our most vital assets. Our President has declared, Religious faith is the prime strength of our nation. Without a true concept of the dignity of man founded upon religious faith, we are sunk. The strengthening of the moral and spiritual life of our Army is the one great aim of our chaplains. It is through chaplains that this spiritual force will become increasingly effective. One of the greatest threats to our security is the attempt to destroy slowly but constantly our faith in God, in our democratic way of life, and in ourselves. The most effective allies of the enemy in the struggle against us are spiritual confusion and moral apathy. It is in fighting these forces, so infernally effective, that the army chaplain directs his greatest effort today.

"Our present responsibilities of world leadership call for strength in great measure—strength borne of physical power and technological skills, and even more, the spiritual strength of our soldier has given him the greatest source of confidence in battle and inspiration in peace. In his service to our Army, the chaplain performs an indispensable role in our nation's security.

"Father Sampson in his book *Look Out Below!* has given a graphic picture of the chaplain at his work in war and in peace. I trust that this book will convey a reassuring message to mothers and fathers, as well as to their soldier-sons, of the complete dedication of the army chaplain. May God bless each chaplain's efforts in the daily battle of life."

> Patrick J. Ryan
> Chaplain (Major General), US Army
> Chief of Chaplains